D1438893

FROM BECKET TO LANGTON

FROM
BECKET TO LANGTON

English Church Government 1170–1213

THE FORD LECTURES
DELIVERED IN THE UNIVERSITY OF OXFORD
IN HILARY TERM 1955

BY

C. R. CHENEY

FELLOW OF THE BRITISH ACADEMY
PROFESSOR OF MEDIEVAL HISTORY IN THE
UNIVERSITY OF CAMBRIDGE

MANCHESTER UNIVERSITY PRESS

Published by the University of Manchester at
THE UNIVERSITY PRESS
316–324, Oxford Road, Manchester 13
1956

Printed in Great Britain by Butler & Tanner Ltd., Frome and London

PREFACE

THE invitation to deliver the Ford Lectures provided an incentive to consider more carefully a question which had long interested me : how did the growth of papal power in the twelfth century affect the Church in England under the first three Angevin kings ? In the past, it has been treated as a question of politics or law, and answered accordingly. But there seems to be room for a broader view of the matter, to embrace the whole administration of the Church and the relations of clergy and people. This I have attempted. No simple formula will suffice for an answer and I can only hope that I have succeeded in giving due weight to Roman and to local influences, to the elements which proclaimed *ecclesia anglicana* to be a part of the Universal Church and to those which declared its unbroken and distinctive history. These lectures, as first prepared, were too long to be delivered in six hours and had to be curtailed. They are printed in their original, longer, form with a few additions and corrections. But they remain in substance lectures and make no pretence of being an exhaustive treatise.

My debts to modern scholars are, I fear, inadequately expressed in the footnotes, and all the less adequately because I have tended to note points of disagreement. But I am no pioneer in this field, and many experts have helped me by their writings and with personal advice. I would like to offer them all my thanks. In a general way I owe most to my three Oxford teachers, R. V. Lennard, F. M. Powicke, and V. H. Galbraith ; but I also recall my pupils of the past ten years at Manchester, the undergraduates in my third-year class and my research-students : they have contributed facts, ideas, and stimulus. Members of my audience at Oxford were good enough to make suggestions and criticisms which I have tried to take into account ; to them also I am grateful. My colleague, Eric

John, kindly read and criticized the whole typescript.   My
wife has submitted patiently to hearing and reading these
lectures in version after version, and the result, however
imperfect, is much the better for her criticism.

I wish to thank the electors to the Ford Lectureship for
the honour they did me in inviting me to lecture in the
University of Oxford.   To the Council of the University
of Manchester I am obliged for sabbatical leave in Michaelmas Term, 1954 ; to my colleagues in the Manchester
History School who relieved me of academic duties during
that term I am deeply grateful.   Without this leisure I
could not have completed the task.   Finally I must thank
the Manchester University Press for offering to publish
these lectures and the Secretary, Mr. T. L. Jones, for his
interest and care.

Documents in Appendix III are drawn from various
collections.   I am grateful to the owners and custodians
of the manuscripts for facilities to use them and for permission to publish them.

CONTENTS

APPENDICES

LIST OF ABBREVIATIONS

ACL . . . Appendix Concilii Lateranensis. (The decretal-collection printed under this name in
Mansi, *Concilia*, xxii. 248 and in earlier editions
of the church councils).

BIHR . . *Bulletin of the Institute of Historical Research*,
University of London.

BJRL . . *Bulletin of the John Rylands Library*, Manchester.

Coll. Wigorn. 'Collectio Wigorniensis', ed. H. E. Lohmann,
in *Zeitschrift der Savigny-Stiftung für Rechts-
geschichte*, Bd. liii kan. Abt. xxii (1933),
35–187.

CRR . . . *Curia Regis rolls of the reigns of Richard I and John*,
7 vols. (H.M. Stationery Office, 1922–35).

Decretals⎫ . *Corpus iuris canonici*, ed. E. Friedberg, 2 vols.
Decretum⎭ (Leipzig, 1879–81).

EHR . . . *English Historical Review*.

Epp. Cantuar. *Epistolae Cantuarienses*, ed. W. Stubbs (Rolls
Series, 1865).

EYC . . . *Early Yorkshire charters*, vols. i–iii, ed. William
Farrer (1914–16), vols. iv–ix and index to
vols. i–iii, ed. C. T. Clay (Yorks. Archaeol.
Soc. Record series, extra series, 1935–52).

JL . . . *Regesta pontificum Romanorum . . . ad 1198*, ed.
P. Jaffe, 2nd ed. by S. Loewenfeld, etc.,
2 vols. (Leipzig, 1885–8).

MIÖG . . *Mitteilungen des Institutes für österreichische Ges-
chichtsforschung*.

Monasticon . Wm. Dugdale, *Monasticon Anglicanum*, ed. J.
Caley, etc., 6 vols. in 8 (1817–30).

MTB . . *Materials for the history of Thomas Becket*, ed. J. C.
Robertson, 7 vols. (Rolls series, 1875–85).

PL . . . . J. P. Migne, *Patrologiae cursus completus : series
latina*.

P.R. . . . Pipe Roll, as published by the Pipe Roll Society,
1884–.

PUE . . . *Papsturkunden in England*, ed. Walther Holtzmann,
3 vols. (Abhandlungen der Gesellschaft der
Wissenschaften zu Göttingen, phil.-hist. Kl.,

neue Folge : xxv, 3 Folge : 14–15, 33 ; 1930–1952).

Reg. antiquiss.   *Registrum antiquissimum of the cath. church of Lincoln*, ed. C. W. Foster and K. Major, vols. i–vii (Lincoln Record Society, 1931–53).

RS . . .   Rolls series (Chronicles and memorials of Great Britain and Ireland during the Middle Ages. H.M. Stationery Office).

SLI . . .   *Selected letters of Pope Innocent III concerning England (1198–1216)*, ed. C. R. Cheney and W. H. Semple (Nelson's Medieval Texts, 1953).

Wilkins . .   David Wilkins, *Concilia Magnae Britanniae et Hiberniae*, 4 vols. (1737).

I

INTRODUCTION

THE jubilee of St. Thomas Becket was celebrated on 7 July
1220 by his successor, Stephen Langton, in the cathedral
church which was the scene of Becket's murder fifty years
before. Becket had suffered exile for six years, and then
martyrdom, for the sake of clerical immunity from lay control ; Langton, before he reached his see of Canterbury in
1213, suffered exile for six years in what was essentially the
same cause. Not surprisingly, Langton (who was probably
old enough in 1170 to be shocked by the assassination)
looked back to Becket to give himself courage in his under-
takings. His fortitude and misfortunes made at least one
contemporary, Gerald of Wales, compare the two archbishops and see in Langton the first true successor of St.
Thomas.

The eminence of the two archbishops and the dramatic
episodes in which they were involved have led recent historians of the Church to look at the intervening period—
between 1170 and 1213—from one or other of its terminal
points. Some scholars, it is true, recognize that it should
not be treated simply as epilogue or prologue. The recent
general works of Dr. Poole and Dr. Barlow examine briefly
the church history of this period for its own sake, so to
speak, free from preoccupation with past or future. But
this has not been the usual tendency.[1]

On the one hand, we are shown the end of an age. Little
conspicuous advance is made in adjusting the claims of
Church and State beyond the settlement of 1172 ; the
bishops have not the same sort of distinction as Becket's

[1] Dom Adrian Morey observed in 1937 : ' The history of the English
Church during the twelfth century has been approached almost exclu-
sively from the political side ' (*Bartholomew of Exeter*, p. 79).

bench displayed ; the papacy, after Alexander III, relaxes control until Innocent III comes with a strong hand in 1198, and even then papal influence on the English Church is seriously impeded between 1207 and 1213. In the years between 1181 and 1215, it has been said, ' the centrifugal, disorderly forces were on the whole preponderant '.[1] During the reign of Richard I, Stubbs wrote, ' the state of religion in the country was extremely bad '.[2] This impression is deepened by reading Augustin Fliche on the state of the Church at large, or Mlle Foreville on England. The earlier work of Böhmer stopped short in Henry II's reign and Dr. Zachary Brooke devoted only a brief epilogue of fifteen pages of his well-known book to the whole period between 1170 and 1216.

Those who approach the history of the Church from the further limit—Langton—see an equally gloomy view.[3] Reaction against the centrifugal forces seems only to come with Innocent III ; and his Fourth Lateran Council of 1215 seems to determine the direction of subsequent reform in the English Church. The episcopate is liberated by the charter of free elections of 1214 ; monastic life is revived by discipline enforced from Rome. From this angle the Church between Becket and Langton appears to be devoid of great ideals, to be only rudimentary in its organization, backward in discipline.

These views from opposite sides of the period seem to me to give its history a false perspective. Becket and Langton have attracted attention precisely because they were exceptional, not typical. That has meant concentration on sources which bear particularly upon their careers and their ideals ; but these sources do not throw much light on the everyday aspects of church life in the intervening time. We

---

[1] David Knowles, *The monastic Order in England* (Cambridge, 1940), p. 314.

[2] *Epp. Cantuar.*, p. cxvii.

[3] M. Gibbs and J. Lang, *Bishops and reform, 1215–1272* (Oxford, 1934), *passim.* Knowles, *The religious Orders in England* (Cambridge, 1948), pp. 3–4.

need to take a frontal view of the strictly contemporary literary and record sources. At the same time, a good many recent studies on particular legal and literary topics will have to be brought into the account. These lectures are confined to a rather broad treatment of church government. In the course of considering the subject I hope to interest you in the nature of the evidence and to suggest lines along which work remains to be done.

What light do contemporary sources throw upon this system of government? First, a word about the narrative writers. The great series of late twelfth-century historians whose works are published in the Rolls Series make as fine a galaxy as any generation of medieval England can show : there are Ralph de Diceto, dean of St. Paul's, Roger of Howden, royal clerk, William of Newburgh, the Austin canon, Gervase, the Benedictine monk of Canterbury, Ralph, the Cistercian abbot of Coggeshall, and others. They are rich in information. Each compensates for some silence or prejudice of the others. For our present purposes their main value is in illuminating ecclesiastical politics, and the story of a few great disputes. But they are tantalizingly imperfect. Then there is Gerald of Wales—of all our sources of illumination the brightest if not the steadiest light. He was a highly educated, intelligent man, who was very well aware of the problems of ecclesiastical government. He knew everybody worth knowing, and he was a fluent and witty *raconteur*. His voluminous, repetitive works (eight volumes of them) cannot be ignored ; for they show, or seem to show, ecclesiastical government at work. But when we use them, we must remember that Gerald was a contentious and disappointed cleric, an irresponsible reporter of rumour, a confirmed glorifier of the past. Moreover, he lived on the Celtic fringe of English affairs and came to prefer Paris and the Capetians to London and the Angevins. His opinion is not an English opinion : it is that of an external—and by no means impartial—observer.

The Rolls Series also contains a volume of *Epistolae*

Cantuarienses edited by William Stubbs in 1865. These 571 documents concern the most celebrated lawsuit of the age— what may be called the Canterbury case. It was fought out between Archbishops Baldwin and Hubert and the monks of their cathedral of Christ Church over the endowment of a collegiate church, first at Hackington, later at Lambeth. The documents, which were put together at Canterbury, give immensely valuable evidence to which we shall want to go back again and again. But it would not do to suppose that bishops and Benedictine houses usually lived in such discord, or that many lawsuits in the Roman curia created equal stir. This is an illuminating source, but it is not typical.

These chronicles and records, together with a certain quantity of papal correspondence and the documents in Rymer's *Foedera*, were the main materials which English church historians had to work on between, say, 1860 and 1880. Stubbs, who edited nearly half of them, was also their best interpreter. Even now his introductions to the Rolls Series, his lectures (which he disliked so much), and Chapter xix of the *Constitutional History*, still provide some of the best and justest historical writing on the Church in the twelfth and thirteenth centuries. I emphasize this because Maitland is commonly supposed to have destroyed Stubbs's picture of Church and State by his brilliant and—be it said— wholly successful attack in the essays reprinted in *Roman Canon Law in the Church of England*. It is too often over-looked, though Maitland made it clear,[1] that he had applied himself to prove one legal point, and one only, in which Stubbs had displayed muddled thinking. He had not des-troyed Stubbs's general view of the relations of the clergy to pope and king.

But it will not do for us simply to re-assert Stubbs. Much more evidence has become readily accessible since he wrote, evidence which is of special interest for the law and practice

[1] *Roman canon law*, pp. 73-5. It was perhaps natural that Maitland did not quote Stubbs's *Constitutional history*, § 389, where Stubbs came much nearer to a correct account of the legal position, but it was un-generous.

of church government and which presents these matters in a new light. Many more papal letters to England have been printed : the three volumes of Dr. Walther Holtzmann's *Papsturkunden* contain over 1,100 of them. Those papal letters, in particular, which were seized upon and copied by contemporary lawyers because of the legal interest of their contents, have been the subject of more systematic study during the past eighty years. The early legal collections of letters are being examined for their historical value. They improve and add to the English material in the *Corpus* of canon law. As evidence of this I may refer to the recent edition of twenty-five decretals concerning the diocese of Lincoln, by Dr. Holtzmann and Canon Kemp.[1] This is the first collection of such records to be published with adequate annotation and index.

On the English side, the records of the Exchequer and Curia Regis have been printed, and some of the earliest examples of record-keeping by English bishops. Every year some new cartulary of a cathedral chapter or religious house is published ; these are supplemented by regional collections of charters, foremost among them the *Early Yorkshire charters* of William Farrer and Charles Clay, and by the collected *acta* of individual prelates, like those of Archbishops Theobald and Stephen of Canterbury which we owe to Dr. Saltman and Miss Major. As more becomes available, we are better placed to submit this sort of material to diplomatic criticism. We can use it more surely. We can make some attempt to distinguish the exceptional from the normal, and observe in the products of ecclesiastical chanceries the progress to order and rule, not only in the chanceries themselves but in the whole organization which they served.

The time has come, in short, to reconsider what was happening in the English Church between 1170 and 1213, and I propose to begin with a brief survey of the state of ecclesiastical government during Becket's pontificate. Secondly,

---

[1] *Papal decretals relating to the dioc. of Lincoln in the twelfth century*, ed. W. Holtzmann and E. W. Kemp (Lincoln Record Soc., vol. 47, 1954).

I shall mention some general features of church history which form the continuous background to the special topics of the later lectures.

By the time Thomas Becket was elected to Canterbury in May 1162 the formal structure of the medieval English Church was complete. That is to say, there was to be no more carving out of new dioceses, no more setting up of new cathedral sees,[1] such as marked the early Norman period. The bishoprics were fixed both in the southern and the northern provinces, even if the see of Carlisle lay vacant for nearly fifty years (1157–1203) and even if the precedence and privileges of Canterbury's suffragans were still matters for dispute.[2] The archdeaconries, too, were all in existence ; most of them already had their later territorial titles.[3] Within their boundaries were the smaller divisions of rural deaneries and parishes. Legatine councils brought English prelates together at various times about the middle of the twelfth century, and stray references in charters show that the bishops held synods, archdeacons held chapters. The monastic orders—except for the Carthusians—were already established in the country, though a great many more houses of Cistercian monks and regular canons were yet to be founded. The evidence already at our disposal provides some indications of the activities of a bishop at the time when Becket became primate. The diocesan supervised the gifts of lands and churches to monasteries, he ordered

---

[1] Except for the short period when Bishops Savaric and Jocelin of Bath established a see at Glastonbury.

[2] Gervase of Canterbury, *Hist. works* (RS), i. 170 ; *PL*, ccxv. 1043 ; *Early charters of St. Paul's Cathedral* (Camden 3rd series, vol. lviii, 1939), pp. 139–42. Cf. Raymonde Foreville, *L'église et la royauté en Angleterre sous Henri II Plantagenet* (Paris, 1943), pp. 479–80, 549–50.

[3] A. H. Thompson, *The English clergy and their organization in the later Middle Ages* (Oxford, 1947), pp. 58–60. For Lincoln diocese cf. *Reg. antiquiss.*, vii. 201–2. In 1175 Archbishop Richard instituted three archdeacons instead of one in the church of Canterbury, but abandoned the experiment after a few years (R. de Diceto, *Hist. works* (RS), i. 403). Innocent III in 1202 authorized Archbishop Hubert to make three instead of one (*PL*, ccxiv. 1029), but we hear no more of the proposal.

enquiries into doubtful rights over tithe, instructed his archdeacons to admit parsons to parish churches, heard lawsuits
over marriages in his synod. During the reign of Stephen
and the early years of Henry II the Crown apparently
expected disputes over advowson and other cases concerning
parish churches to be heard in the court Christian. An
interesting group of Henry II's writs addressed to the bishop
of Norwich order him to give a plaintiff his rights in a church
without delay : ' and if you do not take action, let the archbishop of Canterbury act, so that I hear no more complaint
about it for default of justice '.[1]

By 1164 the church courts were very active. In some
directions they went beyond the customary practice of
Henry I's reign, if we may judge from the terms of the Constitutions of Clarendon. Even if there were no other evidence, we might make some safe inferences from this document. Questions of advowson (c. 1) and even cases of disputed land-tenure (c. 9) were sometimes being settled in
court christian ; bishops claimed sole jurisdiction over
felonous clerks (c. 3), they applied the canon law in respect
of the laity (c. 6, 15) and exercised their power of ecclesiastical censure (c. 5, 7, 10). We might also infer from the
Constitutions that appeals from English church courts to
Rome were common and perhaps growing commoner, since
Henry II and his advisers seem determined to curtail them
(c. 8).[2]

Now all this was certainly no novelty of Becket's pontificate. Already between 1125 and 1151 a series of five
councils of the English Church, held by legates *a latere* or by
English prelates with legatine authority, had laid down lines
for stricter and more strictly ecclesiastical control over the

---

[1] *Register of St. Benet of Holme* (Norfolk Record Soc., vols. 2 and 3,
1932), i. 18, no. 25 (cf. nos. 19, 22–4, 26, 36, 39, 41, 48, 145), and below
Appendix III (ii, iii). See also Stephen's writ for the archdeacon of
Canterbury in *Hist. monast. S. Augustini* (RS), p. 381, and Henry I's
writ in a tithe-case, Hist. MSS. Comm. *Rutland MSS.*, iv (1905), 149.
Dr. Darlington cites the St. Benet cases in *EHR*, lxvii (1952), 564.

[2] Cf. the situation in Normandy. Foreville, *L'église et la royauté*,
p. 118.

Church. They provided that ordinations should be more closely supervised, and legislated against simony, hereditary succession in benefices, the neglect of excommunication by priests, and other matters concerning the clergy ; their rules about marriage and the transfer of tithes showed that the church courts would claim cognizance of disputes over these matters. All this lawmaking represented the Gregorian ideals of moral reform of the clergy and freedom of the Church from lay control. Those ideals were not realized. On the other hand, the laws probably led to tighter supervision of ecclesiastical affairs by the bishops and regular contact with Rome. The bench of bishops in the time of Theobald of Canterbury included energetic, efficient, zealous men ; besides the archbishop there was the great Henry of Blois, bishop of Winchester, Hilary of Chichester, Gilbert Foliot of Hereford, Robert de Chesney of Lincoln.[1] Eugenius III, the Cistercian pope (1145–53), and his English successor Adrian IV (1154–59), had close links with England. One has the impression—though it is only an impression, hard to verify—that English Church government made big advances between Theobald's accession in 1139 and his death in 1161. From the charters and decretals which are being gradually collected and edited, future historians of the twelfth-century Church may discover the way in which a bishop went to work in those days.

Can we discern any further progress as a result of Becket's rule or during his rule over the province of Canterbury ? That question cannot be finally answered until all the remaining acts of the archbishop [2] and contemporary English bishops have been assembled and studied. Meanwhile, no sign is observable of any striking advance towards orderliness in church government. The time indeed was not pro-

---

[1] For these men see David Knowles, *The episcopal colleagues of Archbishop Thomas Becket* (Cambridge, 1951).

[2] His administrative acts are hard to disentangle from those of Theobald, his predecessor. Some are collected by Mlle Foreville, ' Lettres " extravagantes " de Thomas Becket, archevêque de Canterbury ', *Mélanges d'hist. du moyen âge* . . . *Louis Halphen* (Paris, 1953), pp. 225–38.

pitious. The archbishop and some of his suffragans spent
years abroad and most of the bishops were more or less
involved in the bitter dispute of Becket with the king.[1]
John of Oxford, an unfriendly critic, went so far as to say
that the archbishop and his colleagues were not interested
in reforming the clergy. Nicholas of Mont-aux-Malades,
who reported this statement to the archbishop and elaborated
on it, clearly thought the charge had some substance.[2]

We might expect one result of the rupture between Henry
II and Becket to be a lessening of normal traffic between
England and the Curia. In fact, along with heightened
diplomatic activity, churches and individuals continued to
get privileges and letters of grace from the pope, though
probably not so frequently as in the days of Adrian IV.
Several judicial appeals of the time have left records. But
here we come up against a defect of our evidence which
makes it impossible to dogmatize about these matters. The
decretal-letters which show English prelates asking for judgments and advice from the pope and which show the pope's
guiding hand at work are seldom dated in the copies which
survive. When they are dated (according to the usage
which prevailed in the papal chancery until 11 February
1188), they only give the place and the day of the month,
not the year. There is often no internal evidence to compensate for this deficiency, and many of Alexander III's most
important decretals can only be dated by the limits of his
pontificate : 1159 to 1181. Even when an addressee is
named, such as Roger of Worcester, Gilbert of London, or
Bartholomew of Exeter, we still cannot say whether the letter
belongs to the Becket era or to a later time. All that we can
say is that among the dated letters of Alexander III to England a large majority were written after 1170.[3]

---

[1] Roger, bishop of Worcester, when out of the country, seems to have
entrusted diocesan business to Ralph, prior of Worcester, and Matthew,
archdeacon of Gloucester (*The English register of Godstow*, i (Early Eng.
Text Soc., vol. 129, 1905), 131.   [2] *MTB*, v. 146, 149–50.

[3] Dr. Holtzmann's collection contains 75 letters for 4¾ years of
Adrian IV, and of Alexander III 100 assignable to the 11¼ years before

But if the brief and troubled period of Becket's pontificate did not see church discipline strengthened, indirectly his career and fate may have affected the future government of the Church. It made men more acutely aware of the problem to which his murder offered no solution. Not all the clergy of the next generation thought that Becket had acted wisely or rightly,[1] but at least he had exposed the impropriety of lay intervention in matters which had some spiritual content. His dispute with the Crown provoked an intenser study of the canon law.[2] Thanks to his cult the principle of ' the liberty of the Church' was widely advertised. The episode may also have toned down, without suppressing, the reaction of the monarchy to the growing Gregorianism within the Church. The sacrilege of Henry II's knights may have persuaded the Angevins and their servants to act circumspectly.

The known and the unknown alike forbid us to regard 1170 as a turning-point in the government of the English Church. During the next forty-three years, before Stephen Langton was established in his see in 1213, there was a gradual, unsteady movement towards a stricter form of government—a movement almost exactly contemporary with the course of development of Angevin royal government from the Assize of Clarendon to Magna Carta.

England was ruled during these years by three kings, all of them strong-willed, ruthless, unpleasant men, who were very able. Richard I, less of a statesman than either his father or his brother John, was also the least often in England ; but even he was forever busy with the English Church, whether he was at Messina, or at Worms, or at his saucy

Becket's murder, 253 to the following 10½ years ; 93 of Alexander's letters cannot be assigned to one or other of these periods. These figures are indicative, though they have no value as exact statistics.

[1] Cf. William of Newburgh, in *Chron. of reigns of Stephen, Henry II*, etc. (RS), i. 161 ; Caesarius of Heisterbach, *Dialogus miraculorum* (ed. J. Strang, 1851), ii. 139-40.

[2] S. Kuttner and E. Rathbone, ' Anglo-Norman canonists of the twelfth century ', *Traditio*, vii (1949-51), 294-5.

new castle on the Seine.   Meanwhile, at the beginning and
end of this period the Latin Church was ruled by two of the
mightiest popes of the Middle Ages : Alexander III and
Innocent III.   In the sixteen years between the death of
Alexander and Innocent's promotion came five elderly
popes : they were not nonentities, but they could not compare, as rulers of the Church Universal, with these two great
lawyers and theologians who, in General Councils, in legal
judgments, and a voluminous correspondence, dealt with
problems of faith and discipline in masterly fashion.   The
changing climate of the Curia is something to be remembered when one deals with the affairs of the Church in
England.

Of the English hierarchy I shall speak in my next lecture.
For the moment I simply point out that there was no English
head of the English Church : the province of Canterbury
embraced the south of England and Wales, while the province of York included Whithern, or Candida Casa, beyond
the northern border.[1]   The ancient dispute between Canterbury and York was not allowed to die in this period.   The
quarrels of Richard of Dover and Roger of Pont l'Évêque,
and of Hubert Walter and Geoffrey Plantagenet are petty
enough, but they illustrate the disunity of the Church.
Within the southern province Canterbury had been threatened in the middle of the century with the secession of Winchester and Gilbert Foliot was accused of seeking to transfer
the metropolis to London.[2]   Gerald of Wales revived and
maintained for many years the claim of the *ecclesia wallensica*

---

[1] These lectures are concerned with the Church in England.   The
conditions in Wales were sufficiently different to demand separate
treatment.   In the absence of an adequate history of the Welsh Church,
the long and valuable introductions by Dr. J. Conway Davies to
his calendar of *Episcopal acts relating to Welsh dioceses, 1066–1272* (Hist.
Soc. of the Church in Wales, vols. 1 and 2, 1946–8) should be
consulted.

[2] *MTB*, iv. 225–6, vi. 591, 641, vii. 10–11, 40, 41, 43.   Cf. Foreville,
L'église et la royauté, pp. 286–8 and Knowles, *Episcopal colleagues*, pp. 47–8,
160–2.   According to John of Salisbury Gilbert proposed not only to
make himself archbishop of London but to suppress the archbishopric
of Canterbury.

to a separate existence.   It is worth insisting upon this, for
however futile Gerald's claim, however much York followed
the lead of Canterbury in practice (and occasionally submitted to the legatine powers of the southern archbishop),
these divergencies constantly provided a confusing factor in
relations between the papacy, the clergy, and the Crown.

I have suggested that in these years there was a gradual,
unsteady movement towards a stricter form of church government.   If we try to look at the situation as the actors saw it,
this will be seen to be the outcome of innumerable tussles,
differences of opinion translated out of words into action.
No clear-cut division produced two well-organized parties
of churchmen [1] : still less could one distinguish between a
' good ' group of reformers and a ' bad ' group of unregener-
ate maintainers of abuse.   No one big issue divided the
English Church ; but men, good and bad, were taking
sides and arguing about a multitude of matters which engage the human mind and feelings—matters which must
eventually affect the structure and government of the
Church.   The pull of opinion this way and that created
a state of tension which must not be forgotten.   Such tension
in a society is the very proof that it breathes.   It does not
always find expression in open argument, but it is there.

What were the issues ?   They could be described in
general terms favoured by medieval writers : the contrast
of the things that are Caesar's and the things that are God's
—of the way of Mary and the way of Martha—of the
heavenly city and the terrestrial city.   But these contrasts
and conflicts are always with us.   It is more instructive for
historians to look at the particular points where tension arose
in the latter part of the twelfth century.   And since the
whole debate concerns the relations of the Church with the
world, it seems natural to look first at the fortunes of monasticism at this time.

---

[1] Hugh of Avalon, bishop of Lincoln, was the one heroic and intran-
sigent defender of the Church's liberties ; but his influence on public
affairs was comparatively slight.

The monastic orders had perhaps reached the height of their wealth and influence, and their hold upon the laity was very great ; but education of the clergy was less in their hands than it had been of old and among the secular clergy they encountered sharp critics. Roger of Pont l'Évêque, for instance, the archbishop of York who had grown up in the household of Archbishop Theobald, was a confirmed opponent of monks, even on his deathbed. Ancient privileged abbeys such as St. Augustine's, Canterbury, Malmesbury, and Evesham, had to fight for their exemption against bishops anxious to exercise their ordinary rights. Of the monastic cathedral chapters, Canterbury suspected Archbishops Baldwin and Hubert of undermining its position as the metropolitan church, Coventry had to fight for very existence against its diocesan. The Benedictines in general were very sensitive to attack. They had lost some of their popularity in favour of the more austere Cistercians who considered themselves the salt of the earth, so there was no love lost between the Black and the White Monks.

The Cistercians, however, had a name for avarice as well as austerity. Walter Map, archdeacon of Oxford, acidly observes : ' I cannot forget that they are the Hebrews, and we are the Egyptians '.[1] The White Monks still represented an ascetic ideal, their reputation stood high at Rome,[2] they were the chosen confessors of kings [3] : but they were under fire. To judge by the number of new foundations and the patronage of the great, the Austin canons and Premonstratensian canons made a wider appeal than other religious orders in England at this period. Why this should be is not immediately obvious, for their way of life was closely assimilated to that of the monk. Perhaps they attracted support because their houses were smaller, less

---

[1] *De nugis curialium*, dist. 1, c. 25.

[2] The variations of their standing at Rome are discussed by Karl Wenck, ' Die röm. Päpste zwischen Alexander III u. Innocenz III u. der Designationsversuch Weihnachten 1197 ', *Papsttum u. Kaisertum* (Festschrift für Paul Kehr, 1926), p. 433.

[3] Adam of Perseigne, John of Ford, Henry of Bindon.

lordly than the Benedictines', perhaps because their claim to live the apostolic life seemed more plausible than that of the monks, perhaps because they did not withdraw themselves so completely from the world. Be that as it may, it is interesting to see how in the next generation these cloistered priests suggest to the papacy the means of disciplining enthusiasm, of bringing the friars into the approved framework of the religious life. The wranglings of the Orders and the doubts and preferences of the laity in the twelfth century were the signs of a religious ferment pervading the Christian world.[1]

The monastic life apart, there were conflicting tendencies in other matters of piety and discipline. The Third Crusade was the first crusade in which England participated on a grand scale, but in contrast to those who went (with motives however mixed), others were beginning to question the efficacy of pilgrimage and thought these armed expeditions wicked folly.[2]

To take another matter productive of tension in the Church : in the ministry of parishes the Gregorian Church had branded old usages as excesses. But the continued attempts throughout our period to keep the clergy celibate and to oust the hereditary parson from the church in which his father and grandfather had served before him met with stubborn resistance. The programme created a real social problem. Gerald of Wales, for one, doubted whether it was expedient to forbid clerks below the order of deacon to marry. He even suggests doubts about forbidding priests.[3] Ralph of Diceto, dean of St. Paul's, did not think that the

---

[1] See the striking article by Père M. D. Chenu, ' Moines, clercs, laïcs au carrefour de la vie évangelique (xiie siècle) ', *Revue d'histoire ecclésiastique*, xlix (1954), 59–89 ; also H. Grundmann, ' Eresie e nuovi ordini religiosi nel secolo xii ' (in German), in *Relazioni* of 10th Int. Congress of Hist. Sciences (Florence, 1955), iii. 357–402.

[2] G. B. Flahiff, ' *Deus non vult*. A critic of the Third Crusade ', *Mediaeval studies* (Toronto, ix (1947), 162–88), is concerned with Ralph Niger. P. A. Throop deals largely with later evidence in his *Criticism of the Crusade, a study of public opinion and crusade propaganda* (Amsterdam, 1940).   [3] *Opera* (RS), ii. 186–8.

sons of clergy should have their promotion barred.[1] Evidence of another kind on this subject comes from the cartulary of Dunstable Priory : [2] in 1214, after years of litigation, the Austin canons of Dunstable succeeded in evicting from the church of Bradbourne (Derbyshire) a rector and a vicar on the grounds that they were the sons of former incumbents and were imitators of their parents' incontinence. The judges in the case, giving sentence for Dunstable, admitted that ' it seemed very hard to us (*valde durum*) to remove clergymen who had held that church for thirty years and more '. The enforcement of the canon law in such cases as this, and the monastic appropriation of parish churches—to be served thereafter by celibate vicars—cannot have been always an unmixed blessing ; and contemporaries knew it.

Again, the Church undertook to discipline the laity, but ecclesiastical censures were so indiscriminately used that excommunication and interdict lost their terrors. Some prelates argued that people's hearts could best be touched through their pockets and put more faith in fines than in excommunications and penances. To justify that faith someone remarked to St. Hugh, bishop of Lincoln, that the blessed archbishop and martyr Thomas had fined offenders. To whom Hugh replied : ' Believe me, he was not a saint on that score ; for other meritorious qualities have declared him to be a saint and it was not on that account that he deserved to bear the palm of martyrdom.' [3] This question of penalties, comparatively trivial in itself, shows like the other matters of dispute and tension, how difficult it was to achieve a balance between the Church and the world. Some churchmen wanted a stricter discipline, but to attain it they had to arm themselves with secular powers. They used excommunication freely, and when the sentence was

---

[1] *Hist. works*, i. 305. St. Hugh of Lincoln had not been over-particular about the legitimacy of the canons of Lincoln (*PL*, ccxv. 1011), and illegitimate candidates for preferment were often sons of clerks.

[2] Bedfordshire Hist. Rec. Soc. *Publications*, x (1926), 126–32, 166, 233.

[3] *Magna vita S. Hugonis* (RS), p. 188. Cf. the charge against the bishops, *MTB*, v. 146, 150.

ignored the secular arm was invoked to handle the offender.
They claimed immunity for the persons of clerks ; but this
involved the responsibility of criminal jurisdiction over
them, and in the thirteenth century the bishop must build a
safe prison if he would avoid the fine of £100 which the
Crown demanded of him when a prisoner escaped.

Tension was evident in debate about ecclesiastical office.
Was it a prelate's duty to be judge and administrator or
pastor ? The history of society, said John Henry Newman,
' begins in the poet and ends in the policeman '.[1]   There
appeared to be danger that the Church, having begun with
the evangelist, would end with the legist.   Adam, abbot of
Perseigne, King Richard's confessor, observed that nowadays
the road to advancement in the Church lay by way of legal
studies [2] ; and others remarked how the educational system
of the time was moving away from a liberal literary and
philosophical training to the narrow utilitarian discipline of
the law.   Master Mainerius, a Parisian teacher in the middle
of the twelfth century, had said that the prophecy of the
Sybil was fulfilled : ' the days shall come and woe to them
in whom laws will efface the knowledge of letters '.[3]

The law was all the more likely to be the avenue of promotion in the Church when prelates were expected to play
a leading part in civil affairs.   That raised a serious moral
problem.   St. Hugh of Lincoln may not have been the only
bishop to dislike the giving of canonries to courtiers and the
use of canons on diplomatic missions ; but few were so outspoken about it.[4]   St. Hugh did not take any different line
when the bishop's duties were in question, but his colleagues
on the bench did not all see eye to eye with him.   Was a

---

[1] ' Rise and progress of universities ', *Hist. sketches* (2nd ed., 1873),
i. 77.
[2] ' Videmus ad iurisperitos dignitates et bona transire ecclesiae ',
etc. *PL*, ccxi. 667. Cf. William of Malmesbury, *Gesta regum* (RS),
ii. 369 : ' Nullus clericus nisi causidicus.'
[3] Gerald of Wales, *Opp.*, ii. 349. Mainerius is apparently to be
identified with a ' iurisperitus ' who acted as judge in the court of
Louis VII.
[4] *Magna vita*, pp. 126, 260-3. Cf. Gratian, *Decretum*, 2, 11, 1, 47.

bishop justified in dividing his time between ecclesiastical and secular office ? Could he avoid doing so ?

The garrulous Cistercian, Caesarius of Heisterbach, writing early in the thirteenth century, has an anecdote about a clerk at Paris ' a few years ago ' who declared that he ' could believe anything rather than that a German bishop could ever be saved '.[1] When the novice in the dialogue asks why German bishops should be singled out, he is given the answer : ' Because almost all the bishops of Germany hold both swords, that is, the spiritual and the material ; and because they judge in cases of blood and wage war, they have to be more concerned with soldiers' wages than with souls' salvation.' Although in contemporary England bishops did not enjoy equal temporal state, the problem was essentially the same. When Becket refused, at the outset of his career as archbishop, to retain the post of king's chancellor, he was deciding an issue more crucial than any of those over which he and Henry quarrelled during the next few years.[2] This is a question to which I shall revert in lecture II.

The tensions in Church and society, of which I have spoken, are the more striking to a later historian because in one way and another, by design and by chance, new forces were starting to pull violently and produce new disequilibrium in one field of activity after another. With the increasing power of the pope came definitions in matters of dogma and discipline which were not to be lightly gainsaid. At the same time a growing monarchy made heavier demands upon the clergy as citizens, and re-created on a more permanent basis the direct antagonism of lay and clerical aims which Henry II and Becket had somewhat artificially stimulated. A civil service largely composed of clerics multiplied occasions for a conflict of loyalties.

These matters tempt one to speak of a crisis in the Church

[1] *Dialogus miraculorum*, i. 99.
[2] Ralph de Diceto is almost the only contemporary who, in noting the fact, enlarges on it ; he refers to the archbishop-archchancellors of the Empire (i. 307–8, cf. *MTB*, iii. 183).

towards the end of the twelfth century. Admittedly, there is always a crisis in the Church, just as every period of history is a period of transition. But the balance of forces changes, the forces themselves take on different shapes, and we do well to recognize, in studying this particular period, how the forces were disposed. Then we are more likely to see the characters in the story as living men, and not merely as the embodiment of good and evil principles.

II

THE BISHOPS

THE subject of this lecture is the bishops of England in the generation after Becket. Here to begin with is a contemporary's comment : ' I do not say that bishops cannot be saved ; but I do say that in these days it is harder for bishops than for other men to be saved.' One grows so tired of hearing John of Salisbury's doubts about the salvation of archdeacons that it is refreshing to find an archdeacon hitting back. The words are from the *Gemma ecclesiastica* of Gerald of Wales.[1] The office of a bishop in the Middle Ages—as at other times—exposed its holder to many dangers and temptations. These were pointed out with special emphasis by monks who, like St. Bernard, had sought the safety of the cloister and by certain seculars, like Gerald of Wales and Peter of Blois, who had not reached the episcopal bench. The bishop was a servant of the servants of God (for the title was not originally reserved for the pope alone [2]) and he was debtor for the souls of his flock ; but he was also a trustee of church property and a lord. You had only to read Gregory the Great to realize that saintliness without tact, and other-worldliness without what is nowadays styled managerial ability are sorry qualifications for one who has to rule a diocese or province of the Church. In other words, a bishop must have a head for business. Yet he must not let his spiritual fervour be damped. In the twelfth century the difficulty was all the greater since government was becoming more and more complex and required a high degree of professionalism. Kings were prone to make bishops their ministers and to treat bishoprics as rewards for civil servants. It was, of course, a very old

[1] *Opp.*, ii. 359.
[2] St. Wulfstan and St. Anselm used it. See L. Levillain, in *Le Moyen Age*, xl (1930), 5–7.

problem, which Gerald of Wales lays at the door of the
Emperor Constantine.[1]

How was the ideal bishop to be found ? The Gregorian
reformers of the eleventh and twelfth centuries replied : by
the process of canonical election by the cathedral chapter
—free election, subject always to examination of the elect
by higher ecclesiastical authority. Whether free elections
were best adapted to produce bishops able to resist the
temptations of office and involvement in civil affairs is a
nice but hypothetical point. In fact, England under the
first Angevin kings seldom saw an election conducted with
strict regard for the canons. Normally the king controlled
it. It was exceptional for a bishop-elect to get possession
of a see in England or Wales if Henry II or Richard or John
preferred another candidate.[2] The danger of this, as strict
churchmen saw it, was that the king would choose a prelate
solely for secular qualities. The suspicion was not wholly
justified. Henry II, according to William of Newburgh,[3]
made a tart comment on bishops of his time ' who embraced
the world with both arms '. Henry is said never to have
given bishoprics for money, and he took pride in the fact.[4]
Late in life he paid striking tribute to spiritual values by
promoting the Cistercian Baldwin to Worcester and the
Carthusian Hugh to Lincoln. In general, his appointments
were respectable, even when they were made with an eye
to the needs of the State. This is equally true of promotions made by royal influence in the twenty years after
Henry's death.[5]

[1] *Opp.*, ii. 360 and ' De invectionibus ', ed. W. S. Davies, *Y Cymmrodor*,
xxx (1920), 234.
[2] For a witty and scathing satire on the management of elections see
Nigel Wireker's ' Tractatus contra curiales et officiales clericos ' (*c.* 1194),
Anglo-Latin satirical poets (RS), i. 190–8.
[3] *Chron. reigns of Stephen*, etc., i. 281.
[4] Peter of Blois, ep. 10 (*Opera*, ed. J. A. Giles, i. 29) ; *Gesta Regis
Henrici secundi* (RS), i. 346.
[5] Cf. Stubbs on Richard I's bishops : ' It may be said of them all,
that however they came by their promotion, their use of it was wise and
pure.' *Epp. Cantuar.*, p. lxxxi. This is going too far in the case of William
Longchamp of Ely or of Savaric of Bath.

For that matter, cathedral chapters sometimes had in mind the figure their bishops would cut in the world ; and the pope, when he became involved in an appointment, usually recognized that bishops must be chosen who would work harmoniously with the lay power. Archbishop Thomas Becket assured Gilbert Foliot, bishop of Hereford, that clergy, king, archbishop, and pope were all agreed that Gilbert ought to be translated to London ' for the general profit of the kingdom and the church's need '.[1] So, in 1173, Alexander III's legates instructed the electors to the vacant sees in England : ' Choose such men that you honour God in all things and make useful provision for the salvation of your souls and the peace of the realm.' [2] They can hardly have been searching for another Becket. Pope Innocent III's instructions to his legate forty years later were even more explicit : ' Cause to be appointed . . . suitable clergy, who should be men not only distinguished by their life and learning, but also loyal to the king, profitable to the kingdom, and capable of giving counsel and help.' [3]

It was one thing for bishops to attend the councils of kings and to act as diplomatic agents—another thing for them to hold permanent office under the Crown. Bishops were, after all, included in the general prohibition to clerks in Holy Orders to concern themselves in any way with court-sentences involving death or mutilation.[4] Moreover, clerks in Holy Orders were to be discouraged from taking any posts which made them answerable to laymen. As early as 1143 an English church council had forbidden priests, deacons, and subdeacons to act as laymen's tax-gatherers or stewards (prepositi),[5] and in 1172 the pope's

---

[1] *MTB.*, v. 26. [2] R. de Diceto, i. 367.

[3] *SLI*, p. 166 (*PL*, ccxvi. 928). The legate Nicholas went too far in complaisance to the king.

[4] *Decretum*, 2,23,8,30, repeated in Council of Westminster (1175) c. 3 (Wilkins, i. 477).

[5] Wilkins, i. 418 (for date see H. Tillmann, *Die päpstl. Legaten in England bis zur Beendigung der Legation Gualas* (Bonn, 1926), p. 44, n. 1).

legates at Avranches forbade clerks (and Jews) to exercise
the jurisdiction of secular powers.[1] In accord with this
policy the pope, in the same year, 1172, demanded that
Hugh de Champfleury, bishop of Soissons, should vacate the
chancellorship of France, after holding the two offices together for the last thirteen years.[2] Then, in the Third
Lateran Council (1179), the pope decreed deposition from
office for all clergy who undertook the stewardship of manors
or secular jurisdiction under any princes or laymen (c. 12).
Sixty years later Robert Grosseteste put forward forcibly
and fully the supporting arguments in a letter to the archbishop of Canterbury.[3] But the fact that it was necessary
in the mid-thirteenth century to justify this principle suggests
that it had not generally been applied. In the intervening
period bishops had taken various views of the matter. They
continued to do so in Grosseteste's time.

An English bishop of the twelfth century had the temporal
responsibilities of his see, its lands and lordships, as well as
the pastoral care of his diocese. But to what extent he
became involved in civil government depended in a large
measure on the man himself. Contrary to a common impression, many seem to have attended the royal court only
at very rare intervals. Those bishops who previously held
office under the Crown might abandon it on promotion to
the bench. Thomas Becket, it will be recalled, had been
archdeacon of Canterbury and chancellor, and refused to
hold the chancellorship with the archbishopric. Geoffrey
Ridel, Becket's enemy and successor as archdeacon and
chancellor, did as much when he was made bishop of Ely
in 1173. Geoffrey Plantagenet gave up the see of Lincoln
when he became chancellor and gave up that office on
becoming archbishop of York. But these scruples did not
affect the next three chancellors, all of them bishops.

An incident of special interest for the contemporary
comment it aroused is the appointment by Henry II of four

---

[1] *Gesta Henrici*, i. 34.   [2] *PL*, cc. 790.
[3] *Epp. R. Grosseteste* (RS), pp. 205-34.

chief justices on 10 April 1179 : they included the three
bishops of Ely, Norwich, and Winchester, Geoffrey Ridel,
John of Oxford, Richard of Ilchester. Among the letters
of Peter of Blois is an epistle written in the name of Archbishop Richard of Canterbury to Pope Alexander III on the
subject of these appointments.[1] Detractors of the bishops
had been at work in the Curia, and this is a vigorous defence
of them, arguing not only that they are personally honour-
able men but that it is much to the Church's interest that they
should hold office. Whether or no this letter reached Rome
it shows that the archbishop of Canterbury believed in a
closer co-operation between the clergy and the Crown than
the official policy of Rome permitted. Archbishop Richard
of Dover, it should be remembered, on another occasion
received a stinging rebuke from Pope Alexander III for
confirming episcopal elections in the king's chamber : it is
in a famous decretal which opens with the words ' Qua
fronte '.[2] And Richard was accused by Gerald of Wales
of having lost by carelessness, not to say cowardice, all that
St. Thomas had gained.[3] We shall see other indications
that Richard of Dover was not a violent defender of the
liberties of the Church, though he was active in church
government.

Returning to the three bishop-justiciars of 1179 : the dean
of St. Paul's also justified the appointment of these bishops
as royal judges. He explains how the king, having been
let down by judges drawn from other classes, ' turned to
the sanctuary of God ', that is, chose bishops, hoping that
they, with the fear of God before them, deviating neither
to right nor left, would not oppress the poor in the courts
nor twist proceedings by taking bribes.[4] ' Therefore,' says
the dean, ' if the bishops have concerned themselves with

---

[1] Ep. 84, *Opp.* (ed. Giles), i. 252-5. Peter was at the Third Lateran
Council in March 1179. Its decrees cannot have been known in
England when the appointments were made. [2] *Decretals*, 2,28,25.
[3] *Opp.*, vii. 70 and ' De invectionibus ', *loc. cit.*, p. 197.
[4] For Henry II's difficulties in getting honest judges cf. Walter Map,
De nugis curialium, dist. 5, c. 7 (written in 1181).

secular affairs, contrary to canon law, and are indicted on
this account, let them earnestly plead against the rigour of
the law the king's importunity and pious intention and their
own performance, fit to please God and to be praised by
men ; and so the spirit of charity might lessen the offence
of this brotherly crime. They might often consider, however, the laudable conduct of Roger, of happy memory,
formerly bishop of Salisbury (Henry I's minister) who,
though moved by devotion of the same order, did not account
himself justiciar of the realm until this burden had been laid
upon him, in virtue of his obedience, by the Roman Church
and by successive archbishops of Canterbury, Anselm, Ralph,
and William '.[1]

Ralph de Diceto, the dean, was not alone in his attitude
to secular employment. For, with or without dispensation
(and none is recorded [2]), seventeen bishops, or about one-
third of the episcopate during this period, combined the
duties of bishop and royal judge. Maitland, in a famous
passage on those ' popish clergymen ' who converted our
English common law into an articulate system, declares :
' Henry (II)'s greatest, his most lasting triumph in the legal
field was this, that he made the prelates of the Church his
justices.' [3] If the Church claimed to soften and civilize
lay barbarity, this was surely also a triumph for the Church.
The bench of judges was improved by men who not only
had some knowledge of a more refined jurisprudence but
brought to their task a higher standard of Christian conduct.
That this is not an anachronistic way of looking at the

[1] R. de Diceto, i. 435. If this passage was written at the time, Ralph
was not yet dean ; he took office in 1180. The statement about Bishop
Roger is derived from William of Malmesbury.

[2] Did the judges only act after dispensation from the pope, as Mlle
Foreville thinks (L'église et la royauté, p. 475) ? Ralph knew nothing of
it and no contemporary reports it. Surely such a dispensation would
have been well publicized and would have rendered unnecessary Archbishop Richard's apologetic letter. Wireker, writing about 1194, implies that such ' indulgence ' was sometimes sought from the pope
(Anglo-Latin satirical poets, i. 219).

[3] F. Pollock and F. W. Maitland, Hist. of English law (2nd ed., Cambridge, 1898), i. 132, cf. 136.

matter, the dean of St. Paul's comments show. And perhaps this explains the inconsistencies in the writings of a man like Peter of Blois, who frequently touches on the subject.[1]

It explains, too, why the ecclesiastical authorities, and the pope himself, reiterate laws against the secular activities of the clergy but seek rarely to enforce the laws. The Cistercian Baldwin, archbishop of Canterbury, suspended Hugh Nonant from his bishopric of Coventry for holding the shrievalty of Warwickshire and Leicestershire.[2] But when Baldwin came to investigate Hugh's other misdeeds, he was content to entrust the enquiry to the bishops of London and Rochester who were acting at that very time as royal judges. We can cite only one instance of papal intervention in England and the story depends solely on one chronicler.[3] Roger of Howden says that Archbishop Hubert offered in 1196 to resign the justiciarship, on the ground that to rule both Church and State was more than he could manage. The chronicler tells how Hubert changed his mind and condemns his preoccupation with worldly office rather than the ministry.[4] Finally, Roger says, in 1198 Pope Innocent III received reports of Hubert's misdoings as justiciar and asked King Richard to dismiss him. If the request was

[1] Mr. Southern has remarked on Peter of Blois's changing moods (*The making of the middle ages* (1953), pp. 211–13). Cf. ep. 42 against bishops involving themselves in lay government and the retractation in ep. 150 (and cf. also ep. 84).

[2] R. de Diceto, ii. 77. The Pipe Rolls show that Hugh resigned this shrievalty, but again held these counties and Staffordshire in later years. The sheriff's office had peculiar dangers. Howden remarks when Archbishop Geoffrey bought the shrievalty of York (1194): ' he thus became the king's servant and placed himself in the king's power ' (*Chronica* (RS), iii. 241). Ecclesiastics were rarely sheriffs in this period : David the archdeacon, with William fitzRichard, in Beds. and Bucks. in 1170, and Richard Marsh, archdeacon of Northumberland, in Somerset and Dorset in 1212.

[3] Gerald of Wales hints at it (' De invectionibus ', *loc. cit.*, p. 97) and Gervase of Canterbury (i. 551) suggests that Innocent III was prejudiced against Hubert at the beginning of his pontificate. The chief difficulty in accepting the story is the silence of *Epp. Cantuar.*

[4] Hugh of Lincoln taxed Hubert with putting temporal profit first (*Magna vita*, p. 246).

made and acted upon, that was probably because it suited all parties. The pope is said to have asked the king at the same time not to admit Hubert or any other bishop or priest to secular office, and to have forbidden all prelates to take on secular offices (*seculares administrationes*). The injunctions were ignored in England. Never again, to our knowledge, did Innocent III take drastic action against any English prelate on this account. He was even indulgent to those who served the excommunicate King John during the Interdict. This may serve as a reminder that while the interesting questions of principle which we have been considering were under discussion, in any given case the deciding factor might be personal ambition or political interest.

Pastoral care, the duty to defend and enlarge the Church's possessions, the claims of royal government : to what extent were these needs reconciled and what sort of episcopal bench was the outcome of the attempt ? This is an exceedingly hard question. Contemporary comment is often obviously unfair or uncritical. Besides, fully half of the fifty-two bishops of the seventeen English sees received no notice, good or bad, in the contemporary writings which have come down to us ; and the dearth of administrative records of the Church from this period makes it impossible to say how efficiently most of these men conducted diocesan business. To judge them on the fragments that remain would be unjust. It is only when we get an exceptional record of an exceptional man, the *Magna vita* of Hugh of Lincoln, that we hear of a bishop confirming children, dedicating churches, ordaining clergy.[1] But while St. Hugh may have performed these tasks with rare devotion and decorum, we cannot assume that his episcopal colleagues were usually negligent.

A glance at their antecedents may help. No less than

---

[1] *Magna vita*, pp. 140–1, 315 ; Gerald of Wales, *Opp.*, vii. 94. For the dedication of a church by Bishop Eustace of Ely see *Sacrist rolls of Ely*, ed. F. R. Chapman (Cambridge, 1907), i. 114.

twenty-seven had been archdeacons, in England or across
the Channel. Eight had been deans, and two more dignitaries, of cathedral churches, seven had been monastic
prelates (though three of these had been long in office
before 1170 and none was appointed after 1191). In other
words, most of them had already borne the responsibility
of ecclesiastical office.

Among the promotions after Becket's death were eight
men who had been associated with Becket in their younger
days or had earned his displeasure as royal agents.[1] One
of the *eruditi* of his household, Gilbert Glanvill, became
bishop of Rochester in 1185 and survived till 1214.[2] William de Vere, bishop of Hereford from 1186 to 1198, had
been a chaplain of Archbishop Theobald.[3] Some twenty
of the forty-three men promoted during this period (1170–
1213) are known to have served the king in his household
or exchequer or on the judicial bench before they became
bishops. Family origins are often obscure. Most seem to
have belonged to Anglo-Norman families and most were
probably born and bred in England, even if they were partly
educated abroad. They present a more English look at the
end of the period than at the beginning. Among them was
a king's bastard, four or five sons of noble houses (Gloucester,
Bohun, Vere, Braose), three or four sons of bishops, two
bishops' nephews.

Judged by the standards of earlier generations, the conduct of these prelates in regard to the rule of celibacy was
good. None of those promoted after 1170 is known to have
had children. Richard, bishop of Winchester, may have
fathered Herbert and Richard Poore at an earlier stage in
his career, but this is far from certain. Geoffrey Ridel,
accused of incontinence, swore that he had not offended

---

[1] Robert Foliot, Gerard Pucelle, Hugh Nonant, Gilbert Glanvill,
Reginald fitzJocelin, John of Oxford, Geoffrey Ridel, Richard of Ilchester.

[2] His episcopate has been studied recently by John Moule, in an unpublished thesis (M.A., Manchester, 1954).

[3] For his family and career see G.E.C., *Complete peerage* (revised ed.),
x (1945), appendix pp. 114–15.

whilst in Holy Orders.[1]   Gerald of Wales made a scandalous
accusation against Hubert Walter and afterwards withdrew
it.[2]   On the other hand, the charges of perversion levelled
against Roger of Pont l'Évêque and William Longchamp
seem to be more than conventional abuse.[3]

Saints are rare in the annals of the English episcopate,
but this generation had its St. Hugh of Avalon at Lincoln,
who was not only a saint but an efficient diocesan into the
bargain.   Others, too, left a reputation for virtuous living
behind them—Baldwin of Canterbury, Richard of Winchester, John of Worcester (whose body lay long uncor-
rupted), and Richard of London.[4]   Archbishop Baldwin
was also a theologian of some merit and a famous preacher.
A few of his contemporaries were learned men, notably
Bartholomew of Exeter and Gerard Pucelle of Coventry.
But bishops were not being appointed for academic attain-
ments.   The evidence, such as it is, shows them most clearly
as men with knowledge of the world, and legal and administrative training.   If we are to speak of the books they
wrote, beside Baldwin ' On the Sacrament of the altar ' and
William de Vere ' On the life and miracles of St. Osyth '
must be set Richard Fitz Neal ' On the Exchequer ' (although this was written before Richard became bishop of
London).   If the households of these busy administrators
hummed with the disputation of scholars, the disputes (we
may guess) were on nice legal points—between Master
Vacarius and Master Columbus at York, and between
Master Honorius and Master John of Tynemouth at Canterbury.   Literary debates were probably less frequent.   Yet
the old tradition of episcopal patronage of letters was not
dead.   Some bishops' households sheltered men of letters.

---

[1] R. de Diceto, i. 392.
[2] ' De invectionibus ', *loc. cit.*, p. 118, and *Opp.*, i. 426.
[3] John of Salisbury, ep. 305 (*Opera*, ed. J. A. Giles, ii. 261 ; *MTB*, vii.
528–9) ; *Gesta Henrici*, ii. 217, 219 ; Gerald of Wales, *Opp.*, iv. 418,
423 ; *PL*, ccxi. 626.
[4] *Annales monastici* (RS), ii. 70, 245–6, iv. 389 ; Gerald of Wales,
Opp., iv. 38 ; R. de Diceto, i. 415.

Peter of Blois was chancellor to Archbishop Richard. Baldwin's nephew Joseph of Exeter found a place in his uncle's *familia* and dedicated to him his poem ' On the Trojan War '.[1] Gerald of Wales had Baldwin as a patron, and also William Longchamp.[2] Peter of Cornwall, prior of Holy Trinity, Aldgate, dedicated theological writings to his former fellow-student, Godfrey de Lucy, bishop of Winchester, and to Gilbert Glanvill, bishop of Rochester.[3] The evidence is not extensive, but it warns us against dividing the episcopate into mutually exclusive groups of selfish courtiers and pious scholars.

Bishops who had learnt to be business-like in the king's service put their experience to good use in the management of church affairs. To be sure, we cannot say that they always did so, for the records tell us too little about it. But we know something of John of Oxford as bishop of Norwich and Master Eustace as Bishop of Ely. They rose to their responsibilities, and it would be wrong to assume that other royal servants neglected their duty as prelates of the Church. It was, after all, a minority of bishops who were busy in civil government after their promotion. These men knew the law of the Church as well as the law of the State,[4] and even if they were not all like Gerard Pucelle or Gilbert Glanvill professional canonists, they surrounded themselves with *iurisperiti*. We have not, as we have for the bench in Becket's time, great collections of their own letters and their detractors' letters, to invite the composition of character-

---

[1] For Joseph see W. B. Sedgwick, in *Speculum*, v (1930), 49–76.

[2] Gerald of Wales, *Opp.*, vi, pp. xxxv–vi. Nigel Wireker dedicated his ' Speculum stultorum ' to William before the latter became bishop of Ely, and later addressed to Bishop William (for his good) the ' Tractatus contra curiales et officiales clericos '.

[3] R. W. Hunt, in *Studies in medieval history* presented to F. M. Powicke (Oxford, 1948), pp. 143–4, and J. Moule, *loc. cit.*, pp. 295–7.

[4] Celestine III, writing to the bishops of Winchester (Master Godfrey de Lucy) and Chichester (Seffrid II) about a papal provision, addresses them as ' vos, qui iuri sapientes estis et in talibus exercitati ' (H. Singer, *Neue Beiträge über die Dekretalensammlungen vor u. nach Bernhard von Pavia* (Sitzungsberichte der kais. Akad. der Wiss. in Wien, phil. -hist. Kl., Bd. 171 Abh. i (1913)), p. 240, cf. 155–6).

sketches; but such records as remain give the impression of sober men of affairs, men who had high standards of efficiency.

The diplomatic of their official acts shows a marked advance in what we may call chancery-practice during the last quarter of the twelfth century. The men who framed charters and notifications for English bishops in the middle of the twelfth century had no established usage as regarded size of parchment, style of writing, method of sealing. They are fumbling, often with borrowed phrases, towards fixed formulas; but they have not arrived. At the close of the century, by contrast, the charters show a common, business-like format, the writing is good, clerkly work, and the drafts-men begin to be consistent in their treatment of titles, corroborative clauses, and dates. A new form of confirm-ation-deed, the *inspeximus*, is evolved. To the same period belong the earliest surviving formularies and the first traces of a systematic *matricula* or register of the churches in an English diocese.[1] The clerks also compile surveys of the bishop's lands and services, and at Winchester, at least from 1208, they preserve a fair copy of the annual account-rolls of his estates. Evidence of this kind partially compensates for the want of full record of the bishop's activities. It confirms the view of this period as a time of bureaucratic development and definition.

Now, to sing the praises of bureaucracy is never easy. Somehow the subject is the very antidote to enthusiasm. In the twelfth century, as in the twentieth, men watched its growth with revulsion and fear. But moralists like John of Salisbury, satirists like Nigel Wireker, harped overmuch on the more mournful themes. If, as they declared, these bishops preferred the study of law to that of theology, if they did not reach Gerald's standard of latinity, so long as they read their Gratian they would absorb the right ideas about the priestly office and the pastoral care—largely, indeed, in the very words of the early Fathers. We should

---

[1] Cheney, *Eng. bishops' chanceries 1100–1250* (Manchester, 1950), pp. 45–98, 110–30.

remember that the *Decretum* could be described as a theological work.[1] So when the preambles to episcopal charters
speak of the *pastorale officium*, and *sollicitudo* or *utilitas ecclesiastica*, although these are but conventional expressions, they
are conventions deliberately chosen by the bishops' drafts-
men, expressive of a whole background of ideas.

Most of these bishops, as we have seen, had previous
experience of ecclesiastical office. Some had been educated
abroad, some had held preferment in France or Italy. All
were susceptible to the free intellectual intercourse of Latin
Christendom ; all were acquainted with the common European programme of moral and educational reform in the
clergy, and with the ideals and practice of the new international
religious Orders. Not one of them but was accustomed
to use as litigant the system of appeal to Rome, and many
were used as judges-delegate for the working of that system.

Stubbs saw the church history of Richard I's reign as
the record of a few great disputes at law :[2] the Canterbury
case, the St. Davids' case, the Glastonbury case, and so on.
It is well to remember that these disputes arose because
various able men wanted permanent settlements of big
questions. Some of the disputants showed more force of
character than charm, and their methods are not always
edifying to behold. But they raised matters which were of
importance for the government of the English Church, and
the matters were mostly settled once for all. Indiscriminate
condemnation by modern historians, who suggest that the
whole bench of bishops consisted of pliant royal clerks, men
of mediocre capacity, chiefly concerned with the king's
business, is too sweeping.[3] The evidence does not justify it.

So far we have been ranging over the whole period and

[1] See J. de Ghellinck, *Le mouvement théologique du xii⁰ siècle* (2nd ed.,
Bruges, 1948), and the references assembled by W. Ullmann, *The growth
of papal government in the Middle Ages* (1955), p. 366, n. 2.
[2] *Epp. Cantuar.*, p. vii.
[3] Severe judgments will be found in Foreville, *L'église et la royauté*,
p. 481, Knowles, *Monastic Order*, p. 318, and *Episcopal colleagues*,
pp. 155-6, Poole, *From Domesday Book to Magna Carta*, p. 222.

the whole episcopate. Let me for the rest of this lecture focus attention on one man, the third in the series of arch-bishops of Canterbury, Hubert Walter (1193–1205). He is not exactly typical of the bishops of his age. He was too big a man. But there is an exceptional amount of inform-ation about his activities, and they illustrate well the good and the bad, the strength and the weakness, of church government in his day. He deserves closer attention than has been paid to him.

Hubert Walter towers above his English contemporaries. He served three Angevin kings, he met and won the respect of Philip Augustus of France, Saladin, and Innocent III. A nephew of Ranulf Glanvill, the justiciar, he appears as a royal judge and baron of the Exchequer before having high preferment in the Church.[1] Royal influence procured for him the deanery of York in 1186 and the bishopric of Salisbury in 1189. He had the confidence of Richard I on the Third Crusade, where he was a warrior and a diplomat as well as an attentive pastor.[2] Then, in 1193, he became both primate of all England and justiciar. On 18 March 1195 Pope Celestine III made him papal legate throughout England,[3] and during the next few years Hubert wielded both swords, the spiritual and the material.[4] Apparently the strain of multifarious duties told upon his health at this time and it was on this pretext, whether or not he was actually moved by complaints from Innocent III,[5] that in July 1198 he resigned the justiciarship. His legatine

---

[1] He appears first at the granting of a royal charter in the king's chamber, 1182, with Ranulf Glanvill, and next at the making of a final concord at the exchequer, 1184 (Hist. MSS. Commission, *Wells MSS.*, i (1907), 21 and T. Madox, *Hist. and antiq. of the exchequer* (2nd ed., 1769), i. 215*d*).

[2] *Itinerarium . . . Regis Ricardi* (RS), p. 116.

[3] R. de Diceto, ii. 125–6.

[4] *Magna vita S. Hugonis* : ' Magnus ille vir, ut ipse veraciter perhibere solebat, utrumque sibi gladium commissum habebat.' Wireker had said much the same of William Longchamp : ' rex et sacerdos utroque accinctus gladio ' (*Anglo-Latin satirical poets*, i. 215).

[5] *Supra*, p. 25. The royal letter announcing Hubert's resignation is printed in Rymer's *Foedera* (Record Comm., 1816), I. i. 71.

authority had expired with Celestine III at the beginning
of the year. Now he could devote himself to the affairs of
the province of Canterbury. Nevertheless, the next months
were mostly spent in Normandy and France and when King
Richard I died of his wound at Châluz in Limousin the
primate took a leading part in securing the succession of
John, count of Mortain. On the day after John's coronation, the king made Hubert his chancellor and he held this
office for the last six years of his life. No one has ever
denied his services to the State for the space of at least
twenty years. It is unnecessary to enumerate them in
detail. ' He was the acknowledged custodian and expounder
of the law.' [1] Besides triumphs of diplomacy and concilia-
tion, besides notable improvisations to raise the king's ransom
and tap the wealth of the Jews, he left a permanent mark
upon all the business and offices of English government.
The emphatic words of Reginald Lane Poole in the Ford
lectures of 1911,[2] linking Hubert with the development of
the Public Records, has been amply supported by later
study. He is generally recognized to have been ' one of the
greatest of medieval administrators '.[3]

But how did his services to the State affect his conduct as
archbishop ? It certainly produced an anomalous situation.
As justiciar he taxes the clergy whereas the Church teaches
that the clerical order should not be forced to pay ; [4] as
justiciar he receives the king's instructions for organizing a
series of tournaments, a sport forbidden by the canons ; [5]
as justiciar, finally, he shows brutal disregard for the

[1] H. G. Richardson, in *Memoranda Roll 1 John* (P. R. Soc., n.s. 21, 1943),
p. lxxxix.

[2] *The exchequer in the twelfth century* (Oxford, 1912), pp. 186–9.

[3] V. H. Galbraith, *Studies in the public records* (1948), p. 126. The
best modern estimate of Hubert is probably Powicke's, in *Cambridge
Medieval History*, vi (1929), 215.

[4] Cf. A. L. Poole, *From Domesday Book to Magna Carta*, pp. 365–6.
The clergy afterwards obtained a statement from Richard I that their
contribution to his ransom was made 'ex mera liberalitate'.

[5] R. de Diceto, ii. pp. lxxx–lxxxi and N. Denholm-Young, ' The
tournament in the thirteenth century ', *Studies in med. hist.*, pres. to
F. M. Powicke, pp. 240–68.

sanctuary of church-precincts when in 1196 he orders the seizure of a London malcontent, William fitzOsbert, in the church of St. Mary Arches. Chancellor, he is responsible for the issue of writs of prohibition which interrupt suits in courts christian. While Hubert's enemies were quick to comment on these incidents, more friendly critics observed that the archbishop's duties, in court, exchequer, and chancery, left him too little time for ecclesiastical business. This must be true, and yet the scattered records of his pontificate add up to an impressive amount : in mere quantity more than those surviving from any archbishop of Canterbury before the days of Archbishop John Pecham. That simply proves that Hubert had an active office staff and that in his day ecclesiastical corporations set great store by the archbishop's confirmation of their rights and property. For charters of confirmation and *inspeximus* account for the majority of Hubert's *acta* and these imply no personal intervention by the archbishop. But the records also show Hubert or his officials performing almost all the other, more essential, duties of a prelate as conceived at that time.

He is not known to have preached sermons or to have bestowed the sacraments of confirmation and ordination which belong to a bishop's *potestas ordinis* ; [1] but these are all matters which are seldom mentioned in thirteenth-century sources. As for preaching, even if Gerald's gibes at his bad Latin prove nothing, there is the statement of the kinder Gervase of Canterbury that he was not eloquent. [2] On the other hand, he does his duty as supreme ecclesiastical judge of the province, personally giving judgment, acting as arbiter, delegating to local judges cases referred to him on appeal from the dioceses of his suffragans, intervening to

---

[1] He consecrated twelve English and Welsh bishops.

[2] Gerald, ' De invectionibus ', *loc. cit.*, pp. 100–2 ; Gervase, ii. 406, cf. 409. The Carthusian chronicler, favourable to Hubert, writes : ' quia ille venerabilis pater mediocriter literalis intelligencie scientia imbutus erat, viros sapientes et gnaros et totius facultatis ingenue scientia preditos contubernales habere consuevit ' (*BJRL,* xvi (1932), 503).

sequestrate vacant churches and to ordain vicarages. He conducts visitations in various religious houses by legatine or metropolitan authority. In 1195 he held a legatine council for the Northern province at York and in 1200 a provincial council at Westminster : and he took the opportunity on each occasion to issue canons for the control and edification of the clergy.

He was much involved in the later years of his life—between 1201 and 1203—in the canonization of two English saints.[1] The report of miracles at the tomb of Master Gilbert of Sempringham caused the archbishop to set on foot an enquiry.[2] This, besides involving a lot of correspondence for the archbishop, led him to head an investigation by papal authority at Sempringham, conducted solemnly after a three days' fast on 26 September 1202. He came again to Sempringham a year later with the pope's bull of canonization to perform the translation of St. Gilbert's body, on Sunday, 13 October 1202. Meanwhile, Hubert had been to Worcester on political business during Lent 1202 and there he had witnessed scenes of great religious exaltation before the tomb of Bishop Wulfstan, where miraculous cures were daily reported. Again, he paid a second visit to hold a formal enquiry, and Wulfstan was canonized on 21 April 1203. A pleasing account of the archbishop's visits and behaviour will be found in Dr. Darlington's edition of the *Vita Wulfstani* of William of Malmesbury.[3]

In these proceedings and in many others Hubert was the delegate of the pope. Besides the cases in which he acts as judge, papal letters show him concerned with imposing penance on the king, releasing Crusaders from vows, providing for clerks without benefice. There is, in short, so

---

[1] In March 1201 he attended the translation of St. Hildebert of Meaux at Gournai (D. Gurney, *Records of the house of Gournay* (1848), pp. 133-4).

[2] The surviving documents, which are of high interest, have been edited by Mlle Raymonde Foreville in *Un procès de canonisation à l'aube du xiiie siècle (1201-2) ; Le livre de S. Gilbert de Sempringham* (Paris, 1943).

[3] Camden 3rd series, vol. xl (1928), pp. 119-20, 149, 184.

much evidence of ecclesiastical activities that one would not suppose Hubert to have had a political care in the world. Incomplete though the records are, they entirely confirm the statements that Hubert was *industrius*.[1] Considering the double load he carried, he seems to have been amazingly business-like ; and not merely business-like, but genuinely zealous for the welfare of the Church.

It is instructive to see what impression Hubert left upon his opponents in two great lawsuits which he fought at Rome. As the defender of the metropolitan rights of Canterbury over Wales, he drew the fire of Gerald of Wales ; as the promoter of a collegiate church at Lambeth he fell foul of the monks of his cathedral church. In both cases he used his influence with the king and his powers as justiciar and chancellor to impede the process of canon law. He tried to apply his great wealth (derived in part, it must be feared, from his trafficking in wardships and the corrupt acceptance of gifts) [2] to influence his judges.[3] In neither case does he appear in an amiable light. Yet Gerald, when he came in his *Retractationes* to reconsider Hubert's character as soberly as Gerald could, is astonishingly moderate.[4] He was influenced, no doubt, by the consideration that none but a very able man could have beaten the archdeacon of Brecon so soundly : he respected Hubert as a successful adversary. He accuses him of being ambitious, vainglorious, greedy. But Hubert (he says) was also courageous, energetic, generous ; and Gerald allowed that he had curbed the tyranny of his royal masters, had brought peace and comfort to the people, high and low, had been a refuge in time of need against oppression by government. Here, surely, Hubert fulfilled his duty as archbishop of giving Christian

---

[1] Gervase of Canterbury, i. 517 ; William of Newburgh, in *Chron. reigns of Stephen*, etc., ii. 417.

[2] See the chronicle of Jocelin of Brakelond (ed. H. E. Butler, 1949), p. 123 ; *CRR*, iv. 62, 110 and vi. 271 ; *Memoranda Roll 1 John*, p. xxxix.

[3] *Epp. Cantuar.*, pp. 457, 484. But the Cistercian abbots in 1198 said he was incorruptible (*ibid.*, p. 424). See below, p. 68.

[4] *Opp.*, i. 426-7.

counsel to the king. The monks of Canterbury, too, lived in amity with Hubert once the storm about Lambeth had blown over.[1] They received gifts at his hands and wrote kindly of him after his death : ' By his efforts ', one said, ' the affairs of Church and State had been successfully conducted.'[2]

The judicious abbot of Coggeshall, who devotes much space to Hubert's deathbed—for the archbishop's happy ending fittingly conformed with his good life—knew of certain persons' visions, or rather dreams, of torments endured by Hubert after death.[3] These might be caused, he thought, by the archbishop's extreme avidity for land and revenues, money and honours. Hubert had lived magnificently, enriched the archbishopric enormously, and was a lavish host. Had he not aroused King John's anger in 1200 by celebrating Christmas at Canterbury with a pomp equal to the king's ? And had he not atoned for this at Easter following, by entertaining John and his queen at their second crown-wearing ?[4] But against this extravagance, Ralph of Coggeshall sets Hubert's humble and effusive welcome to monks : he would share with them his bedroom and the very straw off his bed. Ralph remembers thankfully how in 1200 Hubert intervened between the Cistercian abbots and the angry King John, and describes the scene in a passage which ranks with parts of William the Marshal's life for the vivid light it throws on the royal court and the

[1] Gerald suggests that there was no love lost between them in 1202 (*Opp.*, iii. 208), but this is not confirmed by Gervase of Canterbury (ii. 412, 413).

[2] Brit. Mus., Add. MS. 38686 fo. 4r : ' Mortuo enim, et ut pie credi debet ad celestia translato, pie memorie Huberto archiepiscopo, seculari sciencia plenius erudito, cuius industria negocia sacerdocii et regni prospere gerebantur. . . .' This occurs in an incomplete account of the exile of the monks and the translation of St. Thomas. Cf. Stubbs in Gervase of Canterbury, ii. p. xvii.

[3] Ralph of Coggeshall, *Chronicon anglicanum* (RS), pp. 159–60. Cf. the preceding note.

[4] Roger Wendover, in Matt. Paris, *Chronica maiora* (RS), ii. 475 ; R. de Diceto, ii. 172. Hubert paid for the king's Christmas festivities at Canterbury in 1203 (Wendover, *loc. cit.*, ii. 484).

king's behaviour.[1] He recalls also the archbishop's intention, frustrated by death, of founding a Cistercian abbey at
Wolverhampton.[2] To Hubert may be credited King John's
vow to endow a Cistercian house, eventually fulfilled with
the founding of Beaulieu Abbey in 1204.[3] Altogether, the
archbishop's relations with the Order were close, at least
from 1195, when he sought the confraternity of the General
Chapter.[4] In 1198 a group of Cistercian abbots wrote a
testimonial to the pope on behalf of Hubert, in which they
spoke of him as a pillar of the Church and a defender of
the weak.[5]

In his earlier days, Hubert seems to have been more
attracted to the Orders of canons. If so, this might well
be the fruits of his East Anglian upbringing and family
connexions. His friends and relations were among the chief
patrons of the regular canons in England.[6] Along with his
own endowment of the Premonstratensian abbey of West
Dereham in 1188 one could enumerate five more abbeys of
white canons founded by his relations ; and when in 1200
he had to give up his plan for a collegiate church at Lambeth,
the compromise provided for a house of Premonstratensian
canons to be established there.[7] Hubert is said also to have
instituted the Order of canons in the church of St. Thomas
at Acre,[8] presumably during the Third Crusade. After his

---

[1] R. de Coggeshall, pp. 159, 104–10.

[2] *Ibid.*, p. 160, cf. *Statuta capit. gen. ordinis Cisterciensis*, ed. J. M. Canivez,
i (Louvain, 1933), 285, 303.

[3] *SLI*, p. 38.

[4] *Statuta*, i. 187, cf. 259, and Knowles, *Monastic Order*, pp. 366–7.

[5] *Epp. Cantuar.*, p. 424.

[6] Ranulf Glanvill founded Butley, Richard de Lucy founded Lessness,
and William Marshal Cartmel. Cf. J. C. Dickinson, *The origins
of the Austin canons* (1950), p. 142. When Geoffrey fitzPeter founded the
Gilbertine priory of Shouldham, Hubert witnessed the foundation charter
(*Monasticon*, VI. ii. 975).

[7] For Hubert's connexions with the Premonstratensians see H. M.
Colvin, *The white canons in England* (Oxford, 1951), esp. p. 135. Gerald
of Wales (*Opp.*, iv. 143–5) speaks of the protection Hubert gave to a
poor Welsh Premonstratensian house (? Talley, Carmarthenshire)
against a covetous Cistercian neighbour (? Whitland or Strata Florida).

[8] *Annales monastici* (RS), iii. 126.

enthronization as archbishop, he adopted at the Austin priory of Merton the canonical habit, an outward sign of his religious intentions.[1] He seems also to have been accepted into confraternity by the Austin canons of S. Salvatore, Bologna.[2]

To patronize the religious Orders was, of course, the ' done thing' among the great administrative landed gentry to which Hubert belonged ; and any one of these items of evidence might be held to show no more than a display of munificence by a man who liked display—or at best a work of conventional piety, imposed upon him by the habits of his class and the claims of his office. The accumulation of details, however, suggests the possibility of a deeper conviction, all the more striking because opposed to much of Hubert's conduct.

Here is one last unexpected ray of light from a fragmentary chronicle of Witham Charterhouse.[3] Archbishop Hubert, it appears, was invited once by the prior to visit Witham on his way from Glastonbury. The prior wanted to soften the archbishop in connexion with a lawsuit that was pending. That job done, Hubert stayed to pray. The sight of the Carthusians' austere life and the stories of his clerks about one of the monks, Adam of Dryburgh, caused an access of religious emotion. When the archbishop attended Mass early next morning not only did he hand over on the spot a chasuble worth 60s. for the poorly-clad celebrant at the altar to wear ; he obtained a private interview with the holy man, Adam, made his confession to him,

---

[1] Wm. of Newburgh in *Chron. reigns of Stephen*, etc., i. 392. He did not, as Mr. Dickinson says (*op. cit.*, p. 254), take *vows*. His act may well have been conscious copying of Thomas Becket. A generation later Edmund Rich became associated with Merton.

[2] A. Allaria, ' English scholars at Bologna ', *Dublin Review*, 112 (1893), 80. This cannot be regarded as evidence that Hubert was a resident and a law-student at Bologna, as Mr. Richardson suggests (*Memo. Roll 1 John*, p. lxii), nor can the story which he cites from the *Gemma ecclesiastica* refer to Hubert.

[3] E. Margaret Thompson, *The Carthusian Order in England* (1930), pp. 74-6 and her ' A fragment of a Witham Charterhouse chronicle and Adam of Dryburgh ', *BJRL*, xvi (1932), 482-506.

D

and taking off his clothes like a little child of Christ (*tanquam
Christi puerulus*), received from him discipline with the rod.
Ever afterwards, so the Carthusian writes, Hubert showed
the prior of Witham special reverence and consideration.
When the archbishop was crossing the sea on affairs of State
and the prior of Witham was going to the General Chapter
of his Order, the archbishop took him in his ship and during
the voyage sat apart with him where they might better
engage in prayer, and solace each other with holy dis-
course. What would we not give to have the record of
those conversations !

This is the man whom Dom David Knowles describes as
' a politician, not a spiritual man ', of whom Dr. Sidney
Painter writes : ' Hubert Walter was thoroughly secular in
his interests.' [1] I cannot but think these statements misleading. Hubert, as he is reflected in the chronicles and
records, shows nothing of the mystic, no power as a theologian, no intellectual refinement of an academic sort. He
has suffered by comparison with those who came before and
after him in the see of Canterbury. The Cistercian Baldwin, despite his defects of temperament, was a learned and
pious man, Langton an academic theologian of high repute.
But in judging a man's quality one must take account of
the circumstances of his upbringing and the opportunities
and tasks of his time. Hubert was trained to be a civil
servant, Langton to be a scholar : the one climbing to the
primacy by steady promotion through ecclesiastical dignities, each regarded as the payment of a civil servant but
each carrying its own responsibilities, the other elevated
suddenly to be primate from the post of a Parisian teacher.
They naturally behaved differently. What is more, they
had different principles of conduct. Doubtless Hubert
looked at his ecclesiastical office through the spectacles of a
civil servant, doubtless that affected his view of his obligations as archbishop. But that does not mean that he was

---

[1] Knowles, *Monastic Order*, p. 334 ; Painter, *The reign of King John*
(Baltimore, 1949), p. 64, cf. 161.

unqualified to hold the office or sacrificed it to his civil duties. We may go further and assert that there is no evidence that Stephen Langton was any more zealous in performing his pastoral duties than was his predecessor.

Hubert was a man of splendid talents and great energy. Without any pretensions to saintliness, he did good work in many directions. He took measures to improve the discipline of the clergy ; he was an excellent steward of church property. If it be asked whether he neglected the government of the Church, the answer can only be that he accomplished much in the time he did devote to her service. He ruled her with dignity. He earned respect rather than affection, respect for ruthless efficiency and success, for statesmanship, for keeping the peace. But he can hardly have provided an inspiration to churchmen in England.

Did he surrender the Church's interests to the claims of the lay power ? That question touches the root-problem of his career and the anomalous position of bishops in twelfth-century society. I doubt whether the question can be answered. But this much can be said. Hubert knew his Angevin masters well and was flexible and firm enough to live with them.[1] He had the sort of qualities they understood and appreciated. On some important matters—for instance, the method of conducting ecclesiastical elections and the type of prelate needed—they may have held similar views. So he was able to hold *regnum* and *sacerdotium* in England in equilibrium while he lived. That in itself was a great service to the Church. Her government, as then constituted, required the service of sinners as well as of saints.

[1] See the revealing letter to King John over the trouble at St. Augustine's, Canterbury (William Thorne, in Roger Twysden, *Hist. anglic. scriptores decem* (1652), col. 1856) and the letter to King Richard about royal action at Christ Church (*Epp. Cantuar.*, pp. 445–6) ; and cf. the remarks of Ralph of Coggeshall (pp. 92–3) and Gervase of Canterbury (i. 544).

III

ENGLAND AND ROME

THIS lecture will be devoted to examining ways in which papal authority was exercised in England. The years from Alexander III's accession (1159) to the death of Innocent III were as important as any comparable period for the advancement of the theory and practice of papal government. To watch this, and to observe at the same time the reaction of Englishmen to a growing system of appeals, indulgences, and provisions—that is the task. I shall treat in this lecture of the law and its application, reserving so far as possible until the next lecture repercussions on the relations of Church and State in England.

First, to say something about the nature of canon law in this age. It is a commonplace that the law-books which mattered in the middle of the twelfth century were those which had grown out of the Gregorian reform movement of the eleventh century. They emphasized the judicial supremacy of Rome. A great majority of the texts which were first incorporated into the legal collections in and after the time of Pope Gregory VII were either papal letters or the decrees of papal synods.[1] Even when these texts did not explicitly stress the pope's authority, they reflected the ideas, the policy, of Rome. But we shall not understand how the law-books came into being, or how readily they were received, unless we look outside them. They did not represent simply the aims of certain ecclesiastical politicians;

---

[1] Z. N. Brooke gave an admirably clear sketch of this development in *The English Church and the papacy from the Conquest to the reign of John* (Cambridge, 1931), pp. 32–43. It is fully traced in vol. ii of the great *Histoire des collections canoniques en occident depuis les Fausses Décrétales jusqu'au Décret de Gratien* (1932) by Paul Fournier and Gabriel Le Bras : in this connexion see, for example, pp. 16–19, 155–63.

their evolution depended on broader currents of thought which were affecting the intellectual history of all Latin Christendom. Putting the matter in its simplest terms : the study of canon law was then and remained for long intimately connected with that of theology, and the two had techniques in common. The connexion has been traced with mastery by the late Fr. J. de Ghellinck,[1] and we shall have to revert to it more than once in these lectures. Its bearing upon the prevailing tone of the law-books is particularly evident in the discussions which arose over the nature of the Church. Here the Gregorian impulse to attribute to the pope the highest disciplinary power was greatly strengthened during the first half of the twelfth century by academic controversy. For even if theology seemed to be concerned with dogmas and the law with discipline, these presented two sides of the same problem. Any definition of the *corpus mysticum* which was the Church must lead inevitably to the question of how the unity of Christian society should be expressed. The circumstances of the time encouraged emphasis both on the directive power of the hierarchy and on the hierarchy's gradations. In Bernard of Clairvaux's *De consideratione* and in his letters are clear and firm statements of the unity of the Church under a head who, as Christ's vicar, enjoys a plenitude of power.[2]

The very methods of theological and canonistic enquiry turned people's attention to the powers of the bishop of Rome. For as scholars accumulated quantities of diverse and even opposing texts, the need became urgent to distinguish between ' authorities '. Pope Urban II declared in 1088 that the stricter decisions in the canons were not always to be applied, if the needs of the times or the quality

---

[1] In *Le mouvement théologique du xii* siècle (first published, 1914 ; 2nd ed., Bruges, etc., 1948). See also the extremely valuable chapter by M. Le Bras on ' Théologie et droit canon ', *op cit.*, ii. 314-52.

[2] De consid. ii. 8, 16 (*PL*, clxxxii. 752), and ep. 131 (*ibid.*, 287). The papal originals of Bernard's contrast between the pope's *plenitudo potestatis* and the *pars sollicitudinis* of other prelates may be seen in *Decretum*, 2,2,6,11 and 12 and 2,3,6,8.

of the persons required milder action.[1] Hence, as M. Le
Bras explains, came the notion that a normal rule of law
might or must be modified in certain circumstances, and this
produced the idea of *dispensation*, 'envisaged above all as a
means of resolving the conflicts of texts '.[2] The subject,
when treated by such writers as Ivo of Chartres or Bernard
of Clairvaux, seemed to be theological, but it plainly raised
a legal question : what authority was competent to dispense ? Late in the eleventh century some were already
inclined to invest the pope alone with the power of dispensation.

It is with these tendencies in mind that one must approach
the history of canon law in the Latin Church in the twelfth
century. It was Roman canon law. That is seen markedly
in the *Concordia discordantium canonum* or *Decretum* of Gratian
of Bologna (*c.* 1140). In the middle of the century this was
the most up-to-date law-book of the Church and it had the
greatest future. It was a guide to contemporary theology.
Its author ' was imbued with Roman doctrines and especially
with the principle of papal monarchy '.[3] In its papalistic
tendency it was not unaffected, maybe, by the civilians'
ideas of the authority of the *princeps*,[4] just as it owed to the
civil law its emphasis on the written legal process, the careful
ordo iudiciarius.

But the law of the Church, as set forth by Gratian in this
magisterial (but not authoritative) work, was not complete,
not fixed for ever in all its principles. The form of the
Decretum, like that of Peter Lombard's *Liber sententiarum*,
invited rather than terminated discussion. More orderly

---

[1] ' Multa ecclesiae principes pro tenore canonum districtius iudicant,
multa pro temporum necessitate patienter tolerant, multa pro
personarum qualitate moderanter dissimulant . . .' S. Loewenfeld,
Epp. pontificum romanorum ineditae (Leipzig, 1885), no. 126, p. 61. See a
later classic discussion of divergent canons by Innocent III in the case
of Mauger of Worcester, *Decretals*, 1,6,20 (*SLI*, pp. 17–21).

[2] Le Bras, *op. cit.*, ii. 337–8, 358. Cf. Ghellinck, *op. cit.*, pp. 488–9.

[3] Le Bras, *op. cit.*, ii. 360.

[4] F. W. Maitland, *Roman canon law in the Church of England* (1898), pp.
16–17. For an example of the papal use of *princeps* see *SLI*, p. 69.

administration discovered and created new legal problems, and certain canons went out of date when the theology on which they depended became unfashionable. Much new legal material was becoming available to lawyers during the pontificate of Alexander III and after. It included, besides glosses and *Summae* based on Gratian, new collections to supplement Gratian with modern pronouncements of the popes. Those pronouncements might be instructions or decisions upon particular lawsuits, which the pope or his delegates had heard, or the pope's answers to specific questions on points of law,[1] or the decrees of papal councils—and two General Councils were held by Alexander III, at Tours (1163) and at the Lateran (1179). The popes of this age did not often utter constitutions, of general force, without synodal backing, but they sometimes did so.[2]

It is still a puzzle to find how lawyers set about making the anthologies of this material which came into circulation between 1170 and 1210. More than fifty distinct varieties are known and none, before the year 1210, was an official compilation. Some of the collectors had access to the papal registers of letters; others probably formed or added to collections at the receiving end—in the provinces to which letters were directed; many simply picked and chose from their predecessors' work. All told, they accumulated more

---

[1] The former was a *rescriptum*, the latter a *decretalis epistola*, according to the usual parlance of the time (Stephen of Tournai, *Summa*, ed. J. F. von Schulte (Giessen, 1891), p. 3 ; cf. *Decretum*, 1,15,4 and 1,19,6). For a 'border-line' use of *rescriptum* see Bishop Roger of Worcester's letter to Alexander III (1166 × 1178) in *PUE*, iii. 374. In modern times the meanings of 'rescript' and 'decretal' are often reversed and often, as in the text above, 'decretal' is used to cover any papal letter which found its way into a law-book.

[2] Cf. W. Holtzmann, 'Die Dekretalen Gregors VIII', *MIÖG*, lviii (1950), 113–23. In the present century much patient study, largely by German scholars, has been and is being directed towards elucidating all this material. See S. Kuttner, *Repertorium der Kanonistik (1140–1234)* : *Prodromus corporis glossarum* i (Studi e Testi 71, Città del Vaticano, 1937), and the writings of Walther Holtzmann, especially ' Ueber eine Ausgabe der päpstl. Dekretalen des 12 Jahrhunderts', *Nachrichten der Akad. der Wiss. in Göttingen*, phil.-hist. Kl. 1945 (1946), pp. 15–36, and briefly in *Papal decretals rel. to the diocese of Lincoln* (Lincoln Rec. Soc., 1954), pp. ix–xvii.

than 1,000 letters of Innocent III's predecessors (713 came
from Alexander III), and the official compilation of Peter of
Benevento, *Compilatio tertia* as it was known, included 483
decretals of Innocent himself.[1] The fact that the collections before 1210 were unofficial meant that they conferred
no new authority on the letters they contained ; they
included some few forgeries ; their diffusion was casual.[2]
None the less, their contents were cited commonly in the
courts and were, like Gratian, the subject of gloss, com-
mentary, and debate by legal teachers. They were making
the common law of the Church.[3]

The greatest centre of legal studies was Bologna, the most
distinguished concourse of practitioners in the law was at
Rome ; but England took a large part in the development
and diffusion of the law. Some fifteen of the earliest
decretal-collections were put together in England in the
1180's and after.[4] Treatises on procedure and formularies
were prepared by Englishmen before the end of the century.
Men like Gerard Pucelle, who became bishop of Coventry
in 1183, and Richard de Morins, prior of Dunstable from
1202, represent successive generations of scholarly prelates
with solid continental grounding in canon law. Honorius,
archdeacon of Richmond, was well able to conduct his own

[1] Many decretals of Innocent III's first twelve years omitted from
Compilatio III are found in other collections.

[2] See the remarks of Stephen of Tournai (*PL*, ccxi. 517) and of Huguccio (cited by W. Ullmann, *Medieval papalism* (1949), p. 35 n. 5) and on
forgeries see *BJRL*, xxxv (1952), 30. Cf. *ibid.*, xxxi (1948), 299 :
Peter of Blois is uncertain whether a decretal is applicable in another
case.

[3] ' In causis quae summi pontificis iudicio deciduntur, et ordo iuris
et vigor aequitatis est subtiliter observandus ; cum in similibus casibus
caeteri teneantur similibus iudicare, nisi forte cum aliquid, causa neces-
sitatis et utilitatis inspecta, dispensative duxerit statuendum.' *Decretals*,
2,27,19 (*PL*, ccxv. 497). Peter of Blois, in the course of a
petition, cites ' decretalis que ab isto papa Innocentio transmissa est
domino H. Cant' archiepiscopo qui nunc sedet.' Hist. MSS. Comm.,
MSS. in various collections, i. 240.

[4] Some small collections such as Holtzmann's ' Wigorniensis altera '
and the decretals in Foliot's correspondence (' Belverensis ') may go
back to compilations made about 1175, but the inclusion of undated
letters makes this hard to prove.

and other people's cases at Rome between 1198 and 1202 : was he not probably the Master Honorius who wrote a *Summa decretalium quaestionum* some ten to twenty years before ? One need not dwell on the English contribution to the canonistic movement since Dr. Stephan Kuttner and Dr. Eleanor Rathbone have written so recently and so learnedly upon it.[1]

To describe the make-up of the law-books is to indicate the kind of contact set up between England and Rome in the sphere of justice.[2] From Maitland onwards, much has been said about the evolution of appeals to Rome. Great stress has been laid on the intense activity of the decade after the settlement at Avranches between Henry II and the pope's legates in 1172. The canonistic material which has been adduced to prove that recourse to Rome became much more frequent after 1172 cannot, for a variety of reasons, be treated as proof. For, in the first place, many decretals cannot be dated : in the little volume of Lincoln decretals are twenty-one of Alexander III, of which two certainly, and nine possibly, date from before 1172. Secondly, the collectors of decretals concentrated on the letters of Alexander III, and those who used the papal registers do not seem to have had access to the volume of his register for the years 1159–67.[3] Thirdly, the decretals contain only cases of legal importance : many mandates were of no interest to the canonist.

Another remarkable fact about this decretal-material emerges from the statistics prepared by Dr. Holtzmann. An absolute majority of the identifiable addressees belong

---

[1] ' Anglo-Norman canonists of the twelfth century ', *Traditio*, vii (1949–51), 279–358.

[2] For the following paragraphs cf. Mary Cheney, ' The compromise of Avranches of 1172 and the spread of canon law in England ', *EHR*, lvi (1941), 177–97.

[3] Holtzmann, ' Die Register Papst Alexanders III in den Händen der Kanonisten ', *Quellen u. Forschungen aus ital.Archiven u. Bibliotheken*, xxx (1940–1), p. 79.

to the Angevin Empire.[1]   What is the significance of this?
Is it that the Anglo-Norman Church, as some have thought,
was backward in learning the law?   Or, to quote a contrary opinion,[2] do the facts suggest 'that as the English
bishops were aware of the deficiencies of the canon law they
were in fact quite well versed in that law, and that they were
among the leaders of canonist opinion in Europe in their
effort to build up a more complete body of law by asking for
rulings and recording them for the benefit of posterity'.
The second seems the more plausible explanation.   But if
the Anglo-Norman collectors were the most active, their
selection of letters may have been weighted in favour of
letters to the Angevin empire.   And even if decretals and
rescripts sent to the Angevin empire were more numerous
(or if they merely had a better chance of survival) than those
sent to other regions, does this provide a measure of the
comparative number of appeals to Rome?   The problem,
if not insoluble, is as yet unsolved.

These problems apart, there are good general grounds for
supposing that cases of first instance, appeals from the
ordinary, and consultations by English judges, came in
increasing numbers to the Curia during the pontificate of
Alexander III, though the process may have slowed up
during the years of Thomas Becket's exile.

Long before this, the clergy of England had accepted the
principle that papal primacy made the pope the Universal
Ordinary ;   and the monks of Durham, appealing to
Eugenius III in 1153, conclude with a graceful reference to
his plenitude of power.[3]   As early as 1128 a lawsuit over the
boundaries of the dioceses of Llandaff and Hereford was in
progress at Rome ;[4] in 1139 the abbot of Evesham pleaded

---

[1] Holtzmann, 'Ueber eine Ausgabe', p. 34 and *Lincoln decretals*,
pp. xvi–xvii. Less exact, but equally suggestive, figures had been
worked out by Maitland and by Brooke.
[2] M. Cheney, *loc. cit.*, p. 187.
[3] *PUE*, iii. 226. They call him 'vicarius Petri'. Cf. John of
Salisbury to Pope Adrian IV, ep. 17 (*Opp.*, ed. Giles, i. 19) : ' de iure
legum et canonum et sanctae ecclesiae Romanae consuetudine, *vestigia
cuius ut iustum est Anglorum ecclesia imitatur*'.   [4] *EHR*, lvi. 178–9.

at Rome against Simon, bishop of Worcester ; [1] and a dispute over manors contested by the churches of York and St.
Peter's Gloucester raged for some time in local synods and
in the Roman Curia before it was settled in 1157 by two
bishops who acted as delegates of Adrian IV.[2] The early
letters of John of Salisbury show litigants appealing to Rome
on matters of no great importance. King Henry II, like
everyone else of his day, accepted appeals to Rome as
being in the order of things and never had any intention
of suppressing the practice.

Likewise, English bishops were seeking the pope's advice
to help them solve the legal problems which arose in synods
and consistories. In 1146, for instance, Jocelin of Salisbury
asked Pope Eugenius III whether a priest who had part
of his hand cut off by robbers might celebrate mass : the
answer came back, No. The florid preamble to the pope's
reply illustrates nicely the idea underlying the practice :
' Knowing as we do that, to those who ask, replies always
flow forth from the apostolic fount to the provinces, we
have thought fit to respond to your attentive consultation,
so that you may imbibe a rule, and obtain certainty in
matters of doubt, at the centre and origin of ecclesiastical
order.' [3] The lesson was generally learnt.

There were several reasons why, as the twelfth century
advanced, occasions should be multiplied for recourse to
Rome. Let me indicate a few : Gratian had done much
to digest for legal purposes the theology of his day relating
to the Church's sacraments, but this was still the subject of
animated debate in the schools and law-courts in the next
generations. Many matters remained obscure. In respect

---

[1] *Chron. abbatiae de Evesham* (RS), p. 99.

[2] *Hist. et cartularium mon. Gloucestriae* (RS), i. 19, ii. 105–7 ; Wilkins,
Concilia, i. 437. For another English case *temp.* Adrian IV see Coll.
Wigorn., vii. 73 (p. 144).

[3] S. Loewenfeld, *Epp. pontificum romanorum ineditae*, no. 199, p. 103.
The bishop had asked various questions which arose from the disorders
of civil war. For later preambles in the same vein cf. *Decretals*, 1,29,10
(Alex. III), 4,1,18 (Urban III) 4,1,23 (Innoc. III).

of both ordination and marriage the law was, one may say, in process of being hammered out afresh.[1] In these circumstances the ordinary, faced with a dubious ordination or a tricky marriage problem, might well feel that it was waste of time to deliver a judgment without first consulting Rome ; and if he did not take this precaution, a party to the suit might make an appeal at any stage in the proceedings. Not only bishops and archdeacons were concerned. Marriage cases lay within the spiritual jurisdiction of a great abbey like Bury St. Edmunds,[2] and Abbot Simon of St. Albans consulted Alexander III on a matrimonial question.[3]

If we turn from cases concerning the sacraments to lawsuits over property—whether land or tithes or patronage of churches—we face the central fact of twelfth-century ecclesiastical history in England : the fact that innumerable rights in these things were becoming the endowments of religious houses. Every grant was a potential cause of dispute, particularly when grants were not recorded at once (if at all) in writing,[4] or could not take effect at once,[5] or ran counter to the customary rights of feudal inheritance. Now, during the reign of Henry I—so Dom David Knowles has calculated —the number of religious houses in England doubled. And by the end of John's reign the number had doubled again. This enormously enlarged the chances of litigation in both lay and church courts.

---

[1] For the problems, which were theological as much as legal, see L. Saltet's classic *Les réordinations* (1907), pp. 290-360, and J. Dauvillier, *Le mariage dans le droit classique de l'église 1140-1314* (1933).

[2] *PUE*, iii. 514, 534. Cf. *Chron. abb. de Evesham*, p. 136. For the employment of Abbot Samson as judge-delegate of the pope see Jocelin of Brakelond's *Chronicle* (ed. H. E. Butler), pp. 33-4.

[3] *Decretals*, 4,7,1.

[4] V. H. Galbraith, ' Monastic foundation charters of the xi and xii centuries ', *Cambridge Hist. Journal*, iv (1934), 205-22. Cf. F. M. Stenton, *Documents . . . of the Danelaw* (1920), p. lxxxix and *Transcripts . . . relating to Gilbertine houses* (Lincoln Rec. Soc. 18, 1922), pp. xvi-xvii.

[5] In 1198 the king's court considered a claim by Lewes Priory to the patronage of a newly vacated church. A jury testified that the last parson was presented *temp*. King Stephen (*Rotuli curiae regis* (Record Comm., 1835), i. 141).

In another way the monastic growth tended more directly to disputes which had to be referred to Rome. Old-established houses sought new privileges, or falsified old ones, or put a new construction on their terms, and then claimed to be exempt from the jurisdiction of the ordinary. The new Orders of Cîteaux and Prémontré and the Military Orders, too, obtained exemption for all their houses. This meant that disputes between the exempt houses and jealous diocesans went to Rome in the first instance.

These general considerations pointing to an increase of English business in the Curia are confirmed by the history of the papal chancery. It is becoming more specialized ; the format of its products is more standardized, its formulas take permanent shape. About the end of the twelfth century were made new regulations governing the scribal work. Innocent III, as one of his first acts, introduced a fixed scale of fees, and reorganized the registration of letters a few years later.[1]

How did the system work ? The evidence on which an answer must be given exposes in a strong light the defects and abuses. We are inevitably led to concentrate more upon protracted appeals than on the pope's responses to consultations. We must be on guard against facile moralizing and anachronistic views of what a judicial system in the twelfth century ought to have provided. It is easy to point to abuse of appeals, less easy to determine the proportion of cases in which Rome gave better justice than could be had in the courts of the ordinary or the metropolitan or the king. Besides the cases in which fraud or violence intervened to upset or delay the decision of the court or which were bedevilled by politics, there must have been countless cases in which the parties compromised or submitted to sentence without difficulty. The pope or judges of the

[1] H. Bresslau, *Handbuch der Urkundenlehre* (2nd ed., Leipzig, 1912–31), i. 329, n. 5 ; F. Kempf, *Die Register Innocenz III* (Miscellanea Hist. Pont. no. 18, Rome, 1945), pp. 123–5.

Curia, or even local judges acting on a carefully-worded commission from the pope, might conduct affairs with stricter regard for the *ordo iudiciarius* [1] than was usual in the synod or in other sessions of the diocesan. Local influences might altogether prevent justice from being done at home.[2] In theory, at least, the system had its advantages.

The papal Curia in the middle and latter parts of the twelfth century was, as befitted a final court of appeal, distinguished by its legal luminaries. Alexander III, Gregory VIII, and Innocent III were all lawyers and so were a good many cardinals. Moreover, just as cardinals begin systematically to sign papal privileges in the time of Innocent II (1130-43) and declare in this way their participation in the government and authority of the Roman Church,[3] so—from about this time onwards—major judicial cases are heard by the pope and cardinals in consistory rather than by the pope in his synod, a more numerous and miscellaneous gathering.[4] An early and extremely interesting and vivid witness to the practice is Abbot Hariulf of Oudenburg, who in 1141 came before Innocent II's consistory, ' where the lord pope sat in tribunal with cardinals at his right hand and Roman noblemen, with curled hair and robes of silk, stood or sat at his feet '.[5] In short, the court was already becoming more specialized, as was to happen in other courts, ecclesiastical and lay, during the next half-century.

It must have been an education for an English lawyer

---

[1] For an early use of the term (1131 × 1134) in an English letter relating to a delegated case, see *EHR*, lvi. 179, n. 1.

[2] So the Christ Church monks claimed in the Canterbury case (*Epp. Cantuar.*, pp. 314, 412, 414, 428) ; but the final composition arranged by English arbitrators seems to have been fair. Cf. John of Salisbury, epp. 6,16 (*Opp.*, ed. Giles, i,7,19) and Arnulf of Lisieux, ep. 132 (*Letters*, ed. Barlow, p. 200).

[3] Bresslau, *op. cit.*, ii. 55 and note 2.

[4] J. B. Sägmüller, *Die Thätigkeit u. Stellung der Cardinäle bis Papst Bonifaz VIII* (Freiburg, 1896), p. 46. In a general way the cardinalate had been steadily acquiring importance since the middle of the eleventh century : cf. W. Ullmann, *The growth of papal government*, pp. 320-5.

[5] *Neues Archiv*, xlviii (1930), 102. Innocent III's consistories, held thrice weekly, are described in *Gesta Innocentii III* (*PL*, ccxiv, col. lxxxi), cf. H. Tillmann, *Papst Innocenz III* (Bonn, 1954), pp. 49-52.

in those days to go to Rome. When the pope delivered judgment in person he commonly discussed the case and enunciated legal principles. When he sent an order to judges-delegate, he would sometimes deliver a little lecture, like that upon legal prescription sent to Bartholomew of Exeter and his colleagues in 1172,[1] or would provide an *expressa forma*, or would give pointers to the judges on the way to proceed.[2] Alexander III, commissioning Roger of Worcester to hear a case between the monks of Durham and St. Albans, adds the caution : ' Be careful to see that Durham enters the case with the bishop's consent '.[3]

As an example of the way in which English prelates consulted the pope, one may cite a decretal of Alexander III to the bishop of Winchester : [4] it answers eight questions relating to the powers of subdelegation possessed by judges-delegate, the procedure when two commissions have been issued in one case, the circumstances in which witnesses are to be excluded, the effect of an appeal about an incidental question on the course of a case before delegates, the power of the delegate to execute his sentence if the diocesan neglects to do so, a problem about church patronage, and the safeguarding of the vicar's portion in a church. The pope's letter begins : ' Although we are involved in a multiplicity of affairs, and occupied with many serious cares yet, besides our general duty, the love and affection which we bear you, brother, obliges us to reply to your enquiries, lest we should leave unsettled those problems which you have wished to refer to us for solution.' With just such a preamble as this, Innocent III sat down in December 1204 to reply to Eustace,

---

[1] *PUE*, iii. 326. The pope quotes the authority of St. Gregory ' que magna est in ecclesia dei '.

[2] E.g., *PUE*, iii. 334-5, cf. 341 ; *Monasticon*, iv. 221 ; and the case of William fitzGodric, below. For the danger of using an *expressa forma*, seeming to bind the delegates in a case where there had been misrepresentation, see ACL, vii. 13 (JL 13950), Alex. III to the bishop of Hereford.

[3] *Decretals*, 2,1,9. Cf. Innocent III on the legal status of the bishop of Durham as abbot of his monks, *PL*, ccxiv. 432.

[4] ACL, vii. 8-10, viii. 6, x. 31, xv. 6, xxxix. 2. It is complete in Coll. Wigorn. vi. 2 (p. 123, cf. p. 76).

bishop of Ely, who had asked for enlightenment on eighteen
distinct points of law on a wide range of topics.[1] This
famous letter, ' Pastoralis officii diligentia ', was at once
widely diffused and every part of it found its way into the
Decretals of Gregory IX.

Let us now approach more nearly the question, how did
the system work, by watching the course of a few lawsuits, so
far as the records permit. The first shall be a case recorded
with unusual detail from the last years of Archbishop Theobald and the first of Becket : the case of Richard of Anesty,
or Anstey, *versus* Mabel de Francheville.[2] This has been
quoted often enough to exhibit the practice of the per-
ambulatory royal court, less often for the light it throws on
ecclesiastical procedure.[3]

In 1158 Richard of Anstey tried to establish in the king's
court his claim to the estates of his uncle, William de Sackville. To do so he undertook to prove that Mabel de
Francheville, William's daughter, was not the legitimate
heir but a bastard. ' The court of that catholic prince King
Henry II ' (I quote John of Salisbury), ' decreed that the
case should be referred to the Church's investigation, where
the question of the marriage might be resolved according to
canon law, which the clergy understand and of which the
laity are ignorant.' So in January 1159 the suit came into
the court of Archbishop Theobald, before whom Bishop
Henry of Winchester testified that he had dissolved the
marriage between William and Mabel's mother twenty

---

[1] *SLI*, pp. 69–78 (*PL*, ccxv. 478–84).

[2] The surviving letters in the case are John of Salisbury, ep. 89
(*Opp.*, ed. Giles, i. 123–32) ; Rymer's *Foedera* (Record Comm. 1816),
I. i. 19 (JL 10662) ; Lena Voss, *Heinrich v. Blois* (Berlin, 1932), pp.
166–7 (*PUE*, ii. 294–5). Francis Palgrave, *The rise and progress of the
English commonwealth* (1832), ii, pp. v–xxvii, lxxv–lxxxvii, printed and
translated Richard's own account of the expenses of the cases in both
courts from P.R.O. Exch. K. R. Accounts various (E.101/505/1).

[3] Cf. Pollock and Maitland, *Hist. of Eng. law* (2nd ed.), i. 158–9.
The ecclesiastical side is brought out by Voss, *op. cit.*, pp. 141–4. Hubert
Hall gave a delightful but partly fanciful and anachronistic account of
the suit in *Court life under the Plantagenets* (1891), ch. vii.

years ago, on the strength of a decretal of Pope Innocent II.[1] But this was not enough. Richard of Anstey did much riding to and fro and 'kept his day' in the archbishop's court twenty times in less than two years. But he could not get his adversary into court and prove the case.

Aggrieved by the delays, he appealed to Rome, after going overseas to get the king's writ permitting him to do so. Then came the business of getting from Theobald's court a suitable statement of the case to forward to Rome. Richard had briefed the well-known Italian counsel, Master Ambrose, and Master Peter de Melide, a canon of Lincoln.[2] The draft letter supplied by the archbishop's chancery was re-drafted by them, only to be altered once more by the archbishop's clerks. It has survived, presumably in its final form, among the letters of John of Salisbury, who was confidential clerk to Archbishop Theobald at the time. Both parties sent their proctors to Rome. When they arrived there, they had not all the evidence and witnesses needed to settle the case. So, on 8 April 1161, Alexander III remitted the case to judges-delegate in England. Hilary, bishop of Chichester, a former clerk of the papal chancery, and Laurence, the business-like new abbot of Westminster, were deputed to summon the parties at fit place and season, to read and hear the arguments, and to take the evidence of witnesses, without allowing any appeal to obstruct them. They were then to decide as justice demanded within three months of receiving their commission. But the pope ordered that if, after the evidence was taken and before sentence was delivered, either party appealed to him, the judges were not

---

[1] This letter, quoted in a letter of Bishop Henry (Voss, p. 166), is also found in ACL vi. 31 (JL 8274).

[2] Ambrose was employed much by the abbey of St. Albans and Richard must have engaged him soon after he had visited the Curia in 1159–60 on the abbey's business (*Gesta abbatum S. Albani* (RS), i. 136–7, 144). Assuming identity with 'Master Ambrose of Watford', other traces of him occur in *Reg. antiquiss.*, ii. 15 ; *EYC*, ii. 33 ; *Decretals*, 3,34,3 ; Singer, *Dekretalensammlungen*, pp. 255, 286. Peter de Melide leaves traces in Lincoln records and was a papal judge-delegate in cases settled in 1179 and 1181 (W. Thorne, in Twysden, *Scriptores decem*, col. 1831 and *EYC*, viii. 164).

E

to proceed to give sentence but should send the whole dossier to him under seal.[1]   Failing such an appeal, the judges' sentence was final.   If either party failed to appear or withdrew from the case, the defaulter was to be excommunicated by apostolic authority.

Richard of Anstey came to Westminster on the day appointed (6 October 1161) with his counsel and friends and auxiliaries (*auxiliis*, an ambiguous term).   But the judges, being busy on royal affairs, kept everybody waiting three days.   At a second session, on 18 November 1161, Mabel de Francheville appealed to the presence of the holy father, and received the date, 16 October 1162, as the time-limit for prosecuting her appeal.[2]   Richard busied himself about gathering his evidence and obtained letters of recommendation to the pope and cardinals from several prominent churchmen—the archbishop of York, and the bishops of Durham and Lincoln—and sent off his clerks with it all to the pope.   Since Alexander III was now an exile from Italy, they only had to go as far as Tours.   There they spent over two months and eleven marks of silver before getting judgment delivered against Mabel, at Christmastide 1162.   Then they brought home to Richard the pope's letters announcing the decision : one for him, one for the archbishop (who was now Thomas Becket), and one for Richard de Lucy, the chief justice.   Unfortunately, the king was vexed because there was not a letter for him, and that cost Richard another fifty shillings in the expenses of a special messenger to Tours. But this was little enough in comparison with the total cost to Richard of the proceedings in courts christian, which he reckoned at £102 6s. 4d. with an extra £24 6s. 8d. in gifts, and £16 15s. 2d. in usury to the Jews, or about £143 in all.[3]

---

[1] For similar instructions in later cases cf. Loewenfeld, *Epp. pontificum*, nos. 348, 356 (1178 × 1183).

[2] The fixing of a date so near the allowable limit of twelve months suggests that Mabel wanted to delay a decision.   In 1160 Richard had proposed a term of less than four months.

[3] These totals are calculated from the original.   Palgrave's text has a very few errors and omissions.   Proceedings in the king's court, including gifts and usury, cost £127 15s. 9d.   In addition, 100 marks to

This case presents several features of interest. It is initiated by an enquiry from the king's court to the court christian. The appeal to Rome is made with the king's permission. The question of bastardy revives a previous judgment by Henry of Blois, bishop of Winchester, then papal legate, in a synod at London about 1141, in which the legate, acting on a directive from Rome, pronounced the marriage of William de Sackville with Mabel's mother to be null. Now this depended on the view taken of an earlier marriage of William *per verba de presenti* ; but even if the first contract were found to invalidate the second, the question still remained : was the child of a second, irregular marriage, contracted in good faith—a putative marriage— necessarily illegitimate ? [1] A nice point in the year 1159 when, as Mabel's counsel took care to point out, there was a princess of France who was the child of the divorced Queen Eleanor and other European notables whose legitimacy it would be indelicate to impugn. [2] And so, although a good many facts were in dispute which could only be ascertained in England, questions of marriage-law and legitimacy were raised to which the English church courts would find no cut-and-dried answers in the law-books. Pope Alexander III, the new pope, had not yet arrived at his final opinion about the indissolubility of marriage *per verba de presenti*, and the notion of a putative marriage with its consequences for the children, which was being newly thought out in the school of Peter Lombard, had not found its way into the law.

There was, then, every reason why Richard of Anstey,

the king and a gold mark to the queen (' queen's gold ') were presumably Richard's relief for the land he had won (cf. *P.R. 11 Henry II*, p. 18). He obtained judgment in July 1163.

[1] See A. Esmein, *Le mariage en droit canonique* (2nd ed., Paris, 1935), ii, 34-8, cf. Pollock and Maitland, *op. cit.*, ii. 375-7. Glanvill (*De legibus*, vii. 13) does not seem to admit of inheritance in the case of a putative marriage.

[2] John of Salisbury, ep. 89 (*Opp.*, i. 130). William de Sackville had held land of Theobald the Great, Count of Blois and Champagne (d. 1152), and counsel for the defendant declared that Theobald, on the advice of the bishops of France, had spoken in favour of Mabel's succession.

advised by professional lawyers, should appeal from Canterbury to Rome.   It could not, after all, be said that Theobald's court was providing swift justice.   But the pope cannot settle the matter without knowing the facts and so remits
the case to local judges of learning and repute.   Even so, he
leaves the door open to a second appeal to his presence and,
for a second time, the litigants' proctors make their way
overseas to plead before the pope.   This time a definitive
sentence is given.   The full account of Richard's expenses—
an unique record—enables us to fix the chronology of the
suit exactly.   It shows that almost precisely two years elapsed
from the lodging of the first appeal to the final settlement.

The case had gone tolerably smoothly, though prolonged
by the dilatoriness of Richard's opponent, and there were
doubtless others like it, where the ruling on some broken
marriage in England helped to determine the matrimonial
law of the Universal Church.   To take a case from the
northern province, recorded in the decretal-collections : it
came to a head in the 1170's.[1]

Many years before this, William fitzGodric, tenant of the
Warenne manor of Wakefield, had been espoused to a little
girl, the daughter of Albreda de Lisours—presumably her
daughter by her first husband, Richard fitzEustace, the
ancestor of the second house of Lascy.   But before the girl
came of marriageable age, she expressed her distaste at the
prospect of marrying William, and the archbishop of York
solemnly annulled their betrothal in full synod.   This was
in the lifetime of the girl's father, Richard fitzEustace, and
therefore before 1163.   Richard died and his widow,
Albreda de Lisours, married a second husband, William de
Clerfait, who died about 1168 and then, being in the ward-
ship of Henry II, she was married to William fitzGodric.[2]

[1] Decretals, 4,2,5. The parties are identified by the readings of
Coll. Wigorn., i. 37 ; cf. *EYC*, iii. 199, 336.   I am indebted to Mr.
Charles Clay for his comments on this case.
[2] William fitzGodric apparently fined with the king (?£100), perhaps
for this marriage, in 1169–70 (*P.R. 16 Henry II*, p. 39, *P.R. 22 Henry II*,
p. 102).

Only after Albreda had borne him children did the archbishop condemn this marriage on the ground that William
had formerly espoused her daughter (who by now had
married another man). But at William's instance, the
archbishop sent him to Rome to consult the pope.

Alexander III issued his instructions to Archbishop Roger.
He is to discover whether the girl was seven years old when
the betrothal took place. If she was not seven, and if the
betrothal had been annulled, then the second marriage may
stand. If she was seven years old, then it is not proper for
William to remain with (*habeat*) her mother. But, writes
the pope, in a passage later omitted from the *Decretals* of
Gregory IX, if it seems that the dispute between the two
families which this second union has healed would arise
again were the couple parted, you may overlook and tolerate
the alliance.[1] In either case, the children may legitimately
succeed to their parents' property, if the Church has once
recognized the marriage. This makes an advance to the
doctrine of putative marriage from the older standpoint
adopted in the Anstey-Francheville case.

Again, this case shows that where matters of fact were in
doubt, the pope could not but throw back the question to the
province. He acknowledges his difficulty with engaging
frankness. ' Cum autem ', says Alexander III, in a letter to
English judges-delegate in 1173, ' neutra pars super hiis que
proponebant fidem nobis facere posset . . .', the case is
referred to persons on the spot.[2] So also, when Hugh,
bishop of Lincoln, had heard some of the witnesses in the
case of the church of Tydd, one of the parties, Thorney
Abbey, appealed to Rome ; but Clement III, ' having
heard the mutual contradictions of the parties ', could make
nothing of the case and had to remit it to judges-delegate.
The terms of his commission, however, were based on a

---

[1] For dispensations ' pro bono pacis ', cf. a decretal attributed to
Nicholas I (*Decretals*, 4,2,2) which appears in Council of Westminster
(1175) c. 18 (Wilkins, i. 479), and a decretal of Alexander III (JL
14169).
[2] *PUE*, iii. 334.

misrepresentation of the case, so that a second commission, to a second trio of judges, became necessary a year later.[1]

We may choose as an example of a different sort a case terminated by Pope Alexander III shortly before 1169.[2] Herlewin, a clerk of Norfolk, had claimed right to tithes in Docking (Norfolk) which were in the possession of the Norman monastery of Ivry-la-Bataille (Eure). The dispute had already dragged on for some time when the pope issued a commission to the bishops of Winchester and London to settle it without possibility of appeal. The princely Henry of Blois and Gilbert Foliot were the two prelates who heard the dispute, in the midst of the troubles of Becket's exile. After hearing all the arguments on both sides the judges found that Herlewin failed to prove his case and they assigned the tithes to Ivry. They sent the written record of their sentence to the pope. But Herlewin appealed against it (notwithstanding the clause *appellatione remota* in the commission to the judges) on the ground that they had failed to deliver sentence within the time-limit imposed in the commission. He betook himself to the papal Curia which was then at Benevento, and the abbot of Ivry went thither in person to oppose him. The pope and cardinals heard Herlewin's appeal and ruled against him. They took into account, the pope says, that Herlewin had himself asked for the commission to include the clause *appellatione remota* and that the bishops (according to their report) had prolonged the hearing of the case with Herlewin's consent : so the bishops' judgment must stand.

The last example of an appeal is chosen from the cartulary of Winchcomb Abbey, concerning the parochial status of a church and the abbey's financial interest in it.[3] At some time before 1187 the abbey claimed and failed to get an annual payment of seven shillings for burial rights from Simon, clerk of Hailes. Whether the abbey first complained

---

[1] *PUE*, iii. 502-3 (4 Jan. 1188), 511-12 (15 March 1189).
[2] *PL*, cc. 512 and *Epp. G. Foliot* (ed. J. A. Giles, 1845), ii. 107-8.
[3] *Landboc sive registrum . . . de Winchelcumba*, ed. D. Royce (Exeter, 1903), ii. 301-2 (also in *PUE*, iii. 538), i. 66-7.

to the diocesan bishop is not certain ; [1] perhaps the first stage
was its appeal to Rome to have the case heard by judges-
delegate. Three judges (the priors of Canterbury, Worcester, and Lanthony) gave sentence against Simon, who
thereupon betook himself to Rome, concealed the fact that
the case had been already settled by papal authority, and
got a commission to fresh judges. He brought into question
not only the seven shillings, but also the tithes of two hides
of land which Winchcomb had long enjoyed. As was usual
in such circumstances, Simon had proposed the names of
judges-delegate, the abbots of Vaudey and Croxton and the
prior of Sempringham. When the abbot and monks of
Winchcomb were cited by these judges, they sent one of their
number whom the judges would not admit to have sufficient
authorization. Thereupon, the monk appealed to the pope
against the judges, as suspect persons, partial to the plaintiff,
and too far distant from Winchcomb. The commission to
the judges which Simon had fraudulently obtained did
indeed forbid an appeal, but it had been decided in other
cases that the clause *appellatione remota* did not bar an exception to suspect judges. [2] None the less, the judges did not
wait to hear the main issue discussed and condemned the
monks in absence.

It was now Winchcomb's turn to go to the Curia for the
second time, and they got (on 9 January 1193) a commission
to three other judges—this time, all secular clergy, the
bishop and dean of Hereford and Master Thomas of Lanthony. They were instructed to renew and enforce the first
sentence for Winchcomb, if Simon was proved to have
obtained the second mandate surreptitiously and if the
second sentence had been delivered after appeal. This
mandate may have limited the enquiry to the question of
possession : the case was only finally wound up a year or two
later by a fourth set of judges—the prior of Studley, the dean

---

[1] Bishop William (1186–90) was in some way concerned with the
dispute (*ibid.*, ii. 300).
[2] Cf. *Lincoln decretals*, p. 53 (JL 14966).

of Warwick, and Master William of Tonbridge.[1] These
decided the proprietary question in a definitive way, establishing the right of Winchcomb to the payments it claimed,
while recognizing the parochial rights of the church of
Hailes. The lawsuit had consumed at least seven years and
had been conducted entirely before English judges in England. Twelve judges had participated in the proceedings.

These cases suggest certain weaknesses in the system.
Let us analyse them and see what the papacy did to improve
matters. The most obvious disadvantage in the government
of the English Church from the Roman Curia was their distance apart. When, as for most of this period, the pope was
at Rome or south of Rome, the traveller from the Curia must
go over a thousand miles by road to reach the nearest
Channel port for England.[2] Ordinary traffic took seven or
more weeks over the journey. If your mission was extremely urgent and the times were propitious you might
manage to cover the ground between Rome and Canterbury
within a month : we know of one passenger who made the
journey in twenty-five days—averaging 43 miles a day.[3]
But that was exceptional.

Apart from delays by bad weather, other obstacles were
to be reckoned with. The intrepid young Samson, sent to
Alexander III in 1161 on business for his abbey of St.
Edmunds, disguised himself as a Scot and smuggled a letter
past the anti-pope's men. A clerk going to the Curia in
those days, he said, was liable to get his nose and lips slit
on the way.[4] In France, under Philip Augustus, English

[1] William was probably of the household of the bishops of Worcester,
and was a correspondent of Senatus, prior of Worcester.
[2] See L. Landon, *Itinerary of King Richard I* (P.R. Soc., n.s. 13, 1935),
pp. 184–91.
[3] R. L. Poole, *Studies in chronology and history* (Oxford, 1934), pp.
263–4. Gervase of Canterbury suggests that the letter of March 1188,
which took 29 days, according to Dr. Poole, took only 25 days to come
from Rome to Canterbury (Gervase, i. 423). In 1187 a letter dated
8 or 9 May at Verona was delivered to Archbishop Baldwin at Bredon
near Tewkesbury on 10 June (*Epp. Cantuar.*, pp. 34, 67).
[4] Jocelin of Brakelond, *Chronicle* (ed. H. E. Butler), pp. 48–9.

travellers were often in danger of molestation. The prior of Canterbury was arrested in 1193 [1] and Gerald of Wales, describing the seizure of Archbishop Hubert's envoys and his own arrest as a subject of King John, as they passed near Châtillon-sur-Seine in 1202, observes that travellers from English territory, whether they were pilgrims, clerks, or monks (save only the Cistercians), were treated as enemies of France because of the war between the kings. Gerald talked himself out of prison, but John of Tynemouth had to be ransomed. [2] Ten years later, three of King John's envoys to the Curia were captured and held at ransom in France. [3] This journeying along hazardous paths a thousand miles in length meant that an exchange of letters between England and Rome would take, given the most favourable circumstances, two months, and more often four months. The inevitable delay in transmitting orders made many of them meaningless by the time they reached their destination. It is with these shortcomings in mind that one must look at the law of the Church and the operation of her courts.

The worst feature of this was the door opened to frivolous appeals and frauds. A man threatened with disciplinary action by his ecclesiastical superior in England had only to appeal to Rome and he was removed out of reach of the local authority in respect of that offence for perhaps a twelve-month. As early as 1159 or 1160 the bishop of Salisbury told the pope that the appeal of Robert fitzWilliam, canon of Salisbury, against an order to perform his canonical residence, was nothing but a subterfuge. [4] Litigants in civil actions before the ordinary or judges-delegate, similarly resorted to what the popes called ' frustratory delays ' if they foresaw defeat. [5] The Anstey and the Winchcomb cases furnish examples. The clause *appellatione remota*, which was commonly put into commissions to judges-delegate, ordering them to hear and finish the case notwithstanding appeal, proved to be but a poor guarantee of finality. Even if the

---

[1] *MTB*, ii. 268.   [2] *Opp.*, iii. 291–6, 307.   [3] *SLI*, p. 131, n. 5.
[4] *Decretals*, 2,28,28.   [5] On frustratory appeals, cf. *SLI*, pp. 9, 73.

clause was not qualified by special conditions, you might still take exception to the judges, as the monk of Winchcomb did, or raise a side-issue and appeal on that,[1] or plead a privilege which gave access to the pope in such and such circumstances.[2] Examples of all these practices can be found in English cases of the late twelfth century. They knocked the bottom out of the clause *appellatione remota*.

Faced with the problem of frivolous, frustratory appeals, the popes could do little. A religious house might obtain, as Kenilworth obtained from Lucius III,[3] a letter to relieve them from answering claims to tithes and other property which were the subject of papal grants, but this safeguard could presumably be circumvented by impugning, on however frivolous grounds, the authenticity of the grants. Alexander III made it clear in the Third Lateran Council (c. 6) that the avenue by which genuine hard cases came to the Curia must not be closed ; and how could one separate the genuine from the false except by judicial enquiry ? Little could be done but make things unpleasant for the proved offender, by the fixing of a time-limit for appeals (as in the case of Robert fitzWilliam),[4] by condemnation in expenses of litigants who failed to appear on the appointed day ; [5] and finally, by stern measures against the positively dishonest. For while many appellants doubtless had faith in the justice of their case, and while some may have thought only of delay, with a vague hope that ' something would turn up ', others misrepresented their case in the Curia, obtained letters based on false information, or forged letters.[6]

[1] ACL, x. 31 (JL 14152).
[2] E.g. *PUE*, iii. 551 (*Gesta abb. S. Albani*, i. 502). An appeal from a subdelegate cancelled the jurisdiction of the delegate : ACL, vii. 1 (JL 13991). For reasonable causes of appeal see Tancred, *Ordo iudiciarius*, ed. F. Bergmann (Göttingen, 1842), p. 297.
[3] *PUE*, iii. 462–3, cf. *Decretals*, 2,30,1 and 2.
[4] Above, p. 63, cf. *PL*, cc. 929 (JL 12253, in *Epp. G. Foliot*, ii. 94–7, etc.), to the bishop of Norwich.
[5] Cf. Bishop Roger of Worcester's action (1166 × 1178) : *PUE*, iii. 372–4.
[6] On forged letters see *Decretals*, 5,20,2 and 4–8. Master Ralph of

It was open to any litigant *tacita veritate* to re-open a case that was closed.[1] Simon the clerk of Hailes had done so. Many years earlier Alexander III had to follow up a mandate to the bishop of Worcester and the abbot of Evesham to hear a case with a second letter in which he said that when the mandate was issued he was quite unmindful of the fact that the case was formerly committed to other judges, who claimed that they had settled the matter.[2] The same pope was prepared to relieve the abbey of St. Edmunds from ever having the archbishop of Canterbury as judge-delegate, but he would not guarantee that mandates would not be issued in future without regard to the fact.[3] In a general constitution of 9 March 1189 Clement III admitted that ' because we cannot keep everything in mind, cases formerly committed to certain judges are committed straightway on the petition of other persons to other judges ; and so commission is frustrated by commission and the Roman Curia incurs the charge of levity '.[4] Despite the fact that the papal chancery had for centuries enregistered letters, it did not usually enregister mandates to judges, and it had no index to the letters it had enregistered. Hence a welter of inconsistent privileges and commands. ' We do not believe we wrote so positively,' says Alexander III to the archbishop of Canterbury, ' and if we did it arose from our being overworked ; and in a letter of this sort this condition is to be understood even though it be not expressed : " if the petition is supported by the truth " '.[5]

Wigtoft, a clerk of Archbishop Geoffrey of York, when dying at Rome in 1196, confessed that he had procured many forged letters (Hoveden, iv. 15).

[1] For an early English case see *Decretals*, 1,36,6.
[2] Coll. Wigorn., vii. 43 (JL 14035) = ACL, xxxvi. 1 which reads ' Norwich ' for ' Worcester '.
[3] *PUE*, iii. 363–4, cf. 470.   [4] *MIÖG*, lviii (1950), 122.
[5] *Decretals*, 1,3,2. The civil law understood this sort of condition (*Code*, i, 23, 7) ; cf. *SLI*, p. 33. Where a second commission had been obtained surreptitiously, and made no mention of the first, the first-appointed judges were empowered to go ahead, according to Alexander III's letter on an English case (*Decretals*, 1,3,3). But in a response to the archbishop of York Alexander ruled that proceedings in such

Suggestio falsi probably played as big a part as suppression of the truth. How tempting it must have been to tell a good story at the Curia when the means of verifying the facts were more than a thousand miles away ! Distance, which we have treated as a disadvantage to the suitor, was good cover for fraud. And how could the pope know the geography of a distant province like England, so as to guard against committing a case to judges who lived eighty miles or more from the defendants, as did the judges whom Simon of Hailes obtained against Winchcomb ? After all, the reference books at the disposal of the Curia did not enable them to know whether or not a house was of the Cistercian Order,[1] or whether it was an abbey or a priory.[2] How could it be otherwise in the conditions of the twelfth century ? The pope could do little to counteract the misrepresentations of petitioners beyond hedging all grants and mandates with a variety of provisos (*si res ita se habet, inquisita veritate,* etc.) which perhaps encouraged litigation as often as they prevented it.

Clement III tried to impede mischief-mongers who obtained mandates to judges, supposedly at the request of another party, but in fact to use the mandates for blackmail or sale. To stop this, the pope declared that the Curia would entertain no petition after Easter Day 1190 unless it was corroborated with an authentic seal and contained the bearer's name.[3] This was a notable reform, if it was enforced. On the other hand little was done to keep better records.[4]

Long journeys and delay had a lot to do with the constant

---

cases should be held up until the pope was consulted (*Decretals*, 1,29,2, cf. Lohmann, Coll. Wigorn., pp. 137–8). All these decisions were available in the decretal-collections for judges to make their choice. For another English case, *temp.* Alex III, see Coll. Wigorn., vii. 73 (p. 145).

[1] *Decretals*, 1,3,6.   [2] *SLI*, p. 186.

[3] *MIÖG*, lviii (1950), 122 ; cf. IV Lateran Council c. 37.

[4] The period is indeed marked by the making of more than one ' Provinciale ' and of the ' Liber censuum ', but these only touched the fringe of the problem.

complaints of expense. But they did not account for all.
Expenses mounted because the ever-growing army of
officials in Church and State—growing in response to the
demand for more government and more professionalized
government—had to be maintained in a great measure on
the fees and presents of petitioners and litigants. Civil war
in Rome and long periods of schism had impoverished the
papacy and cardinalate ; Alexander III left his successors
a heavy burden of debt.[1] There is no trace of fixed sums
charged in his day for the official visitation of pope and
cardinals, or for the putting through of petitions and the
writing and engrossing and sealing of mandates in chancery.
Because fees were not fixed, the door lay wide open to
bribery and corruption. The cardinals lived expensively.
Moved by the news of the fall of Jerusalem in 1187, they
resolved, along with other pious intentions, not to take gifts
from those who had lawsuits in the Curia ; [2] but their fervour
did not last long. Pungent satirists and angry moralists
complained throughout the century of the need to pay all and
sundry if you went to Rome, and said it was useless to go
without the relics of St. Rufinus (red gold) and St. Albinus
(white silver). Unholy jokes were made about it.[3] To
preserve a sense of proportion we must remember that all
law-courts suffered from the same fault. Richard of Anstey's
bill of £71 15s. 5d. spent on two appeals to the Curia is not
excessive when compared with the £71 12s. 9d. he had spent
in the court of Canterbury before appealing or with the
£200 9s. 1d. which his activities in the king's court cost him.
Theobald's next two successors at Canterbury both had to
try to purify their courts.[4] Whether Rome was worse than
Canterbury or Westminster we cannot judge. The fact

---

[1] Cf. Wenck, in *Papsttum u. Kaisertum* (Festschrift für P. Kehr), p. 417,
and Fliche and Martin, *Hist. de l'Eglise*, ix. ii. 179–80.

[2] Peter of Blois, ep. 224 (*Opp.*, ed. Giles, ii. 190, *Gesta Henrici*, ii. 15)).

[3] R. W. Southern, *The making of the Middle Ages* (1953), pp. 152–4,
provides references to the literature.

[4] For Becket see *MTB*, iv. 265 and Gerald of Wales, *Opp.*, ii. 292.
For Richard's efforts see R. de Diceto, i. 436–7.

remains, however, that the outstretched palms at Rome corrupted litigants.

A few important English cases involving metropolitan or diocesan authority came to the court of Innocent III—the Evesham case, the case of St. Davids, and that of Lambeth. In each of these lawsuits the litigants were demoralized by their efforts to win over the Curia. The monks of Evesham joined forces with their villainous abbot and spent over £160 in presents to the pope and others, apart from counsel's fees, to win their case against Worcester.[1] The monks of Canterbury, battling first against Archbishop Baldwin and later against Hubert Walter, show an excess of jealousy, obstinacy, and insubordination which is only matched by the violence and illegal obstruction which the archbishops employed. The pope told King Richard that he would have given judgment for Hubert if he had been susceptible to bribes.[2] Alongside of this we may set the words of the prior of Christ Church to the subprior, describing the presents he has given : ' it would not be reasonable ', he writes, ' when we are ready to stake our souls in defence of our church, to be more sparing in the use of monetary bribes (*in corruptela pecuniae*) ' ;[3] and Prior Honorius was a godly man.   Archbishop Hubert said that his lawsuit against Gerald of Wales had cost him, besides the lives of good clerks and servants, 11,000 marks : the unreliable Gerald says that much of this went in bribes.[4] But the presents did not come from one party only : both sides in this case paved their way with what Gervase of Canterbury calls ' English ointments, gold and silver ', administered to the chancellor, the cardinals, and the *maiores in curia.*[5]

A case conducted by judges-delegate may have cost the

---

[1] *Chron. abb. de Evesham*, pp. 146, 153. The presents were given before the main case opened, and some of the recipients were scrupulous to discover that the giver had no suit actually in progress.   Long accounts of this sordid affair are given by G. G. Coulton, *Five centuries of religion*, ii (Cambridge, 1927), 347–78 and David Knowles, *The monastic Order in England*, pp. 331–45.

[2] *Epp. Cantuar.*, p. 484.   [3] *Ibid.*, p. 197, cf. 457–8.

[4] *Opp.*, iii. 264, 257, 263.   [5] *Ibid.*, i. 308–9 ; Gervase, i. 428.

litigants less than hearings in the Curia ; but the comparative charges of counsel in England and in Rome, the comparative venality of the judges and court servants, are matters which will always remain dubious. It does not appear that in this period a judge-delegate had any approved means of recovering the expenses in which his commission involved him ; presumably the bishop or monastic prelate or beneficed clerk who acted must regard this as a charge on his ecclesiastical revenues.

In these circumstances it is not surprising that prelates groaned under the burden of their responsibilities. Hugh of Lincoln complained, moreover, that this work distracted him from his proper pontifical duties : it was a cross he bore as a matter of obedience.[1] As early as 1141 the bishop of Laon had secured that he should not be involved in other lawsuits.[2] Towards the end of the century Lucius III (1185) promised not to call upon the abbot of Fountains : papal commissions had been a great expense and had brought upon the abbey the wrath of great men.[3] A year or two later the abbot of Osney obtained a like indult on the ground that these tasks distracted him too much from the business of his church. Early in the next century the Cistercians sought the indult for their whole Order, but a *démarche* made in the Curia in 1211 was fruitless.[4]

Fraud, expense, and delays were all in some measure due to pressure of business in an overworked papal court. Bureaucracy had not developed far enough to meet the needs

---

[1] *Magna vita S. Hugonis*, pp. 299–301.

[2] *Neues Archiv*, xlviii (1930), 112.

[3] *PUE*, iii. 470. The pope reserved the right to call on the abbot if it seemed specially desirable.

[4] *Ibid.*, iii. 495 (*Cartulary of Oseney* (Oxford Hist. Soc.), iii. 350). Grants of the kind were made to the Cistercians by Honorius III : see J. M. Canivez, ' Étonnantes concessions pontificales faites à Cîteaux ', *Miscellanea historica in honorem Alberti de Meyer* (Louvain, 1946), i. 505–9, who is unaware of the early cases. The later grants include the clause : ' Nisi forsan obtente ad vos littere de hac indulgentia expressam fecerint mentionem '. The abbot and prior of St. Osyth's (O.S.A.) got the indult in similar terms in 1221 (*Cal. of papal letters*, i (ed. W. H. Bliss, 1893), 81).

of government. That was one of the main roots of the trouble. One remedy was to check unwarranted appeals, and the popes from time to time made efforts in this direction.

One kind of appeal which Alexander III wished to discourage was that of a monk or canon, living under Rule, against the disciplinary action of his monastic superior. A year or two before the general injunction on the subject in the Third Lateran Council (c. 6) he approved [1] the method which the prior and convent of Bridlington had devised for curbing appeals : it was provided that any complaint of a canon against the prior must first be ventilated in chapter. If the canons could not settle the matter quietly, they should call in two or three arbitrators from neighbouring Augustinian houses. If that did not suffice, they should submit the case to their diocesan and only then, if necessary, appeal from his sentence to the Apostolic See. Here, in a single instance, we see an attempt to reduce appeals. There are other indications that the popes were prepared to back up the disciplinary authority of the diocesan over concubinary clerks and the sons of priests who succeeded to their fathers' benefices.[2] Innocent III struck at the right of such offenders to appeal in the Fourth Lateran Council (c. 7).

Not surprisingly, the most comprehensive attempt to reduce the pressure came from an experienced civil servant, Pope Gregory VIII. Albert de Morra, a cardinal of thirty years' standing and papal chancellor for the last nine years, became Pope Gregory VIII in October 1187. He was about eighty years old. A canonist and expert in *dictamen*, he had seen the office work of the Curia develop prodigiously throughout a generation and he knew its defects from the inside. He planned—not mainly the suppression of fraud, though this was present in his mind—but a measure which would relieve the Apostolic See of an intolerable burden of

[1] *PUE*, iii. 371-2.
[2] E.g. Lucius III to the bishop of Paris, 1184 (JL 14972) ; Innocent III to Exeter (*PL*, ccxiv. 1034) and to Winchester (*PL*, ccxv. 724, *SLI*, p. 82).

petty business which clogged the machine. The constitution which he addressed to all archbishops and bishops on 18 November 1187 [1] was designed to safeguard the pope lest he be impeded by the manifold onrush of contradictory claims and complaints, and to permit those who suffer injury to receive justice.

Gregory commanded the archbishops and bishops to disallow evasive appeals from their ordinary jurisdiction to the Curia in suits which involved property of less than twenty marks' value. They must, instead, appoint judges above suspicion within the limits of their own dioceses, and any appeal from them must go to the archbishop or primate. There are other clauses which would deserve to be mentioned if there were any evidence that the constitution took effect. But although it appears in eight of the early, unofficial decretal-collections, it was a dead letter. The pope provided that after the feast of the Purification 1188 the papal chancery would not grant a petition for judges-delegate in these petty cases unless the terms of the constitution were complied with. But the pope had died in December 1187 and too many interests were involved to permit root-and-branch reform.

Yet Gregory's constitution may have been responsible for some indults granted to monasteries in later years. The Austin canons of Kirkham got a letter from Clement III (1187 × 1191) which ordered archbishops and bishops to hear and judge pleas lodged by the canons against malefactors ; in pursuance of this Hugh, bishop of Durham, apparently gave sentence on two occasions. [2] A few years later, Celestine III, in appointing judges-delegate in a suit brought by Reading Abbey against Gilbert Martel, appears to constitute them as a standing commission to deal by apostolic authority with similar cases at the instance of

---

[1] *PL*, ccii. 1553-4. A better text is in *Papsturkunden in Frankreich*, neue Folge, Bd. 2, Normandie, ed. J. Ramackers (Abh. der Gesellsch. der Wiss. zu Göttingen, phil.-hist. Kl., 3 Folge nr. 21, Göttingen, 1937), 383-4 ; and cf. *MIÖG*, lviii (1950), 114.

[2] *PUE*, iii. 521-2.

F

Reading.[1] Comparable commissions were issued by Innocent III in 1198 for the French abbeys of St. Vaast at Arras
and St. Victor at Marseille. In the latter occurs the phrase :
' Because it is not easy for the aforesaid brethren to have
recourse to us each time they are injured . . .'[2]

According to Augustin Fliche,[3] Innocent III reacted
against the centralization of justice which had proceeded so
far in the twelfth century, and wished to leave litigation to
be settled by the local ordinary. But this idea seems to rest
on a confusion between civil and criminal types of case. In
matters affecting the morals of the clergy, Innocent, like his
immediate predecessors, encourages bishops to use their
canonical authority notwithstanding appeal : but that only
touched a small proportion of the cases which flooded the
Curia, and so far as can be seen Innocent's policy contributed
little to diminish the flood. The plenitude of power could
be brought home to the faithful most forcibly in the supreme
court. Innocent believed that God appointed him to be a
judge : ' judge of all men and judged by none '. Appeals
do not seem to have diminished in his day. Records are
known of nearly a hundred cases of first instance or appeal,
taken from England to Rome in the first ten years of his
pontificate. Probably the real total was greatly in excess of
this.

It is instructive to look at the outcome of some of these
cases. A not insignificant number are settled by compromise. Like the final concord of an English court, the agreement before judges-delegates, who have become arbitrators,
can usefully cut short a process before it has ruined both
parties ; and it may be more lasting than a judicial sentence.
What of the judicial sentences ? Did they generally justify
the toil and trouble ? Provincial ecclesiastics often spoke in

[1] *PUE*, iii. 581.
[2] *PL*, ccxiv. 141, 225. The expedient is reminiscent of the later
' conservators of privileges ', but there does not seem to be much evidence
of its use.
[3] A. Fliche and V. Martin, *Histoire de l'église*, x : La chrétienté
romaine (1950), pp. 147–56, especially pp. 148–9.

derogatory terms of the justice meted out in the Curia and in the courts of papal legates : these general statements, though they must be discounted, are not to be written off as worthless. The comments on particular lawsuits, though they may be biased, are instructive. In the St. Davids case, as Gerald of Wales describes it, the Curia does not appear in a favourable light. Gerald seems to expect the judgment to be determined by other than legal considerations.[1] The pope relied on Archbishop Hubert for organizing the Crusade in England and therefore could not afford to alienate him by promoting the archdeacon of Brecon ; whereas the cardinals were interested in raising the status of St. Davids since this would bring them profit.[2] But Gerald, it must be remembered, was the loser. Again, the judgment in the Evesham case was based on doctored documents, inadequately inspected, and if the exemption from the ordinary which was awarded to the abbey enhanced papal power and benefited Rome financially, here as elsewhere it was destructive of discipline.[3]

Then there is the evidence of the Canterbury case. Successive popes vacillated and contradicted each other, until in April 1198 the new young pope Innocent III took a firm line. But the firm line he took on this and on some other occasions had not needed profound legal science or a judicial investigation of the facts ; it simply indicated the determination of a very strong-willed, impatient man to have his absolute power recognized. He received an *ex parte* statement from the monks of Christ Church, Canterbury, that the archbishop had taken action after appeal. Refusing to hear the archbishop's clerks, without holding any enquiry

---

[1] Cf. John of Salisbury's remarks, a generation earlier : *MTB*, vi. 20, 364, vii. 528–9.

[2] *Opp.*, iii. 179, 270, 263.

[3] See David Knowles, *The monastic Order*, p. 344, for trenchant comment on the judicial system as revealed by this case. The so-called privilege of Pope Constantine, produced at the Curia, was a rank forgery ; a copy of it, although written as early as the eleventh century, is not genuine in form, whether or no some genuine document lay behind it (cf. *ibid.*, p. 576, n. 5).

into the facts, and in flagrant contradiction to the latest
decision of his predecessor Celestine III, which he did not
mention and may not have known, he immediately issued a
fierce mandate for the destruction of the chapel at Lambeth
and the revocation of all acts done since the monks appealed.[1]
The pope's account of the case in this letter was found to
have five false statements and two suppressions of fact.[2]   His
more considered judgment, delivered seven months later,
was hardly more equitable, though it showed more respect
for legal procedure.[3]   Two years later it was modified in a
great measure by the English arbitrators to whom the parties
submitted.

In this and other cases the principle of the civil and canon
laws that ' spoliatus ante omnia restituatur ' was applied in
such a way that an appellant who claimed to be deprived of
property or privilege by the ordinary was legally in a strong
position ; and his ordinary was in the wrong if he tried to
exercise ordinary jurisdiction, or took any action, after
appeal.   Contempt of court was one of the major judicial
problems of medieval government, both in Church and in
State.   The pope could not afford to ignore obstructions
which had been put in the way of appellants.   Consequently, his sentence was often determined by the fact that a
judge had failed to allow an appeal rather than by consideration of the main issue.   So it was in the Canterbury case, so
also in a judgment in April 1205 for the canons of Thur-
garton against Archbishop Geoffrey of York, and in a judgment in November 1205 for St. Augustine's, Canterbury,
against the archdeacon.[4]   The legal arguments on the main
issue are brushed aside,[5] and only the affront to papal
authority is considered.   There was danger that the judicial

---

[1] *Epp. Cantuar.*, p. 395, cf. pp. 371–2, 463.   [2] *Ibid.*, p. 425.
[3] *Ibid.*, pp. 459–65. He ordered the return of the *exennia* to the
monks, without entering into the rights of the case or its connexion
with the main issue. Cf. pp. 464, 467, 468.
[4] *PL*, ccxv. 611, 733.
[5] In the St. Augustine's case, the question of custody alone was
decided, ' proprietatis utriuslibet salvo iure '.

system would be maintained as a matter of principle, not for the benefits it conferred on deserving litigants. Innocent III told the prior of Canterbury in 1198 : ' We are sorry for your losses but we are more disturbed at the way in which we are flouted.' [1]

The drawbacks, abuses, and dangerous tendencies of this judicial system are evident. But that is no more than might be said of many judicial systems, especially in the Middle Ages. The reign of law was never established. What prevailed was the reign of lawyers, subject at times to force, bribery, and diplomatic pressure. We ought not on this account to condemn the system out of hand or to suppose that the same canon law could have taken shape in England without the directive force of Rome. Stubbs exaggerated —though not beyond all measure—when he spoke of the ' paralysis of discipline ' in the English Church produced by appeals at the end of the twelfth century.[2] The system, if not particularly successful, if not in its earlier stages of development inevitable, was by now well established. It might still have been reformed but it could not be checked. A backward step was inconceivable at this stage. For the justice administered in the Curia and through its delegates was only one sign of a pervasive papalism, which was coming to be expressed in many other ways besides.

Much of the litigation we have been considering would never have arisen if the pope had not been exercising his prerogative powers in other ways. Apart from cases which involved clerical discipline, or marriage, or the other sacraments of the Church, few suits can have proceeded far before one party (if not both) produced a papal privilege or indult to prove his case. So we are led, in considering the relations of England and Rome, to look at other manifestations of papal supremacy.

In this period, for the first time, the pope's authority over

---

[1] *Epp. Cantuar.*, p. 477 : ' De damnis vestris dolemus, sed magis de contemptu nostro confundimur.' [2] *Ibid.*, p. cxvii.

the English Church extended to control the filling of benefices. I have not now in mind his interest in episcopal elections, which so far arose chiefly in the exercise of judicial
power. But with Alexander III is discernible an interest in
lesser benefices and the filling of them by papal nominees.
This interest is associated, in many of the early papal mandates, with the obligation of the Apostolic See to look
after necessitous clerks.[1] Although papal expectatives
and provisions only attained their final forms and their
wide popularity in a later age, the pope was already
over-riding with his plenitude of power the rights of local
patrons.

Consider first expectatives. In the second half of the
twelfth century (and probably earlier) prelates and ecclesiastical corporations were sometimes induced to mortgage
their patronal rights by promising to an individual that they
would present him to the next church in their gift which
should fall vacant. It is easy to see that such promises or
expectative favours tended to corrupt practices. Talk of
dead men's shoes always has an unpleasant sound. Here
is an early English example which came to the notice of
the pope. Some time between 1173 and 1179, when the
vicarage of St. Mary-outside-the-abbey-gate fell vacant at
Gloucester, the abbey presented a suitable clerk to the bishop
for institution. One John of Coutances intervened to
oppose it. He produced a letter which stated that the abbot
of Gloucester granted him the church which should first fall
vacant in the abbey's gift. The other clerk appealed to
Rome. Alexander III informed his delegates that if John
of Coutances could produce no other title than the promise,

---

[1] This illustrates the intimate link between theology, canon law, and
the growth of papal power, for it depended on the new view taken of
' absolute ' ordination. It requires too long a discussion for a footnote :
the reader may consult Hermann Baier, *Päpstliche Provisionen für niedere
Pfründen bis zum Jahre 1304* (Münster, 1911), pp. 128–32 and V. Fuchs,
Der Ordinationstitel von seiner Entstehung bis auf Innozenz III (Bonn, 1930).
The popes eventually evolved a method of action in cases of ' absolute '
ordination which differed from the normal procedure of provision :
see *SLI*, pp. 35–6 and the references there given.

his case failed.[1] Such cases as this seem to have attracted
attention in England at this time ; for some canons included
in a twelfth-century legal collection and ascribed to Archbishop Richard of Canterbury, include the decree : ' Gifts
of churches and presentations of parsons made during the
lifetime of parsons are null.' [2] In the Third Lateran Council
(c. 8) the pope prohibited expectatives in general, observing
that they were forbidden by the laws of the Gentiles.[3]
Archbishop Hubert reiterated that prohibition for the province of Canterbury, in his Council of Westminster (c. 8)
in 1200.

But too many influences favoured a continuance of the
practice : the fear of overmighty neighbours, the wish to
stand well with a well-connected clerk, the need to recompense a servant without finding ready money. Monasteries
might be protected against themselves with papal indults
which excused them from honouring such obligations,[4] or
the patrons or their presentees might, as in the Gloucester
case, appeal to Rome. But the practice continued. About
1187 the bishop of Worcester held a charter granted to him
by the prior of Deerhurst, contrary to the decree, ' by which
the first of his churches to fall vacant was to be conferred on
one of the bishop's clerks '.[5] That such charters were not
uncommon in England is suggested by an ecclesiastical
formulary of about 1200 which has two forms of grant :
' De prima vacante ecclesia ' and ' Cum datur quid sub

[1] ACL, xlvii. 10 (JL 13952 : Compilatio II (3,7,2) ascribes the letter
to Lucius III (1181–5)). John was probably the nephew of Walter of
Coutances, who later became archdeacon of Oxford, dean of Rouen,
and (1196–8) bishop of Worcester.

[2] Wilkins, i. 475 : ' Donationes ecclesiarum et praesentationes personarum factae viventibus irritae sunt ', which is corrupt (cf. Decretals,
3,24,4). These canons perhaps preserve a draft prepared for the C. of
Westminster 1175 ; Dr. Zachary Brooke made this suggestion : it
seems preferable to the alternative offered in EHR, L (1935), 388.

[3] Cf. Code, 8,38 (de inutilibus stipulationibus), 4 and 2,3 (de pactis), 30.

[4] E.g., Decretals, 3,8,3 to archbishop of York, 1179 × 1181 ; JL 15594
to St. Augustine's, Canterbury, 1186 × 1187.

[5] Lincoln decretals, p. 54. For a later case see PL, ccxv. 1504–5 (Battle
Abbey, 1208).

specie prime vacantis '.[1] There are English instances early
in the thirteenth century of expectatives granted not only
by an abbey,[2] but by the king as custodian of ecclesiastical
property.[3]

Meanwhile, if papal canon law set itself against the practice, the popes were finding that it had its uses. Mgr. Guillaume Mollat has traced the evolution of expectative favours
in papal policy.[4] His earliest papal example takes the form
of a polite request from Adrian IV (1 November 1156 ×
1158) to the bishop of Paris to grant the king's chancellor,
Hugh de Champfleury, the next *personatus* or *honor* vacant
in his cathedral.[5] Within the next twenty years such
requests had multiplied greatly. Alexander III wrote in
1178 to the bishop of Tournai, asking him earnestly and
affectionately to give to a clerk, for whom the Emperor
Frederick had spoken to the pope, ' the first prebend to fall
vacant after those which you have promised at our instance.'[6]
As in judicial matters, the inadequacy of the papal chancery's
records led to difficulties. Incompatible expectatives were
issued. Alexander III (some time in the 1170's) granted to
two applicants letters which led them both to claim the next
archdeaconry to fall vacant in the church of Coventry.[7]

---

[1] MS. Lambeth 105 fo. 271v.

[2] *Cartulary of Eynsham Abbey* (Oxford Hist. Soc., 1907-8), i. 401-2
(1197 × 1208) ; cf. *litere deprecatorie* from King John to Evesham for a
clerk (1207 : *Rotuli litt. clausarum* (Record Comm., 1833), i. 84*b*).
When John was count of Mortain he used his influence with Darley
Abbey to get the living of Bolsover for his clerk, Master Alan (*Cart. of
Darley Abbey*, ed. R. R. Darlington (1945), ii. 627-9).

[3] *Rotuli chartarum* (Record Comm., 1837), p. 96*b* (Westminster, 1200) ;
Rot. lit. patentium (Record Comm., 1835), p. 80*b* (Lincoln, 1208) ; cf.
an interesting letter of 12 Aug. 1202, *ibid.*, p. 16*a*. For the story of a
fraud perpetrated by a royal clerk who held an expectative from Henry II
for a church in royal patronage, see Wireker, *Anglo-Latin satirical poets*,
i. 172.

[4] ' Les graces expectatives du xiie au xive siécle ', *Rev. d'hist. ecclésiastique*, xlii (1947), 81-102.

[5] Cf. above, p. 22.

[6] Loewenfeld, *Epp. pont.*, no. 278 ; cf. French cases in which the
pope's request was ignored and he wrote again peremptorily (*ibid.*,
nos. 303-5 and PL, cc. 592, 806).

[7] *Decretals*, 1,29,12.

Where Rome was concerned, requests had a way of hardening into commands. ' Summi pontificis voluntas decretum est,' wrote John of Salisbury to the bishop of Worcester (1158–60) concerning a request of the pope for a benefice.[1] When the pope wrote ' volumus et mandamus ', he meant to be obeyed.[2] In 1175 the abbey of St. Edmunds, through their messengers at Rome, asked to be relieved of the need to find benefices for certain persons on whose behalf the pope had written. But although, as Alexander III replied, he ' wished and desired to love and cherish the abbot and convent as his devoted and favourite children, and to spare them burdens ', he would not take ' no ' for an answer.[3]

The tendency of the popes to copy the bad examples of others in this matter is seen when Clement III's chancery drafts a new indult for the abbey of St. Benet of Holme on 21 February 1188.[4] It follows in the main an earlier letter, but adds a clause to prohibit expectatives in any shape or form ' unless made on the authority of a papal mandate '. Other evidence of papal expectatives addressed to England in our period is lacking ; but this proves nothing : records were unlikely to remain if the demand were not contested.[5] Expectatives continued, and in due course ceased to be simply requests or commands to a patron to confer the next vacant benefice and became reservations by the pope, the nominee to be instituted by apostolic authority. By the time of Pope Alexander IV the development had reached such a pitch that a church might be charged with more expectatives than the total number of its prebends, and the expectations of their holders were confounded by *non obstantibus*.

Innocent III may have been sparing in his grants of

[1] Ep. 23 (*Opp.*, i. 25).
[2] This is made abundantly clear by the evidence assembled by Baier, *op. cit.*, pp. 204–11.
[3] *PUE*, iii. 350.   [4] *Ibid.*, i. 536.
[5] For examples of obstruction see *PL*, ccxi. 381, 384, 385–6, and Mollat, *loc. cit.*, pp. 84–5.

expectatives and discouraged more consistently than his predecessors the granting of expectatives by patrons ; [1] but this did not mean that he repudiated the papal authority implicit in the practice.[2] Expectatives were but one form of provision, and provisions, in a rudimentary form, were not uncommon. We have not yet reached the stage at which the pope usually supersedes the patron by making a direct collation, although examples may be found by the time of Celestine III.[3] Instead, the pope tells the patron whom to present or collate. But the theory on which his action rests is the same doctrine of plenitude of power.[4]

The evidence for papal provisions in England before the death of Innocent III is various and not always easy to assess. The pope sometimes requests a benefice, specified or unspecified, for an individual clerk : Walter, a notary of Alexander III, obtained a benefice in the gift of St. Edmunds at the pope's request before 1169, and between 1175 and 1181 Alexander got a canonry of Lincoln for his nephew, Gentile.[5] Then, persons are found holding benefices or pensions at the order of the pope : for example, Master Virgil, who was instituted in the church of Meopham by Archbishop Richard at the request of Alexander III,[6] and held it for at least twenty years ; and Peter de Colonna, who was made a canon of Lincoln ' at the instance and petition ' of Innocent III.[7] The form of these records may sometimes conceal an expectative made good ; and

---

[1] Mollat, pp. 89–91.

[2] E.g., *PL*, ccxv. 20–1, 1021, ccxvi. 561, 570.

[3] See the case of Simon of Apulia, below, p. 82 and a case at Cambrai, *PL*, ccxiv. 116 (*Decretals*, 3, 8, 4). Innocent III threatened to collate, through his delegates, to a prebend at Hildesheim (1203), if his requests and commands were not obeyed (*PL*, ccxv. 19–20).

[4] *PL*, ccxiv. 116 (*Decretals*, 3,8,4).

[5] *PUE*, iii. 301–2 ; *Lincoln decretals*, pp. 50–1 (JL 12754).

[6] *Epp. Cantuar.*, p. xlviii, n. 1, 472, 513.

[7] *Reg. antiquiss.*, ii. 41–2. Cf. Powicke's remark about the papal letters on behalf of Peter of Corbeil's collation to a prebend and archdeaconry at York (*Henry III and the Lord Edward*, i. 274–5). It is hardly a wild conjecture that the pope had something to do with the getting of a prebend at York for Stephen Langton.

one cannot distinguish between the request and the command ; but the result was the same in all cases.

Another kind of evidence is rather more copious : Italians are found to be rectors of English churches, usually non-resident.[1] They are mostly nephews of popes or cardinals or are curial officials. Two nephews of Alexander III, one of Celestine III, one of Innocent III, are of the number. It would be wrong to assume that all these are examples of papal provision. The court of Rome was of such importance to Englishmen that patrons of benefices in England were glad to purchase friends at court. According to Gerald of Wales, English prelates regarded expenditure on ' cardinals and their nephews ' as a necessary part of their budget.[2] The king felt the same need. As soon as the chancery enrolments begin in King John's reign, the evidence is there of pensions and prebends granted to Italians. But when all allowance is made for patrons who had an eye to business, the fact remains that their freedom of action was becoming restricted by the pope's intervention.[3]

Religious houses had not only to anticipate encroachment on their rights of patronage. Already in Alexander III's time the pope might require a monastery to accept his nominee as monk. The bearer of his mandate to Fountains Abbey was apparently a penitent who had gone to Rome for absolution and had been recommended, if not ordered, by the pope to compensate for his excesses by entering religion. Here again, the pope was only assuming, by plenitude of power, a right often claimed by kings and bishops and other patrons of monasteries.[4]

---

[1] See Appendix I.   [2] *Opp.*, ii. 332.

[3] Nigel Wireker, writing about 1194, regards the obtaining of benefices ' ad petitionem summi pontificis ' and ' ad instantiam regis ' as equally evil. *Anglo-Latin satirical poets*, i. 171. Stubbs opined that all the Italians in English benefices at this period ' owed their promotion either to the king or to the bishops ' (*Const. hist.* (3rd ed.), iii. 320 § 384), whereas Baier (*op. cit.*, p. 16) attributed all such appointments to the pope. The truth lies between these views.

[4] *PUE*, iii. 401 ; cf. Innocent III to Leicester Abbey, to provide a corrody for a converted Jew (*PL*, ccxiv. 792). For the claims of kings and patrons in England see S. M. Wood, *English monasteries and their*

It would be unsafe to infer that these papal nominees were the cause of widespread resentment ; for, so far as can be judged in the absence of chancery enrolments before 1199 and of bishops' registers before 1217, the clerks and monks for whom provision was made by papal command were not very numerous. There were also plenty of non-resident rectors besides those who owed their benefices to the pope. His action mainly touched cathedral chapters and a few rich monasteries. He steered clear of lay patrons. So the grievance, if it was felt, was usually suffered in silence. Very few cases are recorded in which legal obstructions or violence kept a papal nominee out of his living.[1] The English clergy could not but accept the right of the pope to do these things even though that right was so newly propounded. When Celestine III had heard the disputants for the deanery of York, at Rome in 1194, the lord pope, says Roger of Howden, ' gave the deanery to Master Simon of Apulia, relying on his own power, the amplitude of which it is not lawful to question '.[2]

Papal doctrine was brought to bear in other ways on the discipline of the English Church : by indulgences, dispensations, exemption, reserved absolution, the canonization of saints. Indulgences, devised in the eleventh century, multiplied in the twelfth. Only the pope could grant a plenary indulgence and every grant demonstrated

---

patrons in the thirteenth century (Oxford, 1955), p. 112 and H. M. Colvin, *The white canons*, pp. 95, 163, 304–5, and for the Continent cf. U. Berlière, ' Le recrutement dans les monastères bénédictins aux xiiie et xive siècles ', *Mémoires de l'Acad. Royale de Belgique*, Cl. de lettres, etc., xviii, fasc. 6 (Brussels, 1924), 32–45.

[1] Appendix I and III (xii).

[2] Hoveden, iii. 230 : ' de cuius amplitudine disputare fas non est.' This is how it struck an English clerk. The pope's own letter is interesting for the cautious procedure it displays : ' electione canonicorum non quidem cassata, sed facta resignatione ipsius, quantum ad te, in manum nostram, decanatum eundem per investituram aurei annuli auctoritate apostolica tibi concessimus . . . ita tamen quod ex resignatione praescripta vel ex dicta collatione nostra nullum iuri capituli vel archiepiscopi . . . praeiudicium in posterum generetur ' (*Historians of the church of York* (RS), iii. 94).

the pope's unique authority. Again, the pope, as we have seen, could lawfully give dispensation from the law by his plenitude of power.[1] There had been dispensations in earlier days ; but in proportion to the insistence upon the pope's right to make laws grew the claim to dispense from their observance. In the twelfth century the practice attracted attention from critics of papal policy, but the claim was emphasized more strongly than ever by Innocent III. In his time it became established doctrine that the local ecclesiastical authorities had no power of dispensation where impediments of marriage were concerned : the right to dispense resided with the pope alone.[2] Again, while exemption from the jurisdiction of the ordinary was occasionally granted from the seventh century onwards, the twelfth century saw a tightening of the links which bound exempt monasteries to Rome and recurrent disputes between seven great English abbeys and their diocesans.

In the sphere of penitential discipline, the Second Lateran Council (1139) had published the decree ' Si quis suadente ', reserving certain offences for absolution by the pope. Other irregularities which induced excommunication were added in course of time.[3] Here was another reason for Englishmen to take the path to Rome. By the first years of Innocent III penitents and others seeking dispensations who crowded on the pope from all Christendom were enough to require the appointment of a Cardinal Penitentiary.[4] Along with the sinners came the saints—or rather the promoters of canonization with their evidences and their witnesses ; for with Innocent III it was finally settled that no one might be newly venerated as a saint

[1] PL, ccxiv. 116 (Decretals, 3,8,4) : ' Secundum plenitudinem potestatis de iure possumus supra ius dispensare.' Cf. above, p. 43.

[2] J. Dauvillier, Le mariage dans le droit classique de l'église, pp. 201–8.

[3] P. Hinschius, System des kath. Kirchenrechts, iv (Berlin, 1888), 102–4.

[4] Cf. Foreville in Fliche and Martin, Histoire de l'église, ix. 2. 240 and B. Rusch, Die Behörden u. Hofbeamten der päpstl. Kurie des 13 Jahrhunderts (Königsberg, 1936), pp. 39–46. Clement III and his successors allowed the bishop of Passau by special indult the right to absolve incendiaries (PL, ccxiv. 526).

whose case had not been examined and approved in a
solemn consistory of pope and cardinals.[1]

Most of these developments involved Englishmen in
journeys to the Curia. In the reverse direction came
legates *a latere* and nuncios. Only three legates *a latere*
were directed to England in this period : Hugh Pierleone
in 1175, John of Anagni in 1189, and John of Ferentino in
1206.[2] Though their visits were not without importance
they cannot be said to have had an extensive influence on
the English Church. In this period, too, the English clergy
first experienced the papal nuncio, bringing a request for
direct financial aid to the papacy. Nicholas the subdeacon
in 1173 secured large voluntary gifts from English prelates
for the indigent Alexander III,[3] and in 1184 the nuncios
of Lucius III repeated the process, but this time made their
approach through the king.[4] A tax imposed on the clergy
by the pope in 1199 for a Crusade was the first genuine
direct taxation of the English Church by Rome : to ex-
pedite it Master Philip, papal notary and subdeacon, toured
England, but its collection was left to English prelates.[5]
Serious papal taxation was still a thing of the future.

To conclude this survey of the relations of the English
Church with the centre of church government in Rome :
from Alexander III to Innocent III the canon law of the
Church, as declared and interpreted by the Curia, was
growing and changing. A study of the decretal-collections

[1] The evolution of the exclusive papal claim to canonize is well traced
by E. W. Kemp, *Canonization and authority in the western Church* (Oxford,
1948), pp. 82–106.

[2] See H. Tillmann, *Die päpstl. Legaten in England bis zur Beendigung der
Legation Gualas, 1218* (Bonn, 1926) ; on John of Ferentino see further
Cheney, ' The papal legate and English monasteries in 1206 ', *EHR*,
xlvi (1931), 443–52. The mission of Gerald, abbot of Casamari, in
1204 was purely political.

[3] R. de Diceto, i. 378–9, cf. W. E. Lunt, *Financial relations of the papacy
with England to 1327* (Cambridge, Mass., 1939), pp. 175–6.

[4] Lunt, *op. cit.*, pp. 176–7.

[5] Cheney, ' Master Philip the notary and the fortieth of 1199 ', *EHR*,
lxiii (1948), 342–50 ; *SLI*, p. 46.

shows that England provided a great deal of the judicial business which gave rise to decretals and that Englishmen played a large part in their collection. Rome attracted lawsuits from England increasingly during the pontificate of Alexander III. Although the next generation has left fewer records of lawsuits, it is by no means certain that the tempo diminished. Few cases lasted for fifteen years—as, with some intermissions, did the Canterbury case ; few can have called for so much correspondence : over 500 letters in the *dossier*. But the journeyings to and fro, the briefing of Italian lawyers, the courting of cardinals, the borrowing from Roman money-lenders, constituted an almost permanent bridge over the thousand miles which separated Rome from the English Channel. During the pontificates of Celestine III and Innocent III there seems to be a tendency for more major cases to be heard at Rome, either by the pope or by cardinals appointed *ad hoc* as auditors. This apparent centralization is matched by the limits set upon the legatine powers which archbishops of Canterbury obtained, until Hubert Walter's legateship lapsed with Celestine III's death. Innocent III and his successors in the thirteenth century issued no such commissions.[1]

Meanwhile, other matters besides lawsuits brought Englishmen to Rome. Every religious house sought privileges and indults from Rome and both the number of religious houses in England and the kinds of favour they sought increased. There are one hundred surviving papal bulls obtained by St. Albans between 1159 and 1197— five times as many as the older papal muniments of the abbey.

Not only religious houses, but individual petitioners, clerical and lay, besiege the Curia, desiring the Holy Father to exert his plenitude of power to get them benefices, or to grant them indulgences, or to release them from the consequences of some irregularity or other. As early as 1156

---

[1] Tillmann, *op. cit.*, pp. 30–6. For the later history of the archbishops' legatine title see I. J. Churchill, *Canterbury administration* (1933), i. 157–8.

a north-country gentleman, Askitillus de Ridale, obtains
confirmation of his Scottish estate of Lilliesleaf (Selkirk)
from Adrian IV.[1] In 1190 one Godwin of Chertsey goes
to Rome for confirmation of his tenement with which the
abbey of Chertsey has enfeoffed him.[2]

In 1206 Brother Augustine of Norton Priory in Cheshire
received comfortable words from Pope Innocent III. The
canon had feared that prayers said for his soul, after death,
would be misdirected since he had changed his name from
Henry to Augustine on entering religion. The pope
replied :[3] 'You can with confidence keep the name given
you at the time of your profession, just as we also unhesitat-
ingly keep the altered name which, by the will of God,
was bestowed on us when we undertook the office of apostolic servitude.'—The office of apostolic servitude ! That
finger extended from the Vicar of God to the Austin canon
on the banks of the Mersey is not merely quaint. It sym-
bolizes the pastoral obligations of the pope and the belief
of humble men in remote places that he is the holy father.
It should remind us that when men went to Rome they
went to the threshold of the Apostles. Gerald of Wales
devotes several chapters of the *Speculum ecclesiae* to a des-
cription of the chief churches of Rome, their dimensions,
and the relics they contained. Every man was a pilgrim,
even if he had his little temporal axe to grind. However
much we may approve, in their context, Maitland's incisive
words, ' The medieval church was a state ', political considerations alone will not explain the allegiance men gave
to the particular form of church government which we
are considering. The structure raised by the theologians
and canonists of the twelfth century, exalting the position
of the pope over the universal Church, was built on deep
foundations.

[1] *PUE*, iii. 255, cf. 295, 435, and Rymer, *Foedera*, I. i. 43.
[2] *PUE*, i. 562.   [3] *SLI*, p. 83 (*PL*, ccxv. 955).

IV

CHURCH AND STATE

To be in a position to examine the subject of Church and State we have had to consider first the legal relationship of the English Church with Rome and the way in which the papacy exercised its power over the English clergy. That was the theme of the last lecture. Now we must envisage the matter in a broader way, to take into account the king's relations with the pope, the attitude of the English clergy to Rome, and the extent of their freedom from lay control.

I do not propose to consider systems of political theory. The classic rhetoric of John of Salisbury, the polemics (as unfavourably reported) of Alexander of St. Albans, the majestic pronouncements of Pope Innocent III—these all have their importance for historians ; but this lecture is concerned with the issues of Church and State as they arose in the day-to-day working of English church government, when dogmas were somewhat diluted with considerations of expediency and philosophic ideas bruised by hard fact. We shall be concerned not only, or mainly, with two opposing schools of thought each of which finds it needful to make certain concessions, but mostly with men who believed in compromise as a matter of principle and who would draw the line in various places to make the boundary between *sacerdotium* and *regnum*, ecclesiastical and royal government.

I translate *sacerdotium* and *regnum* as ecclesiastical and royal government, for this seems to be the usual meaning of the terms when they appear conjoined.[1] According to Stephen, the twelfth-century bishop of Tournai, *sacerdotium*

---

[1] The letters of Innocent III provide abundant examples of this meaning. A monk of Canterbury writes of the alliance of king and archbishop against Christ Church in 1188 : ' Regnum et sacerdotium suas in ipsam exacuere sagitta, publica videlicet potestas, sacerdotalis dignitas ' (*Epp. Cantuar.*, p. 190).

is the hierarchical power or *principatus* which rules the clergy, *regnum* the royal power which rules the laity. ' Give to each its due ', says Stephen, ' and all will agree '.[1] He expressed a pious but unhelpful doctrine. For it ignored the plain fact, which Stephen as a French prelate knew perfectly well, that while the king is not concerned solely with ruling laymen, the hierarchy of the Church counts both clergy and laity, prince as well as prelate, within its jurisdiction.

What was the attitude of the Angevin kings of England to this complex situation ? If they were to exercise even partial control over their clergy, they must reckon with the authority of Rome. And they were not heretics or infidels, even though Henry II once threatened to embrace Islam and John was reported to have moved in that direction.[2] They recognized that the pope was in a real sense the head on earth of the whole Church, including England. The English Church—one must remember—had no constitutional unity within itself, no one member of its hierarchy which controlled it.[3] At times when *regnum* and *sacerdotium* fell out and then made peace, the agreement was between the king and the pope or his legates.[4]

The Constitutions of Clarendon of 1164 present a scheme of what Henry II and his advisers thought to be reasonable working relations between Church and State in England ; we may guess that at least as many wakeful nights went to its drafting as to the assize of novel disseisin. It is a business-like statement. Some of the clauses on judicial matters will call for comment later. For the moment let us concentrate on one or two clauses which affect nearly

---

[1] Quoted, C. Mirbt, *Quellen zur Gesch. des Papsttums* (5th ed., Tübingen, 1934), p. 172 and R. W. and A. J. Carlyle, *Medieval pol. theory in the west*, ii (Edinburgh, 1909), 198.

[2] *MTB*, vi. 406 ; M. Paris, *Chronica maiora* (RS), ii. 559.

[3] Cf. Maitland, *Roman canon law*, pp. 113-14.

[4] In 1172 and 1176 the king came to terms with papal legates, although the terms had been drafted by local clergy. In 1215 the royal charter on ecclesiastical elections was sent to the pope for confirmation.

the obedience of the English clergy to the pope, and see how they influenced Anglo-papal relations in the next few decades. They do not suggest, I think, that the king had the idea of segregating the English Church from the common life of Christendom or even from the law and administration which had their centre in the Roman Curia. But the clergy's contact with Rome must not endanger the king's control over them. In all matters affecting temporal interests the king must have the last word. This was, of course, obnoxious enough to the exponents of ecclesiastical freedom, and was contrary to papal policy. For that reason, the Angevin kings, while they tolerated intercourse with Rome, showed marked distrust of the Curia's intentions.

This is best illustrated by the Constitution that ecclesiastical appeals should only go to the pope in the last resort and with the king's assent.[1] Nothing indicates that it was intended to put an end to appeals to Rome. Henry II denied the intention.[2] He simply was aware of the manifold abuses of appeals ; [3] and, above all, he meant to safeguard his interests as temporal lord of England. There were lawsuits in which Henry allowed, and even co-operated in, the activities of judges-delegate, both early and late in his reign.[4] But there were also cases which concerned the possession of land, or which implicated the king's barons or an abbey of royal foundation,[5] or which touched the

---

[1] The canonical view is expressed by Tancred, *Ordo iudiciarius* (ed. Bergmann, pp. 292–3) : '. . . dominus papa, ad quem potest ab audientia cuiuslibet iudicis appellari . . . et hoc ideo quia iudex est ordinarius singulorum.'

[2] *MTB*, vi. 79 (1165 or 1166). Cf. Davis, in ' England and Rome in the Middle Ages', *H. W. C. Davis, a memoir*, ed. A. L. Poole and J. R. H. Weaver (1933), pp. 117–18.

[3] The reason alleged by Gilbert Foliot in 1167 (*MTB*, vi. 272). Gervase of Canterbury (i. 541) makes Henry II denounce the encouragement given by the Romans to litigation (*c.* 1185).

[4] For the dispute over Mildenhall church between Battle Abbey and Leeds Priory (1154 × 1159) see *Chron. monast. de Bello*, pp. 113–15 and for an interesting case between Reading and Gloucester Abbeys (1177) see Morey, *Bartholomew of Exeter*, pp. 140–2. See also Appendix III (v), below.

[5] E.g. *Gesta abb. S. Albani*, i. 145, 159–66.

king's dignity : these were not to go freely to Rome. Moreover, Henry II ordered Archbishop Theobald, after Alexander III's election, to settle cases in England so long as
schism lasted in the Roman Church.[1]

The settlement at Avranches in 1172 whittled down the
rule declared at Clarendon, so that appeals were now
allowed freely ' in ecclesiastical cases so long as, if any
persons were suspect to [the king], they would guarantee
not to seek to harm him or his realm '.[2] It is doubtful
whether this meant a change in the royal attitude. The
great Canterbury lawsuit provides a little evidence. The
dispute broke out between Baldwin and the monks of his
cathedral church towards the end of Henry II's life, and the
king advised the pope by letter not to entertain the appeal
of the monks.[3] A little later he tried to get the monks to
settle the matter by reference to him rather than to a papal
legate. When they objected, Ranulf Glanvill, the justiciar,
exclaimed angrily : ' You only ask for Rome, and Rome
alone will be your ruin.'[4] Henry II took the line that
he was patron of Baldwin's proposed chapel and protector
of its clergy and that the monks' resistance was tantamount
to treason.[5] Then, Richard I, in November 1189, told
the monks not to trust in the papal legate but submit to
arbitration by English bishops and abbots.[6] In 1198, when
the pope had given judgment for the destruction of the
archbishop's chapel at Lambeth, the king urged two cardinals
to persuade the pope that he had been misled and that
sentence should be suspended.[7] On this and on other
occasions the pope's dignity will be preserved by the
assumption that he has been misinformed.[8] It sounds
deferential ; but the letter to the cardinals concludes :

[1] See the writ, discovered by Dr. A. Saltman, with his comments,
in *BIHR*, xxii (1949), 154–5.
[2] *Gesta Henrici*, i. 32. [3] *Epp. Cantuar.*, pp. 172–3.
[4] *Gervase*, i. 448, cf. 442. [5] *Epp. Cantuar.*, p. 117, cf. 295.
[6] Gervase, i. 476.
[7] *Epp. Cantuar.*, p. 404, cf. 406 citing the civil law.
[8] *Ibid.*, p. 406 and Wm. Thorne in Twysden, *Scriptores decem*, col. 1852.

'We would like you to know that we cannot allow a mandate of this sort, which has been issued to the prejudice of our dignity and of the liberty of our realm, to be put into effect in our realm.' [1]

In other directions Richard I did his best to obstruct appeals to the Curia. He tried unsuccessfully, while captive in Germany, to stop an appeal by Archbishop Geoffrey of York against his cathedral chapter. [2] During his reign, too, the king's court ruled that a question of bastardy, which admittedly was a matter for courts christian, must not go to Rome but must be settled in the court of the ordinary. A similar objection to an appeal ' de bastardia extra Angliam ' seems to have been raised in 1207. By Bracton's day this had become a rule which Bracton illogically explained by the argument that it might lead to the pope's indirect cognizance of a suit of lay fee. [3] It contrasts with the state of affairs in Henry II's reign, when Richard of Anstey and William fitzGodric had no difficulty in taking their cases to the pope.

Reverting to the Canterbury case : the monks tried to draw the pope and cardinals to their side by suggesting that the king was in league with their adversary, the archbishop, to stop all appeals from England to Rome. [4] Pope Celestine III was told that the projected college at Lambeth would produce a new Curia, in which the suffragan bishops of Canterbury would be cardinals and the archbishop pope.

---

[1] I assume that ' libertatis nostrae et regni nostri ' should read, as in the letter on p. 406, ' dignitatis nostrae et libertatis regni nostri '. King John claimed that the royal dignity was prejudiced by Innocent III's judgment in the Bath-Glastonbury case in 1205 (Adam of Domerham, *Hist. de rebus gestis Glaston.*, ed. T. Hearne (Oxford, 1722), ii. 425).

[2] Hoveden, iii. 222–3, 229–30, 283. The pope's decision was satisfactory to the king.

[3] *Rot. curiae regis* (Record Comm.), i. 56–7 (1194) and *CRR*, v. 48 (1207). Bracton, *De legibus*, fo. 420 ; he may have had in mind Alexander III's letter of 1 Oct. 1178 (*Decretals*, 4,17,7 cf. Diceto, i. 427–8 and Morey, *op. cit.*, pp. 68–70) in which the pope disclaimed the intention of adjudicating in an action over lay possessions ; but cf. Pollock and Maitland, ii. 665–6.

[4] *Epp. Cantuar.*, pp. 68, 165, 185, 241.

Every plaint or appeal would stop there. King Henry had planned it with the approval of several bishops, so that they might disburden themselves of the yoke of the holy Roman Church.[1] The monks' hysterical allegations were almost certainly unfounded ; but if they had been anxious to provoke general disagreement between king and pope, they would hardly have gone about it in a different way.[2]

That clause of the Constitutions of Clarendon which forbade prelates and beneficed persons to go out of the realm without the king's leave was applied in the following period in much the same way as the clause relating to appeals. The king would not isolate the clergy permanently ; but he claimed and occasionally exercised the right to prevent their departure on unauthorized missions. When Henry II allowed his bishops to attend the council summoned by Alexander III at Tours in 1163, he extracted from the pope an assurance that this would not be taken as a precedent.[3] Few English prelates went to the Third Lateran Council. They alleged, so Howden says, a privilege by which only four English bishops need attend a Roman council.[4] Richard I began his reign by asserting control over *exeats* : he would not let the envoys of Geoffrey, the elect of York, go to the Curia to fetch the pallium for their master, and they had to go home.[5]

As the king meant to control *exeats*, so he controlled the entry of papal representatives into his dominions. Under Henry II legates and nuncios come to England and pass through England only after undertaking to do nothing to the detriment of king or realm.[6] When Cardinal Vivian landed in 1176 on his way to Scotland, he was rapped over

---

[1] *Epp. Cantuar.*, p. 380.
[2] As the bishops warned Innocent III in 1198 (*ibid.*, p. 422).
[3] Rymer, *Foedera*, I. i. 44. Cf. Henry I and the Council of Reims, 1119 (Orderic Vitalis, *Historia*, lib. xii c. 21, ed. A. Le Prévost, iv. 373).
[4] Hoveden, ii. 171.
[5] *Gesta Henrici*, ii. 92.
[6] See Tillmann, *op. cit.*, pp. 77–81 and cf. *Gesta Henrici*, i. 118, 206, 209, 264. Some came at the king's request : Hugh Pierleone in 1175, Octavian and Hugh Nonant (for Ireland) in 1187.

the knuckles by Henry II for entering England without leave. Permission was, however, never withheld. These men did their business unmolested. With Richard I there arose obstruction. The legation of John of Anagni is fully recorded in the Canterbury correspondence. One of the monks reports an interesting conversation between the king and the cardinal in Normandy in 1189. Richard gave the legate several reasons why he was not wanted. He would in no circumstances have him at the coronation, lest the Roman Church might claim some right in it thereafter.[1] When the cardinal legate did eventually land, the old Queen Eleanor forbade him to proceed and Gilbert Glanvill, bishop of Rochester, enunciated the rule that ' before he has the licence of the lord king to enter the realm, he cannot be legate '.[2] John eventually was able to transact some legatine business, but was effectively excluded from the affairs of Canterbury which were the chief occasion of his coming.

By contrast to this episode, the early years of King John's reign show several papal legates and nuncios in England, and in no case do the records speak of safe-conducts or oaths taken or obstruction offered. Nevertheless, among the complaints of the pope against the king in 1203 is the allegation that he had recently ' prohibited his people from attempting to receive a legate or nuncio of the Apostolic See anywhere in his realm, and especially in England '. The pope added that the king ' afterwards withdrew this decree as being thoughtlessly issued '.[3] Evidently the Angevin leopard had not changed his spots.

Considering that a disputed election to the see of Canterbury was the spark which caused the explosion in John's reign, it is at first sight surprising that appeals over disputed elections in England did not cause serious friction between king and pope until 1207.[4] The reason why trouble did not arise sooner seems to be that usually royal

---

[1] *Epp. Cantuar.*, p. 300, cf. 296. [2] *Ibid.*, p. 318.
[3] *SLI*, pp. 49-50 (*PL*, ccxiv. 1175). [4] *Ibid.*, pp. 50-1.

influence was so strong, or king and chapter were so much of one mind, that there was no dispute and therefore no appeal.[1] But in 1206 Innocent III quashed two irregular elections at Canterbury ; he persuaded a group of Canterbury monks at the Curia to elect as archbishop Cardinal Stephen Langton, and later consecrated him in the king's despite. The king complained of ' the damage to his royal right and dignity '.[2] He might be unable to prove canonically that Langton's election was canonically irregular, but he could claim that he had a real interest in getting the right man as archbishop, and he could as a matter of fact keep Langton from his see for six years, whatever the canonists said. His attitude recalls the response of his father Henry to Hilary of Chichester, fifty years earlier, when Hilary declared that only the pope could sanction the deposition of a bishop. ' The king stretched out his hands and said : " It is quite true that a bishop cannot be deposed but he can be pushed out by outstretched hands, so." ' And it is clear from the later reported remarks of the king that his threats of force were sustained by a sense that God had given him his royal prerogatives and he had royal dignity and ancient privileges to guard.[3]

There is no sign that in these doings the king's heart was ever troubled by threats of papal censure. For political reasons he might have to notice them : more often, not. The pope threatened many times in these years to lay an interdict on lands of the English kings, but only once did interdict fall on England. That was when Innocent III caused interdict to be laid on England and Wales in March 1208 for King John's offence. It was rigorously applied : but the king did not take it lying down.[4] He took reprisals

---

[1] The appeal of the young Henry against his father's appointments in 1173-4 was heard in the Curia and rejected.
[2] Gervase, ii, p. lxiii.   [3] *Chron. monasterii de Bello*, pp. 91-2.
[4] Cheney, ' King John and the papal interdict ', *BJRL*, xxxi (1948), 313-14, and ' King John's reaction to the interdict on England ', *Trans. R. Hist. Soc.*, 4th series, xxxi (1949), 129-50.

and proclaimed his case against the pope with, it would seem, some popular response. Then, in November 1209, he was excommunicated. For three and a half years he remained in that condition and nevertheless continued to receive faithful service from two of the English bishops, several Cistercian abbots, and countless clerks and laymen. And during these years he performed acts of piety appropriate to a Christian king.

The episode is instructive. It shows the king prepared to reject plain and repeated commands of the pope and, while he accepts the reality of papal censure, doing his best to annul its consequences. The dispute had arisen over the king's claim to control his clergy—to be precise, to influence the election of an archbishop of Canterbury. We can hardly help drawing the same conclusion from this and from the Constitutions of Clarendon : the king is determined to control his clergy to the very limit of their tolerance, and papal jurisdiction over them will be contested if ever it affects adversely the king's interests. It may seem to us illogical for the king to recognize the jurisdiction of the papal Curia by allowing appeals to it and by pleading in it and then to override and obstruct its decisions ; but a logical distinction between law and politics really had no place there. The pope was not only a supreme judge of ecclesiastical cases and the most holy father : he was also the head of a State.

A recent historian of the Becket controversy refers to the cause for which Thomas Becket fought and the case made out for Henry II.[1] The clash of these two vigorous and intelligent men raised big issues in which both sides could appeal to important principles. What was the king's case, or the cause which he defended ?

On this and on other occasions which have been mentioned Henry II and his sons talked of their honour and dignity. These terms cannot be brushed aside as empty

---

[1] Knowles, *Episcopal colleagues of Thomas Becket*, p. [viii], cf. R. W. Southern, in *EHR*, lxvii (1952), 88.

words. They were full of the ideas of 'kingship by the grace of God' which Fritz Kern and others have indicated as potent forces in early medieval times. Kingship was office. If the king did not think so, others thought so for him. The office of an anointed king was to look after all his people, without distinction of clerical and lay persons. He represented the whole community, from which the clergy came and to which they belonged. The churches of God were committed to the king's protection in a general way, and he and other laymen had special responsibilities towards churches of which they were founders or hereditary patrons. There was nothing ignoble in the idea. It was in some ways opposed to the main current of twelfth-century ecclesiastical thought and produced in practice some unfortunate results : that was all. 'High Church men' wished to take the initiative away from the king and thought this theory of regality out of date. Whether they were right about that it was for later generations to show.

And now to view the position from Rome. The papal claims to control over the English Church were, if not limitless, extensive and unpredictable and in them was implicit a claim which might at any moment undermine the authority of the Crown. But in practice the popes moved cautiously. They were obliged by circumstances to overlook rudeness of the lay power and insubordination of the clergy. They were more successful in piling up authoritarian statements than in exacting wholehearted obedience to their commands. While the papal chancery was tireless in sending diplomatic notes, those notes seldom produced tangible results until Innocent III laid the interdict on England. Of the reaction to that interdict I have already spoken. In disputes which arose between the courts christian and the king's court in England, the popes recognized another problem of great complexity.[1] Occasionally Alexander III or Innocent III may tell English ecclesiastical

[1] Cf. above, 91, n. 3 ; *SLI*, 106, n. 7, 205.

judges to go ahead despite action in the lay court;[1] Innocent III may write to the king to intercede in a case of prohibition,[2] or to complain against prohibitions in general.[3] But even Innocent does not enter the field often and the best that he can ever achieve by intervention is a compromise in fact, with a safeguarding of principle.

Faced with the problem of serving two masters, how were the English clergy to conduct themselves? Would they show reluctance to obey the orders of king or pope? What choice would they make when they were forced to choose between two incompatible systems of law? These questions naturally concerned the prelates most of all, but the rectors and vicars of churches and even unbeneficed clerks might find themselves on the horns of a dilemma. Sometimes it seemed to be a moral problem but as often as not seemed to be a matter of expediency. The late Dr. Zachary Brooke, summing up the development which took place in the relations of the English Church and the papacy, said: ' The English Church starts in 1066 with the view of its master, King William I; it has come by 1215 to the view of its new master, Pope Innocent III.' [4] While this may do well enough as a simplified statement of the way in which the canon law grew during the twelfth century, it is positively misleading if it is understood to mean that the English clergy in 1215 recognized but one master: the pope. We may add that there can have been few matters of ecclesiastical politics on which Innocent III's views were shared by any considerable body of English clergy.

Not that the English clergy were anti-papal. Their conception of the Church required a Church of which the pope was doctrinal head and in which government involved

---

[1] ACL, x. 26 (JL 13931, tithe); Coll. Wigorn., iv. 48 (p. 118, patronage) ; PL, ccxiv. 804 (vicarage) ; PL, ccxiv. 850 (SLI, p. 15, parsonage).

[2] PL, ccxv. 747 (on behalf of the abbess of Caen, in a case of frankalmoin), cf. CRR, iii. 223, iv. 3, 172, 300.

[3] SLI, p. 50 (PL, ccxiv. 1175).

[4] The English Church and the papacy, p. 29.

constant intervention by Rome in the affairs of the provinces.
There must be a pope and he held the plenitude of power.
As we have seen, the English clergy recognized that his
power could be exercised in the hearing of lawsuits, both
of first instance and on appeal, by the granting of dispensations, indulgences, absolution.

A letter to King John from Eustace, bishop of Ely, and
Abbot Samson and Prior Herbert of St. Edmunds shows
the predicament of the clergy and the reaction of three
distinguished clerics.[1] The king had forbidden them to
execute a papal mandate, by which they were instructed
to excommunicate royal servants who had done violence
to the monks of St. Augustine's, Canterbury. It was a
situation foreseen in the Constitutions of Clarendon, c. 7.
Bishop Eustace and his fellow-delegates, in their reply,
state firmly that the king's servants had acted illegally and
not according to the custom of the country. They conclude :
' Your lordship may take it as certain that we are ready
with promptness, good will, and determination to preserve
your rights and royal dignities in all things and to obey
your commands as the commands of our most dear lord,
so far as our order permits, and the obedience by which
we are absolutely bound to the lord pope. It is common
knowledge, however, and you are not unaware, that we
can be obliged to no one except with a saving of the obedience by which we are bound to the Roman Church. And
therefore your royal highness should not be angry if we
proceed on so strict an order from him whom we cannot
rightfully resist, especially since, as it has seemed to us, it
is not opposed to the royal dignity and is consonant with
propriety.'

But a prelate might hold these principles and still feel
alarm, rage, and even the will to resist, when papal omnipo-
tence threatened his interests or took on a new form. There

---

[1] Wm. Thorne's chronicle in Twysden, *Scriptores decem*, col. 1853. I
have used and revised Dr. A. H. Davis's translation of the *Chronicle*
(Oxford, 1933), pp. 151-2.

are signs that English bishops feared that their own authority
was being undermined by the policy of Rome. What the
pope did was undeniably lawful ; but was it fitting, was
it expedient ?

Peter of Blois wrote to the pope in the name of Archbishop Richard of Canterbury to condemn, humbly but out-
spokenly, the papal policy of granting monastic exemptions.[1]
Archbishop Baldwin is credited with opprobrious remarks,
made in private, about the papacy as a court of appeal.[3]
Ten years later Archbishop Hubert complains of the in-
justice of Innocent III's procedure and notes that the pope
is assailing other metropolitan sees besides Canterbury.[2]
The bishops protest to the pope in 1198 that hitherto canon
law and English custom alike permitted a man to erect a
conventual church in his own fief, by authority of the
diocesan : now the pope is over-riding that right.[4]   When
the dispute arose between King John and the pope over
the Canterbury election, a great many clergy, as well as
almost all the laity, were (according to one monastic reporter) on the king's side.[5]   The suffragans of the southern
province cannot have been pleased at the pope's definitive
sentence (December 1206) against their long-standing claim
to participate in electing the archbishop.

Sympathy with King John, at least in the early stage
of this dispute with Innocent, may have been due to the
feeling that the pope had not given enough weight to English
custom in the matter of elections.   If we study the canon
law we see that the popes from Alexander III to Innocent III
allowed only a closely restricted space to local custom and
held always in reserve the right to overturn it by a pro-
nouncement that the custom in question was *potius corruptela*.[6]

[1] Ep. 68 (*Opp.*, ed. Giles, i. 203) : a condemnation which has a
parallel in Peter Cantor's *Verbum abbreviatum* (*PL*, ccv. 139). See also
Wireker on exemptions (*Anglo-Latin satirical poets*, i. 207). Cf. Peter's
letter (ep. 75, i. 224) against the dispensations from paying tithe granted
to Cistercians.

[2] *Epp. Cantuar.*, pp. 80, 241.   [3] *Ibid.*, pp. 394–6.
[4] *Ibid.*, p. 422.   [5] *Annales monastici* (RS), i. 28.
[6] Cf. F. M. Powicke, *Stephen Langton* (Oxford, 1928), pp. 84–5.

Moreover, the papal claim to override custom did not only cover old provincial usages of the English Church, but also the common law of England where it touched the Church.[1] And an older theory of society and kingship had included much that concerned the Church within the sphere of common law.

We detect among the English clergy of this period no trace of unorthodoxy, no failure to recognize in theory the plenitude of papal power. But even the greatest—perhaps most of all the greatest—among them were sometimes unwilling and resentful servants of the pope, tempted to submit readily to royal protection against their spiritual head.[2]

An important factor in the situation was the growth of nationalism in England and the Curia. The regionalism which was implicit in the social structure of medieval Europe already tended to produce a sense of nationality. Despite all the obstacles to unified government and the lack of coincidence between political boundaries and linguistic or racial frontiers, despite the narrow horizons of the average small man and the broad view of Christendom taken by the most elevated, Western Europe in the twelfth century was acutely aware of the common traditions and customs of groups of people, still more of their common sentiment in the presence of foreigners. Quite often people thought and talked of Englishmen, Frenchmen, and Germans (though we cannot always say what they meant). Ironically enough, it is the great counter-attack of Western Christendom upon Islam in the Crusades which reveals the regional differences most clearly to the modern historian.

---

[1] See T. F. T. Plucknett, *Legislation of Edward I* (Oxford, 1949), pp. 6–8.

[2] Cf. H. W. C. Davis, *loc. cit.*, p. 111 and see Mr. Pantin on the attitude of the fourteenth-century bishops (*The Eng. Church in the 14th cent.* (Cambridge, 1955), pp. 69–71). Wireker implies that many clerics took an Erastian view (*loc. cit.*, i. 187) ; for one who was devoted to Thomas Becket, he takes a remarkably detached view of the conflict between *regnum* and *sacerdotium* : ' utrumque vult praeesse et neutrum subesse ', etc. (*ibid.*, i. 225).

In the field of academic learning and in the monastic Orders there was, to be sure, an international exchange which has happily endured into modern times ; and it was assisted in the twelfth century by the general use of Latin. These are the aspects of the twelfth century most copiously recorded in literary sources. But the literate classes, if they wrote mostly in Latin, spoke a vernacular tongue or two ; and often, we may believe, their Latin limped lamely behind the vernacular. In the middle of this century the clergy in England had perhaps been less disposed to think about their Englishry than at other periods, for they were often educated in France or Italy, many of them were of French origin, they looked for ecclesiastical preferment both at home and abroad. Nor did the political troubles of Stephen's reign denote a unified England. But under the rule of the Angevins England, the one realm in their empire, becomes a political unit and finds in France a permanently un- friendly neighbour. The loss of Normandy in 1204 sharpens the division. English education becomes more self-sufficient as English cathedral schools and the schools of Oxford grow, even if many English scholars still go to France and Italy.[1] While English-born clerics continue to make their careers abroad, fewer men of continental extraction reside in English benefices and occupy English bishoprics.

These circumstances encouraged national sentiment to grow in the English Church precisely at the time when, as we have seen, links with Rome in law and administration were being strengthened.[2] When Richard I protested to Pope Innocent III about his handling of the Canterbury case he spoke of the damage done to the church of Canter- bury ' which is the mother and teacher of all Christian people in my realm '.[3] The letter was presumably drafted by a

---

[1] Cf. R. W. Hunt, ' English learning in the late twelfth century ', *Trans. R. Hist. Soc.*, 4th series, xix (1936), 23-4, 28.

[2] See the remarks of V. H. Galbraith, ' Nationality and language in medieval England ', *ibid.*, xxiii (1941), 123-28, especially pp. 122-4.

[3] *Epp. Cantuar.*, p. 403. Stephen Langton used similar words in 1227 : ' inter alias ecclesias Anglicanas optinet principatum, utpote que

cleric in a chancery over which Eustace, bishop of Ely, presided. The Bedan tradition of a united Anglo-Saxon Church seems to live on in these words ; and one wonders whether the scribe chose them by a calculated indiscretion, when the pope was fond of saying that ' the Apostolic See was constituted as the mother and teacher of all Christ's faithful '.[1]

Stirrings of national sentiment were stimulated by what was happening to the Papacy. ' The cosmopolitan but Roman Church ', as Maitland called it, was ruled in the middle of the twelfth century by an English pope, and for a brief period there were several distinguished Englishmen in the Roman Curia. But as the century drew to its close, as the popes re-established their patrimony after the trouble of the Schism, the Curia became more and more of an Italian institution. The college of cardinals had become of great importance in the determining of papal policy,[2] and while we do not know enough about the cardinalate to say just how many cardinals were Italians, it is certain that by the time of Innocent III they were in an overwhelming majority.[3]

The enlarged organization of papal chancery and *camera* meant a larger staff of Italian clerks. Now it was unfortunately true that the relations of English clergy to the Curia were generally those of debtor to creditor, and as everything, including justice, sold at a high price in Rome, the Curia incurred obliquy on all sides. Differences of national temperament played their part, if they were not the root of the trouble. A monk of Canterbury at the

aliarum mater est et magistra ' (*Acta S. Langton*, ed. K. Major (Cant. and York Soc., vol. 50, 1950), p. 130). Cf. Theobald to Henry II : ' Ipsa est enim caput regni vestri et vobis et toti regno fidei parens in Christo ', John of Salisbury, ep. 44 (*Opp.*, i. 46).

[1] *SLI*, p. 10, n. 2.

[2] See the flattering words of the Christ Church monks in 1198 : *Epp. Cantuar.*, p. 434.

[3] J. M. Brixius states the origin of less than half in the period 1130–81 ; 54 out of 70 of known origin were Italian (*Die Mitglieder des Kardinalkollegiums von 1130–1181* (Berlin, 1912)). Cf. Jean Rousset de Pina in Fliche and Martin, *Histoire de l'église*, ix. 2. 231–46.

Curia in 1188 wrote home : ' To tell the truth, at Rome I have found that all are Romans, and the lord pope (Clement III) is Roman both by birth and by nature. No wonder the natives are Roman since, from the character of the Curia, even foreigners become Romans '.[1] The next year Cardinal John of Anagni was described as ' a man in whom we have confidence so far as his nationality allows '.[2]

The attitude of English prelates to legates and nuncios was equally unfriendly,[3] and Italians appointed to English benefices cannot have been welcome. Both sentiment and interest made such visitors unpopular. Sentiment and interest also made the English clergy look suspiciously at papal attempts to extract money from them. When Innocent III tried to collect Peter's Pence in full, instead of allowing bishops and archdeacons to pocket their pickings, he met with stubborn resistance.[4] *Ecclesia anglicana* was not a legal entity, *primas totius Anglie* was the hollowest of titles, but there was a strong and persistent tradition of solidarity and separateness in the English Church.

And yet those English clergy who from prejudice or bitter experience or self-interest were tempted to resist papal government were not necessarily at one with the king in his view of the relations of Church and State. They knew how to play off one master against the other as opportunity offered. Having got royal protection against papal taxation, they were capable of calling in the pope to justify their refusal of a royal tax. A good deal of that probably occurred. But it was not inevitable. For those who most disliked the trend of papal government might yet hold high views of the sacred nature of their office. And it really is not possible to generalize about the clergy as a whole, or even to be sure that an individual was consistent in his

[1] *Epp. Cantuar.*, p. 194, cf. pp. 212, 214, 230. On the venality of the Curia see also above, p. 67.
[2] *Ibid.*, p. 286, cf. p. 294.   [3] E.g., R. de Diceto, ii. 168-9.
[4] *SLI*, p. 173.

H

attitude ; even if he was clear in his own mind, he must respond to pressure from one side or another.

This celibate clergy, along with its sentiments as a class apart, retained natural links with lay society. These men had spent their childhood as a rule in lay households, high and low, and they did not shake off all traces of their origin. On the episcopal bench in 1200 were a king's son, a justiciar's son, the nephew and protégé of another justiciar, and sons of two great marcher lords. These were exceptionally illustrious ; with them were others who came from every rank of free men. They all brought into the clerical class their diverse traditions.

It is also well to remember, as contributing to their diversity of outlook, how various were the careers open to those who took Orders and what a high proportion of male adults became clerks or monks.[1] With these considerations one may be tempted to doubt the existence of a distinctive class feeling in the clerical order. The Carthusian in his cell, the Benedictine in the cloister, the bishop, the parish priest, the civil servant : what had they in common ?

Such doubts would be unjustified, at least so far as concerns the large majority. The twelfth century did much to sharpen the distinction between clergy and laity, and to emphasize it legally and theologically. To begin with, every clerk was tonsured and whether monk, canon, or secular, was supposed to wear distinctive clothes. Again, the clerk was literate, the layman—at least by definition —illiterate. Charters might be addressed in general terms to *literatis et laicis*.[2] An encyclopaedist of the thirteenth

---

[1] A plausible calculation sets the proportion in the thirteenth century at about 2 per cent. of the whole population (J. R. H. Moorman, *Church life in England in the thirteenth century* (Cambridge, 1945), p. 52).

[2] O. Morel, *La grande chancellerie royale* (1900), p. 55, n. 3 (1201) ; cf. T. Madox, *Formulare anglicanum* (1702), p. 155 (early 13th cent.). Appendix III (xiv) below : ' iuvenis litteratus quidem sed nescio si ordinatus '. Jocelin of Brakelond refers to ' magnates abbacie, tam laicos quam literatos ' (*Chronicle*, ed. H. E. Butler, p. 26). He also uses *literatus* sometimes in a more restricted sense, as is usual with an academic scholar like John of Salisbury (e.g. *Polycraticus*, lib. 7, c. 9).

century will derive *laicus* from *laos, lapis,* ' whence *laicus* = *lapideus,* for he is hard, and a stranger to book-learning '.[1] The fact that the distinction was not a real one makes it, from our present point of view, more rather than less significant.

These were old distinctions. Now, the reformed papacy was making a special effort to keep the clergy from the entanglements of family life and from laymen's work and hobbies. It demanded celibacy, forbade hunting and shooting. And the clergy claimed special protection for their persons. Men who laid violent hands on a clerk were not only answerable to the civil power for breach of the peace but must also go to the pope to get absolution. Clerks could not be tried and punished by laymen for criminal offences.

Meanwhile, Catholic sacramental doctrine attached more and more spiritual prestige to the priest, by giving the sacrifice of the Mass a more important place in the devotions of the people and by intensifying its mystery with the dogma of transubstantiation. Again, although theologians of the twelfth century held diverse opinions about the sacrament of penance (some assigning more, some less, to the part of inner contrition), and although they disagreed about the implications of priestly absolution, the general trend was unmistakable : confession was not complete unless it was made to a priest. The Church, taught by the theologians that the priest has the power of the keys—the power to bind and loose—, underlined that by requiring at least annual confession to a man's own priest.[2]

---

[1] Quoted by G. Paré, A. Brunet, P. Tremblay, *La renaissance du xiie siècle* (Ottawa, 1933), p. 62.

[2] IV Lateran Council c. 21 ' Omnis utriusque sexus ' (*Decretals,* 5,38,12). The priest had at least a declaratory power, according to the school of Peter Lombard. Adam of Perseigne writes : ' Solvant [sacerdotes] denique a metu poenae, quos absolvit caritas a vinculo culpae, hoc est enim sacerdotem solutos ostendere quos per se dignatio divinae pietatis absolvit.' (*PL,* ccxi. 682, quoted by A. Teetaert, *La confession aux laïques dans l'église latine* (1926), p. 98, n. 5, who also quotes Langton : ' Auctoritate sua sacerdos tamen dimittit ostensione et ministerio quare ostendit ea dimissa quantum in se est apud dominum sicut sacerdos legalis mundabat.' Cf. *ibid.,* p. 182, n. 1. (See, in general,

Finally the theology of ordination could not but submit
to change when other sacraments, in all of which the clergy
were concerned, came under discussion. The schisms of the
twelfth century raised questions of validity of orders which
were long debated. Pope Lucius III incurred the blame
of the canonist Huguccio by causing to be re-ordained
clergy ordained by schismatic bishops who had been themselves ordained by schismatics.[1] Gradually the Church
came round to the opinion of Huguccio's school that ordination by schismatics was irregular but not null. The sacred-
ness of ordination, the fact that, once performed, it could
not be reiterated, was emphasized when the Third Lateran
Council (c. 5) revised the old law of the Church about clerks
who had been ordained without title.[2] Various enactments
treated subdeacons along with priests and deacons,[3] and
with Innocent III the subdiaconate was finally counted
among Holy Orders, not minor Orders.[4] The clergy, in
short, were being encouraged to take a high view of their
office. However many shades of belief and opinion might
be found within the clerical order, there was no doubt of
its separateness from the rest of the world.[5]

Now all this had a direct bearing on the harmony of
Church and State in contemporary England. The Con-

Teetaert, pp. 85–197, and the important work of Paul Anciaux, *La
théologie du sacrement de pénitence au xiie siècle* (Louvain, 1949).

[1] Saltet, *Les réordinations*, p. 329.

[2] Cf. *Decretum*, 1,70,2, which declared ordinations without title to be
invalid.

[3] III Lateran Council, c. 12 (*Decretals*, 1,37,1), concerning secular
occupations ; *PL*, ccxiv. 68 (*Decretals*, 3,5,16) concerning ordination
without title and cf. *SLI*, p. 35.

[4] *Decretals*, 1,14,9, cf. Hinschius, *System des kath. Kirchenrechts*, i (1869),
7, n. 1.

[5] Cf. Powicke, *The Christian life in the Middle Ages* (Oxford, 1935),
p. 11 : ' As an ecclesiastical system the body of Christ was becoming
the most intricate administration which the world had yet seen ; as
a society the Church affected and was affected by every form of human
endeavour. From the one point of view the distinction between lay
and clerical is all-important ; from the other it is irrelevant.' I am,
of course, only concerned with the ecclesiastical system.

stitutions of Clarendon brought into the open, along with questions of papal control, questions of local ecclesiastical jurisdiction. There lay the debatable land which Henry chose for his battlefield with Becket, in which cases partook of two natures, spiritual and temporal. It was possible to look at them from two points of view. Argument as to who should hear these cases was more likely to crop up if bishops and clergy were withdrawing from the shire-court, and were discouraged from acting as royal judges, and were discouraging intervention by the laity in synods.[1]

The most notorious dispute concerned felonous clerks. Here Becket posthumously won his point—at least in principle—and clerks escaped hanging ; but it was not long before a bargain between king and legate in 1176 brought forest offences of clerks into the king's court. At the same time, murderers of clerks were subjected to temporal pains as well as spiritual. A wise letter from Archbishop Richard of Canterbury to his colleagues of Winchester, Ely, and Norwich (those bishops who, three years later, became chief justices) argued for justice rather than logic, for punishment by both Church and State and, in general, for co-operation between *regnum* and *sacerdotium*.[2] It is an important record of the spirit of compromise at work in the English Church.

The Constitutions of Clarendon had mentioned various civil pleas which became matters for discussion and settlement : advowsons (c. 1), frankalmoin tenure (c. 9),[3] debt (c. 15).[4] While the jurisdiction over testaments and tithe

---

[1] Cheney, *Eng. synodalia of the XIIIth cent.* (Oxford, 1941), pp. 28–33. Cf. below, p. 156.

[2] For the agreement of 1176 see Diceto, i. 402–3, 410, etc. Richard's letter is Peter of Blois, ep. 73 (*Opp.*, ed. Giles, i. 217–19 ; *MTB*, vii. 561–4). Cf. Foreville, *L'église et la royauté*, pp. 426–8, 436–7.

[3] In 1175 Darley Abbey and Hubert fitzRalph were in dispute before delegates of Alexander III over the manor of Crich. They reached a compromise duly ratified by Bishop Roger of Worcester as judge-delegate (*Cartulary of Darley Abbey*, ed. R. R. Darlington, ii. 538–41).

[4] Cf. Glanvill, *De legibus*, lib. 1, c. 3. For a writ of prohibition in a case of debt (1201) see *CRR*, ii. 28. For a case of debt settled by composition before delegates of the papal legate (1213–14) see *Cart. of Darley Abbey*, ii. 537.

was not in question at Clarendon, these matters also had
to be faced. During the past thirty years Pollock and
Maitland's classic exposition of these subjects has been
enlarged by valuable studies, mostly by American scholars,
on particular topics : Miss Gabel on benefit of clergy, Miss
Kimball and Mr. Thorne on frankalmoin and the assize
utrum, Miss Adams on tithe.[1] So far as we can now see,
Church and Crown recognized that they had different
interests : each was determined not to be over-reached ;
neither was prepared to proceed to extremities. The so-
called compromise of Avranches settled nothing ; but the
next generation was a period of effective adjustment, with
give and take between the two jurisdictions. Testaments
are drawn into the church courts [2] but they cannot dispose
of heritable land. The Church holds the felonous clerks,
but the sheriff holds on to his chattels.

Let us for a moment forget the conflict of laws and regard
these two judicial systems simply as competing public services. The question arises : which offered the swifter and
surer justice ? It is a matter worth enquiry, if only it leads
to the discovery that no answer is possible. I will only say
this : recent studies of the working of the royal court of the
Angevins—by Sir Cyril Flower and Lady Stenton and Dr.
Poole—do not present it in a very favourable light. And
in 1229 a stubborn layman of Northampton, summoned to
say why he had started a plea of chattels in court christian,
had the courage to tell the king's justices that it was ' because
he could get justice more quickly there '.[3]

The history of church patronage illustrates the ways in

[1] Leona Gabel, *Benefit of clergy in England in the later Middle Ages*
(Smith Coll. Studies in History, xiv. 1929) and cf. A. L. Poole in *Hist.
essays in honour of James Tait* (Manchester, 1933), pp. 239-46, and C. R.
Cheney in *EHR*, li (1936), 215-36 ; Elizabeth G. Kimball on frankalmoin in *EHR*, xliii (1928), 341-53, and xlvii (1932), 1-12 ; S. E. Thorne
on *utrum* in *Columbia Law Review*, xxxiii (1933), 428-36 ; Norma Adams
on tithe in *EHR*, lii (1937), 1-22.

[2] Cf. Glanvill, *De legibus*, lib. vii c. 5-8. In this direction the English
Church extended its jurisdiction farther than did other provinces of
the Church.

[3] *Bracton's note-book*, ed. F. W. Maitland (1887), no. 351.

which the English clergy looked at the conflict of laws.
The first sentence of the Constitutions of Clarendon declares
that disputes over advowsons and the presentation of churches
should be heard and settled in the king's court.[1] The Crown
never withdrew this claim ; and the papacy never abandoned the contrary assertion of Alexander III to Henry II
that ' cases of patronage of churches are so connected and
bound up with ecclesiastical cases that they can only be
decided by judgment of the Church and settled before an
ecclesiastical judge '.[2]

At some time undetermined during Alexander's pontificate, the pope delegated to the archbishop of Canterbury
a case of patronage which had been started in the court of
the bishop of Exeter, from whom the lay party concerned
had appealed to the pope.[3] On another occasion, Alexander ordered his delegates to enforce a judgment they had
given about the patronage of a chapel, despite the attempt
of a third party (who was to be threatened with anathema)
to re-open the question in the lay court.[4] Unfortunately,
we cannot tell whether these cases arose before or after the
Constitutions of Clarendon. The local clergy moved warily.
In 1175 Archbishop Richard of Canterbury ventured to
condemn illicit practices concerning advowson and presentation, in his council of Westminster, at which King Henry II
was present. His decree has the unusual and significant

[1] There might be a possessory assize if the church was vacant, and a
proprietary action by grand assize was possible when the church was
full (Glanvill, lib. iv, c. 6–9 ; cf. *CRR*, i. 32, 187, 273, v. 43). The
proprietary action, if it turned on advowson, was not supposed to be
heard in court christian (cf. Foreville, *L'église et la royauté*, pp. 443, 455–6).

[2] ACL, xlvii. 4 (*Decretals*, 2,1,3, a slightly modified text) ; the date
cannot be determined. So also a letter to the prelates of France or
England denouncing those who hold patronage or benefice by judgment
of a secular court : ACL, L. 33–34 (*Decretals*, 3,38,21).

[3] Singer, *Dekretalensammlungen*, pp. 270–1. The appellant is described
as ' J. de Valle Dei ', *recte* J. de Valle Torta, his opponent as ' Plumtim.',
recte Plympton (priory, O. S. A., Devon), and the church as ' Sint.' or
' Sintime ', *recte* Sutton Vautort, in Plymouth. If, as is probable, the
appellant is Juhel de Vautort, who appears on the pipe rolls at intervals
from 1171–2, the case may well be dated after 1164.

[4] Coll. Wigorn., iv. 48 (p. 118).

clause ; ' armed with royal authority as well as our own, we ordain . . .', etc.[1]

In theory the pope never admitted that it was lawful for the lay court to hear a case of advowson, and English prelates a hundred years later will go no further than concede that it is a practice they cannot prevent.[2] But in fact, Maitland tells us, the king won ' the fight for the advowson'. ' While it lasted', he says, ' it must have been sharp ' ; but somewhat inconsistently he goes on to suggest that the clergy were glad that such cases were ' withdrawn from the sphere of ecclesiastical law, Roman influence, and begging letters that were almost " provisions ".' [3]

A closer examination of the matter shows more activity in the church courts touching questions of patronage than Maitland supposed.[4] First, note that on the pipe roll of 1183-4 the bishop of Durham was charged 500 marks ' because he held a plea of advowson of a certain church in court christian '.[5] It was an enormous, exemplary fine, but it was not taken seriously, for it remained unpaid after Bishop Hugh's death and was pardoned to his successor, Philip, in 1198.

The writ of prohibition to court christian first appears in the late 1170's, though it may have been devised in the preceding decade.[6] A few writs in patronage cases are recorded during the next thirty years.   Some time in King

---

[1] Wilkins, i. 478.

[2] C. of Lambeth, 1261 : ' de patronatu, cuius cognitionem rex de facto exercet ' (ibid., i. 748).

[3] Roman canon law, pp. 62, 73-4.

[4] Cf. Foreville, op. cit., pp. 420-1 and R. R. Darlington, EHR, lxvii (1952), 564-5 ; see also Mary Cheney, ibid., lvi (1941), 191-5 and C. R. Cheney, BIHR, xxv (1952), 21.

[5] P.R. 30 Henry II, p. 37, P.R. 10 Richard I, p. 28.

[6] So G. B. Flahiff (Med. Studies, vi. 271-2) and Poole, From Domesday Book to Magna Carta, p. 217.   See Fr. Flahiff's important studies, ' The use of prohibitions by clerics against eccles. courts in England ', Mediaeval Studies (Toronto), iii (1941), 101-16 and ' The writ of prohibition to court christian in the 13th cent.', ibid., vi (1944), 261-313 and vii (1945), 229-90.   There are earlier references on the pipe rolls than Fr. Flahiff indicates (iii. 103) : a doubtful reference in P.R. 23 Henry II, p. 171 and a clear reference in P.R. 26 Henry II, p. 41.

Richard's reign, a claimant to the patronage of Bucksworth church (co. Huntingdon), having lost his case by an assize of darrein presentment, obtained a papal letter to implead his opponent, and the king prohibited the plea.[1] In 1199, at the height of the dispute between the archbishop of Canterbury and the monks of Christ Church, the justiciar served writs of prohibition in the cases of advowson which the monks were pursuing as part of their main action in the Curia. The archbishop, who was now chancellor, was doubtless responsible for these writs ; but he dexterously avoided the embarrassments of his ambiguous position by allowing the question of advowson to be settled by the ecclesiastical arbitrators in the main action.[2]

If writs of prohibition were few, the fact admits of two interpretations. Either few disputes were taken to the court christian or defendants in court christian seldom sought writs. It is not safe to assume that every disputant in a case of patronage preferred to sue in the lay court or was frightened into so doing. If the plaintiff preferred the church court, there would be no writ of prohibition unless the defendant sought it.[3] We have no means of telling how many cases were heard uninterrupted by ecclesiastical judges. That they were numerous is suggested by the fact that an overwhelming majority of the assizes of darrein presentment which appear on the rolls of the king's court before 1213 either concern laymen only or show a layman as plaintiff.[4] It was not proper for clerks to bring such actions to the king's court ; St. Hugh, bishop of Lincoln, forbade clerks to bring clerks to judgment in a lay court in an ecclesiastical case.[5]

Granted that advowson was to be adjudicated upon in the king's court, bound up with it were other matters—

---

[1] *CRR*, v. 173. For a prohibition of 1205 cf. *ibid.*, iii. 293.

[2] *Epp. Cantuar.*, pp. 499, 506, 508, 513. Writs were directed both to the judges and to the plaintiff. Cf. an earlier episode, *ibid.*, pp. 342–3.

[3] Flahiff, *loc. cit.*, vii. 232, 282.

[4] *CRR*, i. 24, 282, 288, 431 provide examples of ecclesiastical plaintiffs in the king's court in cases of advowson.   [5] *Gesta Henrici*, i. 357.

the rights of parish churches over chapels, the possessory or proprietary rights of the incumbent, or the right of a third party to a pension. Suitors might easily be in honest doubt about the court to which a plea should be referred. Mr. J. W. Gray's valuable study of the technicalities of the *ius praesentandi* [1] shows how complicated it all was.

The Crown tried from the first to bring disputes between rival patrons into its court, and sought, as time went on,[2] to attract suits between clerks which affected indirectly the rights of their patrons. But where the right of a presentee to a living was concerned, the king's court could not fail to recognize that possession only became legally valid by canonical admission and institution.[3] Consequently, procedure in one court tended to be duplicated or to call for complementary action in the other court. A plaintiff in the king's court on a writ of darrein presentment (which only operated during a voidance) might find that an exception of plenarty removed the matter, at least temporarily, to the ecclesiastical authorities. However anxious the king's court may have been to retain complete control over the case, it could not usually settle this exception on its own.[4] Moreover, if the plaintiff won his case on the writ, he might still find his possession obstructed because the bishop, following the Third Lateran Council's decree (c. 17), had collated to the vacant benefice after the lapse of four months consumed in the dispute. This was a fruitful cause of trouble.[5] Then again, if the plaintiff sought a writ of right (generally in respect of a church which was filled), he could not, when he was successful, straightway exercise his patronal right until the church had been ' disencumbered ' by the diocesan : this might involve suing the incumbent in court christian.[6]

---

[1] ' The ius praesentandi in England from the Constitutions of Clarendon to Bracton ', *EHR*, lxvii (1952), 481–509.

[2] After 1180, Mr. Gray thinks (*loc. cit.*, pp. 486–7).

[3] *Ibid.*, pp. 490, 501, 508.　　　　　　　　[4] *Ibid.*, pp. 496–8.

[5] Mr. Gray cites two cases, in 1194 and 1200, when the bishop's right to collate on lapse was contested by the writ ' Quare incumbravit ' issued after judgment on the assize (*ibid.*, p. 495).

[6] *Ibid.*, pp. 488, 504, 506.

So writs of prohibition were sometimes countermanded,[1] and the parties to a plea arising from the writ sometimes withdrew.[2] In 1205 the abbey of Sallay promised the king ten marks and a palfrey ' so that he will not allow them to be disseised of their church of Tadcaster unless by judgment of Holy Church or of the king's court '.[3] The Crown, then, recognized that in certain legal conditions Holy Church could judicially effect the transfer of patronal rights.

Confusion about the nature of the action might arise where a monastery claimed that a church was appropriated to it. For then the monastery was patron and parson combined. English cases were heard and settled before judges-delegate in the years after Avranches in which a layman claimed as tenant of a fief to control the patronage of a church in that fief, although the church had formerly been granted to a monastery.[4] A decretal of these years speaks of vicars who set themselves up as rectors.[5] In 1202 Guisborough Priory established by sentence of judges-delegate that they held appropriated the church of Skelton (Yorkshire) against the demand of Archbishop Geoffrey that they should present a rector to the parsonage. But the canons armed themselves for any conflict of laws by paying heavily for a writ to have an inquest (' convocato clero et populo ') and inspection of their title-deeds.[6]

[1] *Rot. de oblatis et de finibus* (Record Comm.), p. 291 (*cf. P.R. 7 John*, p. 168 and *Rot. litt. patentium* (Record Comm.) p. 129).

[2] *CRR*, iv. 132.

[3] *P.R. 7 John*, p. 60 (cf. another case, *ibid.*, p. 85). In this case the Crown's chief interest was apparently financial : next year the king accepted ten palfreys from Sallay's adversary ' so that the king shall not concern himself with the church of Tadcaster ' (*P.R. 8 John*, p. 209). For the later history of the church see *Chartulary of Sallay Abbey* (Yorks. Archaeol. Soc. Record Series, 87, 90), ii. 114–16, 124–31.

[4] M. Cheney, *loc. cit.*, pp. 190–3. Two other cases concerning the canons of Kirkham and Drax, who may have claimed to be parsons, were heard by judges-delegate in the 1170's and the judges' sentences confirmed by Alexander III (*PUE*, iii. 418–19, 434–5).

[5] *Decretals*, 5,31,6 (to the bishop of Norwich), reproduced in C. of Westminster (1175) c. 12 (Wilkins, i. 478 cf. *ibid.*, 475, c. 27).

[6] *Cartularium . . . de Gyseburne* (Surtees Soc., 86, 89), ii. 126–9, cf. 134–5 and *P.R.4 John*, pp. 64, 67. The canons' patronage was apparently not contested.

Where two monasteries both claimed to hold a parish church appropriated it was common, we may suppose, for the case to go to the court christian. Such a case arose between two Oxford houses, Osney and St. Frideswide's, concerning the parish church of St. Mary Magdalen. The church had been claimed by St. Frideswide's in the church courts in 1147 and 1151. Another lawsuit began in 1173 and dragged on under various papal commissions of judges until 1177. Then Osney was awarded proprietorship and possession of the church. St. Frideswide's re-opened the case in 1200 with an appeal to Rome, but had to submit.[1] Not only did the Crown tolerate this procedure ; but when the case was re-opened in 1200 and it appeared that the king's interests might be damaged by a decision in favour of St. Frideswide's, the sheriff, on behalf of the king, entered an interlocutory appeal to the pope.[2] This litigation could be regarded as a dispute between two rival corporate rectors. The words ' advowson ' and ' patronage ' are avoided in the documents which survive.[3] But it will be evident that the decision by judges-delegate of the pope judicially determined what had happened in the past to the advowson of the rectory, and determined for the future who should present a vicar to this church.

Another way which sometimes avoided the lay court was an action brought against the incumbent of a church as an intruder.[4] One such action was settled, *mediante concordia*, by Gilbert Foliot, bishop of London, before 1177. Ramsey Abbey claimed the church of Burnham Deepdale against a *soi-disant* rector. They got the man's supposed patron into court, where he resigned all right, recognized

---

[1] *Cartulary of Oseney Abbey* (Oxford Hist. Soc.), ii. 214–16, 219–30. The case is summarized by Morey, *Bartholomew of Exeter*, pp. 56–9. For a similar case, 1176, see *PUE*, i. 418–19.

[2] *Ibid.*, ii. 227. His letter to the judges concludes : ' Valete et tantum faciatis ut domino regi debitum honorem deferatis.'

[3] ' advocatio ' occurs once in the report of the judges of 1200, but not in the principal clause of the settlement (*ibid.*, ii. 228).

[4] Two cases of 1177 occur in *Reg. Malmesburiense* (RS), i. 372–3. Some of the varying circumstances are described in Glanvill, lib. iv, c. 9–12.

that the *ius patronatus* belonged to Ramsey, and swore not to contest it in future. Then the priest resigned the benefice into the hands of the bishop who awarded ' both the right of advowson and the church itself' to Ramsey.[1]

A concord of this sort had the advantage of avoiding the formality of a judicial sentence. Numerous cases of advowson pure and simple, and of disputes over parochial rights, were brought before ecclesiastical judges and then settled by compromise out of court.[2] An unusual form of compromise was sponsored by Bartholomew, bishop of Exeter, between 1180 and 1183 : Tavistock Abbey and William de Lega both claimed the patronage of Legh chapel. The parties agreed to abide by the sworn decision of six men, three priests and three laymen, who swore unanimously, in the presence of the bishop, to Tavistock's right.[3] However such arbitrations were conducted, no definitive sentence was declared and the king's right to contentious jurisdiction was unassailed. When ecclesiastical judges confirmed a concord by apostolic authority, it had the same validity in canon law as a judicial sentence.[4]

The Church also had her say in many cases of advowson settled by final concord in the king's court. For the fine often provided for a pension to be paid to the losing party, chargeable upon the parochial revenues. Now a decretal of Alexander III forbade the charging of new pensions on churches without the bishop's approval,[5] and the king's court respected this requirement. It referred final concords of this kind to the bishop for ratification. For instance, when in 1188 John Lestrange recovered the patronage of

---

[1] *Cartularium mon. de Rameseia* (RS), ii. 192–3.

[2] E.g., *Ancient charters*, ed. J. H. Round (P.R. Soc., 10), pp. 74–7 (1178) ; *Cart. of Oseney*, vi. 135–7 (1175 × 1183), iv. 441–2 (1189 × 1191) ; *Cart. of Darley*, i. 186 (*c.* 1200), ii. 574 (1164 × 1179). And see below, Appendix III (vi).

[3] Morey, *Bartholomew of Exeter*, pp. 157–8.   [4] Cf. *Decretals*, 1,43,9.

[5] *Ibid.*, 3,39,8 to the bishop of Worcester (1164 × 1179. Part of the decretal ' Meminimus ', found in full in *Epp. G. Foliot*, ii. 99–102). III Lateran Council c. 7 forbade the imposition or augmentation of charges on churches, without mentioning the bishop's powers in the matter.

Holme against Ramsey Abbey by a final concord before the justiciar, it was John, bishop of Norwich (who happened to be one of the judges) who gave and granted to Ramsey, with John's consent, a mark of silver to be levied each year in Easter week on the parson of Holme.[1] In 1196 Theobald Walter made a fine with Shrewsbury Abbey by which he got the advowson of Kirkham church and the abbey a pension ; but an endorsement on the foot of the fine shows that it is held up (' quasi in sequestro ') until the archdeacon of Richmond arrives and ' it is known from him whether he will give his consent : because then it will be all settled ("omne erit stabile ") '.[2]

For another dispute over an advowson, take the case of Harlton (Cambridgeshire). The monks of Longueville, at the beginning of Richard I's reign, claimed the advowson of the church and further claimed to be its parsons, by virtue of a pension of twenty shillings from the incumbent, whom they called a vicar. The lord of the manor, Roger of Huntingfield, claimed that he was the patron and the incumbent parson. This dispute was first ventilated in the diocesan synod of Ely in 1191 : the synod pronounced that the monks and their vicar should possess the church. But this could not prevent Roger from taking his case in 1196 to the king's court. The justiciar, Archbishop Hubert, heard it and Roger was awarded the advowson. The monks were to be solaced by a pension of forty, instead of twenty shillings, and the parson was to pay it if the diocesan agreed. But the next diocesan, who was the royal chancellor, Eustace, would not agree, and the patron, Roger, became liable for the difference.[3] It is an illuminating example of the courses open to litigants.

---

[1] *Cart. mon. de Rameseia,* ii. 383. The bishop also gave a separate notification of the pension which does not mention the final concord (ii. 191).

[2] *Feet of fines, Henry II and Rich. I* (P.R. Soc., 17), pp. 97–9 ; cf. *Feet of fines, 7–8 Rich. I* (P.R. Soc., 20), p. 64 ; J. Thorpe, *Registrum Roffense,* p. 496 ; *CRR,* i. 137, 365.

[3] *Newington Longeville charters* (Oxfordshire Record Soc., 3), pp. xxxv, 72–9.

To sum up the evidence on advowsons : both the spiritual and temporal aspects of the matter remained constantly in view. Whatever declarations of principle emanated from Rome, the English clergy did not persistently and publicly oppose the jurisdiction of the king's court. The Crown, on its side, did not stop a case in the court christian until a defendant sued a writ of prohibition ; nor did it stop compositions from being recorded before ecclesiastical judges ; nor did it regularly prevent cognate cases from being heard by ecclesiastical judges, although writs of prohibition might sometimes be invoked against them ; nor did it control pensions from churches, which were subject to the bishop's sanction.

These proceedings about benefices are significant. In this and in other disputable matters the clergy display a strong corporate desire to retain a sphere of jurisdiction marked out for them by the canon law. They even extend the bounds into the field of testamentary cases. They emphasize, that is, the ecclesiastical and spiritual aspect of actions which also affect laymen's rights and temporal possessions. This is not disproved by the occasional recourse of clergy to the lay court whenever, as we may surmise, necessity or self-interest led them to it. On the other hand, the Crown and its judges consider the earthy aspect of benefices and lay inheritance. They devise the writ of prohibition which pulls up short the ecclesiastical judge when he is deemed to encroach upon the territory of the common law of England. Whatever the complaints of distressed churchmen, these writs served the same ends as appeals to Rome, offering an alternative mode of action and at times an opportunity for the dishonest defendant to evade immediate defeat. It was for this reason that they became so insidious a danger to ecclesiastical justice. But although, in the future, prohibitions to courts christian were to be very harmful to the Church's claim, in this period they are a tool rather than a destructive weapon : a powerful wrench kept for occasional use in a normally gentle process of adjustment. Church courts and king's court compromise, partly by drawing subtle legal distinctions, partly by the exercise of restraint on both sides.[1]

When the chief officers of state and many of the judges on the bench were prelates and dignitaries of the Church, it was not to be expected that there would be persistent wrangling over questions of principle in these matters which concerned things spiritual and temporal.[2] But it is remarkable that the peace was kept without utter surrender either to the canon law or to the law of the realm. It called for a lot of legal learning and a good deal of statesmanship. The higher clergy, judged by their works, seem to have thought that the need of their time was peace, in which to develop orderly diocesan government. Though they were not blind to the traditions of the English Church or to contemporary canonistic opinion in Europe, they would not disturb the harmony of Church and State in England by impolitic assertions of high gregorianism. There was a time for firmness and a time for pliancy. Their caution procured more, maybe, for the Church than martyrdom would have procured. Neither the Angevin kings nor Popes Alexander III and Innocent III were mild men who willingly renounced a right. It is owing to the clergy who had masters both in England and in Rome that the dispute between king and pope, when it flared up in 1207, was confined to ecclesiastical elections.

[1] Mr. Gray's study of *ius praesentandi* suggests that the king's court gradually tightened control over benefices after 1180.

[2] Cf. Stubbs, *Constit. Hist.*, iii (3rd ed., 1884), 336–7, 353–4, (§§ 390, 399), and Powicke, *The thirteenth century* (Oxford, 1953), p. 458.

V

THE DIOCESE

WE have been led inevitably, from considering the relations of the English Church with Rome, to look at the problem of Church and State. That is a subject which has a fatal fascination. It throws into high light certain episodes which offer the spectacle of grand ideas in conflict, plenty of incident, colourful and accessible records. Much that passes for church history is concerned with these episodes to the exclusion of all serious study of what churchmen did when they were not wrangling with the lay government. But the history of church government, properly speaking, includes much more. And in our chosen period a great deal was happening in the government of the English Church : not only in the papal direction of it from above and without, but in the steady establishment of the diocesan's authority over his flock and in the elaboration of administrative offices and procedure in diocese and province.

Without this development, be it noted, there would have been far fewer appeals to Rome, far fewer consultations of the pope on points of law, and a slower growth in the common law of the Church. The advance in papal control over the Church is both cause and effect of what the bishop does in his diocese. The diocese—the bishop's parish—was the unit of ecclesiastical government and the bishop was the ordinary long before Rome and its bishop exercised any regular over-riding jurisdiction. So let us turn to the diocese.

The earliest organization of the Church had associated the bishop very closely with the clergy of his cathedral see, and the link still held in the twelfth century. It was among the cathedral clergy that the bishop found his

principal helpers and he usually saw to it that his archdeacons were provided with stalls in the choir and seats in
the chapter. Sir Frank Stenton, commenting on a 'fine
and concord' issued by Bishop William de Warelwast in
his synod in the new church of St. Peter at Exeter, on
14 June 1133, observes that the bishop confirmed the
document by his authority and the 'counsel' of his whole
church, while he called upon the synod merely to witness it.[1]

During the period we are concerned with, the number of
members of the cathedral chapter busied with the bishop's
affairs seems to have been narrowing to an important professional group. The men in this group, who commonly
witness the bishop's acts, often bear the title of *magistri*,
which denotes an academic training. A passage in the
Magna vita of St. Hugh of Lincoln shows what was going on.[2]
The author describes Hugh's exertions, on becoming bishop,
to surround himself with men who would help him to rule
clergy and people and administer ecclesiastical justice :
these he installed in the bosom of his church—that is, he
gave them prebends. Among them, he attracted the future
dean of Lincoln, Master Roger of Rolleston, from the service
of Archbishop Baldwin. The chapters of monastic cathedrals contributed to their bishops' households,[3] but their
Rule made monks less suitable as assistants. If, towards the
end of the twelfth century, the archbishops of Canterbury
and the bishops of Coventry and Rochester wanted to set
up secular chapters [4] (in contrast to the policy which had
produced nine new conventual cathedrals in the early
Norman period), this might be attributed in part to the
limited value of monks for administrative office.

---

[1] 'Acta episcoporum', *Cambridge Hist. Journal*, iii (1929), 10. Note
that 'my archdeacons' are the first witnesses.

[2] *Magna vita S. Hugonis*, pp. 121–2, cf. 124.

[3] E.g., Benedict, chancellor of Archbishop Richard of Canterbury,
and Ranulf of Wareham, official of Bishop John de Gray of Norwich.

[4] For the well-known cases of Canterbury and Coventry see Knowles,
The Monastic Order, pp. 318–330, and for Rochester see J. Thorpe,
Registrum Roffense (1769), p. 53. An anti-monastic party among the
bishops was no novelty : cf. *Anglo-Saxon chronicle*, *s.a.* 1123.

The decades around 1200 saw great activity in statute-
making in the English secular cathedrals. Although their
constitutions had undergone some re-shaping soon after the
Norman Conquest, the process was slow,[1] and there are no
codes of cathedral customs or statutes earlier than the last
decade of the twelfth century. From Lichfield comes the
earliest surviving code, with an addition made by Archbishop Hubert's authority in 1195.[2] Lincoln, London, and
Chichester, all yield ordinances made during the next few
years.[3] Then in 1214 Salisbury produced the important
Nova constitucio and Lincoln prepared a digest of its customs
for the information of the Scottish church of Moray.[4]
These statutes and other documents show that some of the
cathedral dignities were only now taking shape and receiving
endowments.[5] Late in the twelfth century vicars choral
appear in the cathedrals 'for the increase of divine worship'.[6] In this movement towards definition and orderliness the bishops played their part.

Cathedral chapters, monastic as well as secular, were all
the more important in the government of the Church at
large because they enjoyed patronage in parish churches
and a 'peculiar' jurisdiction over the clergy and people of
these churches.[7] The history of the churches belonging to

---

[1] Dr. Kathleen Edwards's *The English secular cathedrals in the Middle
Ages* (Manchester, 1949) has transformed our view of this process.

[2] Wilkins, i. 496–501.

[3] *Lincoln Cathedral statutes*, ed. H. Bradshaw and C. Wordsworth,
i (Cambridge, 1892), 300–6 ; *Reg. antiquiss.*, i. 260, 261, cf. 254–5 ;
Reg. statutorum . . . S. Pauli, ed. W. S. Simpson (1873), p. 63, cf. pp.
109–10 and R. de Diceto, i, p. lxvi ; *Statutes and constitutions of the cath.
church of Chichester*, ed. F. G. Bennett, etc. (Chichester, 1904), pp. 1–3,
and an ordinance for the provostry of Wells c. 1212, Edwards, *op. cit.*,
p. 117.

[4] *Statutes and customs of . . . Salisbury*, ed. C. Wordsworth and D.
Macleane (1915), pp. 40–53 ; Wilkins, i. 534–8.

[5] Cf. Edwards, *op. cit.*, ch. i, and pp. 186–7 for the emergence of the
office of chancellor. For the office of precentor at London cf. *SLI*,
pp. 121–2.

[6] Edwards, *op. cit.*, pp. 268–73.

[7] St. Paul's seems to have controlled the establishment of vicarages
in its churches in 1181 (*Domesday book of St. Paul's Cathedral*, ed. W. H.
H. Hale (Camden Soc., 1858), pp. 146–7). Bishop John de Gray

Durham shows what a complicated legal situation had arisen and how much was being done in this period to clarify it.[1]

Great abbeys, too, like St. Albans and Bury St. Edmunds, had their archdeaconries and deaneries in which they replaced the ordinary,[2] just as they enjoyed temporal liberties which ousted the sheriff. This was an age when such rights as these, founded usually in custom, were being questioned by diocesan bishops and defined by agreement or by papal judgment. In a compromise made between Archbishop Richard and St. Augustine's, Canterbury in 1183, the abbey 'lost the right of instituting and removing rectors and vicars '.[3]   Why did the abbey's chronicler, William Thorne, regard this loss as something of a disaster ?   The answer is simply that it profited the abbey to have entirely free disposal of its churches.

And so we come to the core of the matter : the control by the bishop over the parochial clergy, who were immediately responsible for ministering to most of the population. In general, by the middle of the twelfth century bishops had established their right to supervise appointments to parochial cures and to prevent a patron from dismissing an incumbent at will.[4]   Numerous charters from this time record institutions to benefices made under the bishop's eye.   Even so, in the time of Alexander III and after English bishops were still finding it desirable to reinforce their right with papal

allowed the monks of Norwich to serve their churches by removable chaplains (see Appendix III (xv)). Innocent III allowed the prior and convent of Holy Trinity, Aldgate, to serve their neighbouring church of St. Botolph's and its chapels by canons of the priory removable at the prior's will (*Monasticon*, VI. i. 156 note).   For peculiar jurisdiction cf. *BJRL*, xx (1936), 98–9.

[1] See Frank Barlow, *Durham jurisdictional peculiars* (Oxford, 1950).

[2] E.g., *Cart. of Darley Abbey*, ii. 596, *Chron. mon. de Bello*, p. 192, *Chron. abb. de Evesham*, p. 210, G. Oliver, *Monasticon Exoniense* (1846), pp. 138–9 (for Plympton Priory). And see the two preceding notes.

[3] Twysden, *Scriptores decem*, col. 1837.

[4] For early decrees see C. of Westminster (1102) c. 22, (1125) c. 9, (1127) c. 9 (Wilkins, i. 383, 408, 410) ; also the first of canons ascribed to Archbishop Richard (*ibid.*, i. 474, cf. above, p. 77, n. 2).

letters.[1] The bishop of Salisbury gets a letter to monks and canons who have patronage in his diocese, rebuking them for installing clerks on their own authority and forbidding them to increase the pensions (*census*) they draw from their rectors without the bishop's leave.[2] The papal policy is also declared in the privileges to religious houses which, as a matter of common form, provide that a monastery shall present suitable clerks to the bishop for institution to the churches in their gift, who must answer to the bishop in things spiritual and to the monastery in things temporal.[3]

There are these two aspects, spiritual and temporal. Parish churches were *beneficia*, or livings, in the gift of somebody or some corporation which might take or give away a pension from the incumbent. In the legal documents these terms occur more often than ' the cure of souls '. No sooner was the endowment of the parish church accumulated than it began to crumble and disperse. For the canon law, like the common law of England, regarded the church as so much material property ; it could be divided, and all or any of it might be devoted to purposes outside the parish, so long as somebody was found to take on the cure of souls. The dispersal should not be condemned out of hand. It could be justified by the great wealth of some benefices, in excess of local needs, and—on the other hand—by the lack of endowment for archdeacons, bishop's officials, and other useful people. But abuse was only too easy.

To be patron of a benefice can be directly profitable, by yielding you a pension, and indirectly profitable by providing a living for your nominee—a younger son, maybe, a

---

[1] *Decretals*, 3,38,5 and 8 and 13 and 20 ; ACL, xv. 22 (JL 14085).
[2] ACL, xlvii. 6 (JL 14096), cf. above, p. 115.
[3] *PUE*, passim ; cf. a general injunction to regulars in the province of Canterbury, *Epp. G. Foliot*, ii. 68 (no. 346 : JL 13829). A more precise formula, requiring provision for the vicars, is used by Lucius III, 1183 (*PUE*, iii. 456-7, cf. ii. 462). Nicholas de Sigillo, archdeacon of Huntingdon, stipulates (probably during a vacancy of the see of Lincoln, 1182 × 1183) that the monks of St. Neots shall present their vicars to him for institution ' sive fuerint perpetui sive temporales ' (Brit. Mus., Cotton MS. Faustina A. iv, fo. 37r).

private secretary, or any cleric whom you wish to gratify. You may also alienate some part of the tithe-revenue in favour of a religious house and acquire merit thereby.

To be rector—although it imposes some obligations—can be still more profitable. For then you may perform the ministry of the church yourself and take all the revenues, or you may install your nominee to be the pastor, and then receive from him either a substantial proportion of the church's profits, or a fixed pension. To take a simple example from the beginning of our period : Walden Priory was patron of the church of Aynho and received an annual pension of two shillings from the rector. The rector, who was Master Ralph de Diceto, later dean of St. Paul's, did not reside or take the revenues of the church : he installed a perpetual vicar (Turbert, son of Turbert, served the church for at least twenty years). The vicar took the revenues, discharged all the obligations of the cure, and paid Master Ralph two gold pieces a year.[1]   To take an example from a later generation. In 1205 the abbey of St. Benet of Holme had the patronage of Stalham (Norfolk) and received one pound of incense as annual pension from the parson. Master John of Wormgay, the parson, received fifty shillings a year from Master Clement of Stalham, who was perpetual vicar.[2]

No wonder that the pope and bishops had to watch for non-resident and underpaid parish clergy. No wonder that they had to forbid the buying and selling of advowsons.[3] And no wonder that ecclesiastical corporations tried to acquire by lawful gift the patronage of churches. While the Church dared not disturb the legal rights of lay patrons,[4] she preferred to see patronage in ecclesiastical hands.

[1] R. de Diceto, ii. pp. lxviii–lxix. As at Aynho, a vicar may be instituted on the presentation of the rector with assent of the patron, or on the presentation of the patron with assent of the rector (e.g., *Cart. mon. de Rameseia*, ii. 179 (1183–4)).

[2] *Register of . . . St. Benet of Holme*, i. 59.

[3] Paul Thomas, *Le droit de propriété des laïques sur les églises et le patronage laïque au moyen âge* (1906), pp. 149–51.

[4] *Ibid.*, pp. 116–18.

Monks were the *pauperes Christi* and could, almost by definition, plead poverty and the need for gifts. Having acquired patronage of a church, they often saw no reason why they should not appropriate the revenues to themselves —become, as it were, corporate rectors—and engage a clerk to look to the cure of souls. These processes of transfer of patronage and appropriation were in full swing before Thomas Becket died ; and his contemporaries and their successors had to ensure that through this transference the parochial ministry did not suffer.

The parochial system in the twelfth century was just about as unsystematic as the feudal system, and for much the same reasons—economic, social, and legal. And in so far as the idea of the cure of souls was overshadowed by the idea of the benefice, the parish church could be integrated into the law and custom of feudalism. The pattern of English parish churches, in fact, and of the rights and duties in them, was of extreme complexity. Their history is yet to be written. When it is written it must include some account of the many chapels which were being set up in outlying parts of parishes.[1] Let us hope that one day there will arise a student sufficiently well equipped in the canon law, the common law, and economic history to do justice to this important subject.

Complicated though the position was, the bishop had a fairly simple object in dealing with all sorts of parochial structure. Whatever the division of rights and revenues, he must see that it did not proceed so far as to leave the parishioners untended or the minister impoverished. Also, he must have the last word in the appointment and dismissal of the minister. With this main object a bishop was concerned chiefly with four problems : (1) the problem of the benefice regarded in the feudal way as an hereditary

---

[1] For a picturesque account of the growth of Windlesham (Surrey), within the parish of Woking, until a chapel was established there in or before the reign of Henry II, see *Bracton's notebook*, ed. F. W. Maitland, no. 769. For typical obligations of such a chapel, see the arrangements made *c.* 1200 at Osmaston, in the parish of St. Peter's, Derby (*Cart. of Darley Abbey*, i. 20). Cf. below, p. 166.

possession, held by priests who married and passed on their
living to their sons ; (2) the problem of the rector whose
income was reduced by obligations to his patron or to a
third party ; (3) the problem of the living divided between
several rectors ; (4) the problem of the non-resident rector,
of which a special type is the monastery which appropriated
a rectory and became a corporate non-resident rector.

As early as 1102 Archbishop Anselm's council at Westminster ruled (c. 8) that the sons of priests should not be
heirs of their fathers' churches, but the practice persisted
throughout the twelfth century.   In some parts of England
there were parish churches richly endowed with lands where
the lord of the manor was not merely patron of the church
but parson as well.   He married although he was a priest
and transmitted his church to a son who also took Orders.
Whalley in Lancashire, is a notable example : Scarborough
in Yorkshire, may be another.[1]   Besides this hereditary
' squarson ', as he was termed in a later age, countless other
livings descended from father to son by the tolerance of the
patron or by the family's absorption of the patronage.   To
old-fashioned people there was nothing disreputable in the
practice.   Ailred of Rievaulx, born at Hexham about 1110,
' came of a long line of married priests, learned, respectable,
conscientious '.[2]

Objections arose partly out of the campaign for a celibate
clergy, partly because the system interfered with the rights
of monasteries as patrons or appropriators, partly because it
placed appointments beyond the control of the diocesan.
A very large number of letters were directed to England by
Alexander III and his successors to eradicate the custom
whereby, as Alexander said, men sought to gain possession

---

[1] For Luton, acquired with its great endowment by St. Albans in
Stephen's reign, see *Gesta abbatum S. Albani*, i. 113–19, 276–7.

[2] F. M. Powicke, *The life of Ailred of Rievaulx* (1950), p. xxxiv.   Cf.
F. M. Stenton : ' The feeling that the benefice should be hereditary
lasted long and died hard ' ; see the case of Edlesborough (Bucks.)
1163 × 1167, which he cites (*Camb. Hist. Journal*, iii (1929), 5–6).

of God's sanctuary by hereditary right. Archbishop Richard forbad hereditary succession in the Council of Westminster 1175. But the custom was evidently very well established. Bishops, it is plain, never heard of some vacancies where the son of the last incumbent stepped into his father's shoes without formality. That appears to have been the situation in the Norfolk village of Dunston where jurors declared in 1194 ' that they never saw any parson presented to the church, but always the parsons held it, one parson after another from father to son down to the last parson lately deceased '. He left a daughter, Alice, and the king's court ruled that she should hold the patronage : ' Let the bishop receive a parson at the presentation of the said Alice.' [1]

Although monasteries were as a rule anxious to protect themselves against the sons of incumbents and bring actions to evict them, throughout the twelfth century we find the religious sometimes ready to tolerate hereditary succession in return for a pension. Thus, Battle Abbey, early in Henry II's reign, undertook to admit to its church of Mendlesham (Norfolk) Nicholas, the son of the existing priest, Wihtgar, on condition that the pension which the abbey drew from the church should be raised from 10s. to 40s. [2] Roger of Howden, the chronicler, was admitted by Archbishop Roger of York to the church of Howden on the resignation of the rectory by his father Robert c. 1173 × 1176. [3] Guisborough Priory in 1196 allowed a father and son to continue to serve one of its benefices in consideration of an increased pension. [4]

Where bishops could be trusted to enforce the canons, the best safeguard lay in institutions by the bishop recorded in writing. So Alexander III instructs Bishop William of Norwich (1160 × 1174) : ' Fortify the parsons of churches

---

[1] *Rot. curiae regis*, i. 37–8.

[2] *Chron. mon. de Bello*, pp. 122–3.

[3] F. Barlow, ' Roger of Howden ', *EHR*, lxv (1950), 355–6, 359. This practice, whereby a parson made over his church to his son in return for a pension, is found in churches of St. Benet of Holme (*PUE*, i. 486, 535 and *Register of . . . St. Benet*, i. 41–2).

[4] *Cart. de Gyseburne* (Surtees Soc.), ii. 287–8. The arrangement was ratified by papal judges-delegate.

in your diocese with authentic documents from you and from the lord of the fee, so that when one of them dies neither the son nor the vicar of the deceased, nor anyone else, shall be able by any device to forestall your opportunity of conferring the parsonage of the vacant church on a suitable man.' [1] As a supplementary precaution bishops begin to keep lists or *matriculae*, registers of benefices with particulars of their patrons and incumbents.[2]

In a letter to Roger, bishop of Worcester, Alexander III ordered that the sons of priests were not to be allowed to minister in their fathers' churches, but were to be removed.[3] This injunction seems to lie behind the first decree of the Council of Westminster 1175, but that council watered down the rule so as to prohibit only future succession. Lawsuits in both the king's court and courts christian in the next generation show that the intrusion of sons into their fathers' livings continued, and in Innocent III's early years the bishops of Exeter and Winchester both obtain general indults to displace the son and heir from benefices.[4] No doubt the rule was all the harder to apply because it sometimes penalized excellent parish priests and destroyed a happy and close relationship in the compact social unit of the village. Moreover, some influences may have been too strong to counter. Was a bishop like John de Gray of Norwich likely to resist King John's presentation of a royal clerk, Master John of Bridport, to his father's living of Hingham, Norfolk? [5] It is noticeable that many instances are only known to us because someone else wants the living. The claimant to the benefice has probably informed against the son and heir at Rome and brings a papal mandate for the diocesan to enforce. Nevertheless, the constant

---

[1] *Decretals*, 2,28,4.
[2] Cheney, *Eng. bishops' chanceries*, pp. 112–19. These records responded to various needs, e.g., the information required in an assize of darrein presentment (cf. *EHR*, lxvii. 499).
[3] *Decretals*, 1,17,3.
[4] *PL*, ccxiv. 1034 ; ccxv. 724 (*SLI*, p. 82) ; cf. Appendix III (ix).
[5] *The book of fees*, i (Stationery Office, 1920), 280.

pressure of the Church authorities took effect : in the thirteenth century hereditary succession appears as an occasional abuse, no longer as a deeply-rooted social habit. The critical time of change was the generation after Becket.

Wihtgar, parson of Mendlesham, whose son Battle Abbey undertook to admit to the living, was to pay the abbey, his patron, forty shillings a year as a pension. This, in proportion to the total value of the living, was no great sum. But elsewhere a benefice might be seriously impoverished by substantial pensions—not only to the patron, but to third parties [1]—or by alienation of tithe in favour of some religious house.[2] Alexander III provided that new pensions should not be imposed nor old ones augmented without the diocesan's permission.[3] He and his successors sent various injunctions to the same effect to English prelates, in some instances evidently at the addressee's request. Archbishop Hubert obtained one such letter from Celestine III and another from Innocent III.[4] He reiterated the rule in his council at Westminster (c. 8). Whether bishops generally took effective action is another matter, which requires investigation. Perhaps the legislation was a little behind the times, for the largest pensioners were monasteries and these, when they wished to enlarge the profit from their churches, were tending to get appropriation of the rectory.

The result of treating patronage as partible inheritance or as a subject for compromise after disputes where its ownership was disputed was to produce divided rectories. Rectors are presented to fractions of churches : not only halves, or moieties, but thirds, fourths, fifths and sixths. In

[1] Often as the result of a final concord or a compromise (see above, pp. 114–17). The bishop was sometimes granted a pension when he allowed appropriation by a monastery.

[2] In 1199 Innocent III authorizes Archbishop Hubert to restore tithes to churches from which they have been alienated (*PL*, ccxiv. 672, cf. IV Lateran Council, c. 56).

[3] *Decretals*, 3,39,8, cf. above, p., 115 n. 3.

[4] *PUE*, ii. 480 (1197) and *PL*, ccxiv. 672 (1199). See Innocent III's ruling on the bishop's powers, *SLI*, p. 75 (*Decretals*, 3,10,9).

the Danelaw, where villages were often divided between several manors, each lord of a manor had his share in the church. ' There is every reason to believe ', says Sir Frank Stenton, ' that when a church was to be built in one of these villages, the lords of all the manors within the village shared in the cost of its erection ' ; [1] and it seldom happened, as at Willingale (Essex), that two lords both built churches within one churchyard. The division of both income and responsibility often produced doubt and litigation : but the canon law gave no clear directive, although authorities might be cited for deprecating the division.[2] In 1222 Langton at Oxford forbad the creation of fractional benefices and provided for the gradual extinction of existing ones.

But already in the preceding half-century we find a few attempts to prevent the division of the office of parson. Patrons might be induced, especially if the patronage were in dispute, to make a joint presentation ; [3] or to present to the one moiety, when it fell vacant, the rector of the other : Hubert Walter had obtained such a settlement in the church of Okeford (Dorset) when he was bishop of Salisbury (1189–93).[4] The bishop of Norwich came into the king's court in 1203 to show cause why he had not admitted a suitable person to the moiety of the church of Erpingham on the presentation of Robert of Erpingham, and he came and said: ' although the advowson is divided he does not wish to divide the parsonage '.[5] In 1211 the advowson of a Yorkshire parish was divided by concord in the king's court ' if it could be done with the archbishop's agreement ' ; if the archbishop objected to dividing the parsonage, then the two parties were to have alternate presentations to the parsonage.[6] A like arrangement for alternate presentation was reached in the following year between two claimants to the church of Wootton Rivers (Wilts.).[7] Whether these

---

[1] F. M. Stenton, *Documents illust. social and econ. hist. of the Danelaw* (1920), p. lxxvii.

[2] E.g., *Decretum*, 2,7,1,41. [3] *CRR*, vi. 308, cf. p. 97.

[4] *Ibid.*, v. 178. [5] *Ibid.*, ii. 211.

[6] *P.R. 13 John*, pp. 29–30, cf. *CRR*, vi. 150. [7] *CRR*, vi. 251.

instances indicate a general attack upon moieties could only
be proved by more evidence. They simply show that
Langton's legislation was not the fruit of an altogether new
idea.

But although these legal complexities created a problem
for the bishop, his main difficulty arose from the increase
of non-resident rectors. He had to see to it that if a properly
qualified rector did not reside in the parish, a second benefice
was created in the church, alongside of the parsonage,
called a vicarage,[1] permanent, with a guaranteed income.
It is a little like the process of subinfeudation, though the
analogy cannot be pressed closely. The bishop must oblige
the non-resident rector to provide adequately for his vicar
and once a rector has assigned a portion to the vicar with
the bishop's approval, the parson's successor may not
remove the vicar or reduce his portion.[2] A letter obtained
by Peter des Roches, bishop of Winchester in 1205, suggests
that some rectors in his diocese were installing vicars who
did not themselves reside but who took a vicar's revenues
and deputed the service of the church to another ill-paid
substitute.[3] When a monastery appropriated a parish
church it became its non-resident rector. The bishop, in
approving the act of appropriation, was supposed to ' ordain
a perpetual vicarage ' : that is, he was to establish in a
written ordinance that there should be a vicar, instituted
by him, with security of tenure and with either a fixed
income or specified portions of the church's revenues from
glebe and tithe and offerings.[4] The man was known as a
perpetual vicar.

The notion has gained ground among modern historians
that the perpetual vicar, instituted by the diocesan, was

[1] Innocent III ruled in 1214 that a perpetual vicarage was a benefice
(*PL*, ccxvi. 954, *Decretals*, 1,3,27).

[2] *Decretals*, 1,28,3 (Alex. III to the bishop of Winchester).

[3] *PL*, ccxv. 723. Another situation is seen at Ludlow in 1200, when
the vicar farmed his vicarage (which consisted of a moiety of the church)
to the rector (Cheney, *Eng. bishops' chanceries*, pp. 157–8).

[4] E.g., Appendix III (xi).

chiefly a product of the thirteenth century, consequent on
Pope Innocent III's decree on the subject in the Fourth
Lateran Council of 1215 (c. 32). All admit that a few
earlier examples of the later practice can be found, but it
is usually implied that these were spasmodic, unsystematic ;
that the pope's legislation made all the difference.[1] I
believe that this is a misconception. It is based on the
mis-reading of one most remarkable record and the neglect
of a great deal of less conspicuous, scattered evidence.

The manuscript known as ' the old book of ordinations of
vicarages of the time of Hugh Wells, bishop of Lincoln ',
is still preserved in the Lincoln diocesan archives and was
privately printed by Alfred Gibbons in 1888. This contains some 80 deeds of appropriation and details of nearly
300 perpetual vicarages,[2] supposedly ordained by Bishop
Hugh de Wells. Hugh was bishop of Lincoln from 1209
to 1235 ; but he was absent from his see until 1213. Many
of the vicarages in this book are said to be ordained ' by
authority of the Council ' ; this can be shown to refer to
the Fourth Lateran,[3] which Bishop Hugh attended.

The value of this extraordinary record is enormous. It
shows Bishop Hugh's intense activity in providing adequate
recompense for vicars. What it does not show is the extent
to which Hugh was an innovator in the diocese of Lincoln.
By comparing this book with other records, one discovers
fifty or so perpetual vicars installed in churches of the
diocese before the time of Hugh de Wells. The earliest is
the vicarage of Aynho, Ralph de Diceto's church, established by Bishop Robert de Chesney (1148–64). Moreover,

[1] R. A. R. Hartridge, *History of vicarages in the Middle Ages* (Cambridge,
1930), has been generally followed. Morey, *Bartholomew of Exeter*,
p. 74 and Poole, *From Domesday Book to Magna Carta*, p. 227, recognize
that the prevailing view needs modifying.

[2] There are about 373 vicarages indicated, but many entries are
incomplete. The book omits the archdeaconry of Leicester, for which
another record remains (*Rotuli Hugonis de Welles*, i (Canterbury and
York Soc., 1904), 238–72).

[3] E.g., *Liber antiquus*, p. 103 ; the term refers to a vicarage dated
16 Dec. 1220 ; so it cannot mean the Council of Oxford (1222) which
fixed the five-mark minimum.

the nature of the evidence suggests that very many more of the vicarages normally regarded as creations of Hugh de Wells may in reality have been set up by his predecessors.[1] His ordinations may often have been reassessments.

The pontificate of Hugh de Wells may nevertheless have marked a new departure. In his time it seems to be more usual than before for the vicarage to consist in a portion of miscellaneous revenues, of which the appropriating monastery takes the lion's share. Not that this arrangement was unknown in earlier days ; but a vicar often took all the revenue, bore all the burdens, and paid a sum of money ' as a pension ' (*nomine pensionis*) to the corporate or individual rector. Where individual rectors were concerned (and the *Liber antiquus* did not deal with their arrangements), a cash payment was probably generally to be preferred. Appropriating monasteries, on the other hand, may have come to find it more profitable to take a rectorial portion of the revenues than a pension fixed long ago : fixed, maybe, when the transference of patronage was made over the head of the incumbent and the quondam rector became the monastery's vicar ; for the pension could not be raised without the diocesan's consent. It is noticeable that the status of perpetual vicars who paid only a pension often gave rise to doubt, and unless the rector, corporate or individual, had clear title deeds, the vicarage of one generation might become a parsonage in the next.[2]

If we leave the diocese of Lincoln, to look for evidence of vicarages elsewhere, we find a few indications in the middle of the twelfth century and many in the last thirty years. The evidence is of three sorts : sometimes the pope or bishop provides that a monastery possessed of a church shall present a clerk to the diocesan for institution ; sometimes the order is added that he be given proper means of livelihood ; sometimes an actual ordination of his vicarage is recorded. The earliest evidence is contained in a charter of Archbishop Thomas II or Archbishop Thurstan of York

[1] E.g., Appendix III (x).   [2] See Appendix III (vii).

(1109–14 or 1114–40) who grants four churches to the priory of Holy Trinity, York, ' saving in those churches a competent vicarage to be assigned to him who serves in them '.[1] The phraseology is a most remarkable anticipation of later usage. For a generation there seems to be no more light on the practice. Then, in the 1150's, the complete arrangement is seen in being at Winchester. The great Bishop Henry institutes Robert the chaplain to a perpetual vicarage in Christ Church, Twinham, on the presentation of the prior and canons, and confirms to him the various items of his annual income, which the former vicar, Hucgred, had and which are set out in detail : ten shillings in cash, a daily corrody for himself and a servant from the priory, offerings at confessions, mortuaries, mass-pennies, oats for his horse, and so on.[2]

Nothing quite like this can be found elsewhere at so early a date, but a few other references to vicars deserve mention. Robert de Warelwast of Exeter, between 1155 and 1160, appropriating Milton (Abbot) to Tavistock, demanded that a perpetual vicar be appointed to whom enough should be assigned from the revenues of the church for him to maintain himself decently and meet the demands of his superiors.[3] This corresponds with the arrangement made by Bishop Robert of Lincoln between 1151 and 1154 in churches of Newport Priory, although the terminology of his charter is less precise than that of his colleague at Exeter.[4] Some time before 1161 Archbishop Theobald approved the provision made for a perpetual vicar in the church of Norton, belonging to Rochester.[5] In the diocese of Hereford, before 1163, Bishop Gilbert Foliot settled ' sufficient and decent maintenance ', to the value of ten marks, on the ' chaplain

[1] *EYC*, vi. 82–4.

[2] Voss, *Heinrich v. Blois*, pp. 159–60. He appointed a perpetual vicar in the chapel of Binsted *c.* 1150 (*CRR*, iii. 119). The bishop also assessed four more vicarages in churches belonging to Twinham (1161 × 1170), safeguarding tenure and revenue (*ibid.*, 161–2).

[3] *EHR*, lxii (1947), 358, cited by Poole, *loc. cit.*

[4] See Appendix II and cf. the Aynho case, above, p. 124.

[5] Thorpe, *Reg. Roffense*, pp. 507–8.

or vicar' who was to serve the church of Cowarne, when
its appropriation to Gloucester Abbey took effect.[1] The
next generation of bishops has left clearer indication of a
widespread, consistent policy.

Roger, bishop of Worcester (1164–79), twice complained
to the pope that monastic rectors were shirking their duty
to maintain perpetual vicars. His complaints drew two
important decretals from Alexander III. One letter dealt
with the particular case of Ralph the priest. He had been
presented by the priory of Kenilworth to the bishop to serve
the church of Salford (Warwickshire). The bishop had
instituted him as perpetual vicar on securing a verbal undertaking that Kenilworth would assign a suitable portion of
the revenues to his maintenance. The prior tried to wriggle
out of the arrangement. To avoid further trouble, he
declared that Ralph was an annual, not a perpetual, vicar
and tried to eject him. Ralph appealed, putting his benefice under the protection of St. Peter, and set out for the
Curia. The pope instructed Bartholomew, bishop of Exeter,
to look into the matter and assess the vicarage, saying : ' We
do not wish annual vicars to be appointed in God's churches,
but perpetual vicars.' [2] It was an important statement of
principle.

The second reply elicited from Alexander III by Bishop
Roger is in a lengthy decretal.[3] This sets out clearly the
bishop's duty both to admit perpetual vicars to appropriated
churches and to see to it, when he admits them, that they
are assigned, in his presence, a portion which will meet
their obligations towards the bishop and provide them with
' decent and sufficient maintenance '.

These two statements, if they were widely recognized as
binding, went a long way towards ensuring a minister for
parishes where the rector did not reside, and provided vicars
with both security of tenure and adequate maintenance.

[1] *Hist. et Cartularium mon. Gloucestriae*, i. 252. There is no explicit
provision for the man to be presented to the bishop for institution.
[2] Coll. Wigorn., iv. 42 (p. 116).
[3] *Decretals*, 3,5,12 (*Epp. G. Foliot*, ii. 99–100).

K

But they were not general enactments, and although they found their way into books of decretals, these were not as yet official collections. That papal policy remained unaltered is shown by numerous letters of Alexander III and his successors which safeguard vicarages. If at the same time certain monasteries get papal privileges which specifically or by implication allow them to serve churches by removable clerks, not answerable to the diocesan, they are exceptions. Bishops, who (after all) had a fiscal interest in parish churches, make the policy of establishing vicarages their own. By about 1184 we find perpetual vicarages in more than half the dioceses of England.[1] Nor is there evidence that this was generally resisted.[2] And in the thirty years after 1184 the practice proceeds *pari passu* with the great increase of appropriations. Archbishop Hubert, in his Council of Westminster, 1200 (c. 14), required that in every church canonically appropriated by religious to their own use a vicar should be instituted to whom the bishop should assign a decent and sufficient maintenance from the property of the church. There was no special stimulus from Rome. Mr. Hartridge's statement [3] that ' Pope Innocent III sent many mandates to English bishops on the subject ' is just untrue. The decree of the Fourth Lateran Council (c. 32) did not create a new system, though it stimulated bishops to extend the system and to augment existing vicarages. But for England, before 1215, there remain records of two to three hundred vicarages at least, which bear witness, though imperfectly,[4] to the activity of the bishops in the preceding fifty years.

It was no small achievement of the bishops to get control

---

[1] I have noted them in Canterbury, Bath, Chichester, Coventry, Exeter, Lincoln, London, Norwich, Winchester, Worcester, York.

[2] Particular assessments of vicarages were sometimes resisted by monastic appropriators : e.g., St. Augustine's, Canterbury, 1215 (*SLI*, p. 193), St. Albans, 1219 and 1228 (*Gesta abbatum*, i. 275–9).

[3] *Op. cit.*, p. 35. The only clear example is the one he cites ' for instance ' : *PL*, ccxv. 723.

[4] The records are extremely incomplete. A bishop did not always

over the appointment of parish clergy, and to get, also, in
the squabble for church endowments, a share of the spoils
for the minister on the spot. But this was not enough.
The Church demanded of her ministers celibacy and a
modicum of book-learning. In this period she had difficulty
in obtaining either.

Innocent III stated the objection to a married parish
clergy in a decretal to Bishop John de Gray of Norwich, in
1203.[1] 'We have heard', he wrote, 'that certain clerks of
your diocese who have solemnized marriage before the
church (*in conspectu ecclesie*) strive to hold on to ecclesiastical
benefices, though in their conduct the harp accords ill with
the psalter. Since, therefore, a man thinks how he can
please his wife and is thereby impeded from pondering on
divine matters, and since he is divided in two and is not
completely free to serve fully Him whose wages he receives,
we grant that you may by authority of this letter deprive
such clerks of the ecclesiastical benefices which they have
got in your diocese . . . especially as such persons commonly waste church property.' Gerald of Wales colours
the picture more vividly. As archdeacon of Brecon he had
closer personal acquaintance with the facts than had the
Supreme Pontiff. 'The houses and hovels of parish
priests', he says,[2] 'are full of bossy mistresses, creaking
cradles, new-born babes and squawking brats'; and he
complains that the bishops connive at this state of affairs.
It is certainly true that although decrees of councils [3] and
decretals throughout this period condemned the marriage
and concubinage of the clergy, they were only half-heartedly

note in his appropriation-deed the creation of a vicarage : that might
be the subject of a separate act, e.g., *Charters and records of Hereford
Cathedral*, ed. W. W. Capes (Hereford, 1908), 40–2 ; *Early charters of
St. Paul's Cathedral* (Camden 3rd series lviii, 1939), pp. 51–3 ; *Cart. of
Darley Abbey*, ii. 605–8.

[1] *PL*, ccxv. 110 (*Decretals*, 3,3,5).

[2] *Opp.*, iv. 313. On the cost of keeping wife and family see *ibid.*,
ii. 277–81.

[3] In England, Westminster 1175 and 1200, York 1195 (Wilkins, i.
477, 502, 507).

applied. A strictly celibate clergy must have seemed as remote an ideal in Langton's day as in Becket's.

Gerald of Wales is equally outspoken concerning the ignorance of the rank and file of the clergy (to say nothing of his stories about archiepiscopal Latin). Again, we have decrees and decretals to set alongside of Gerald's good stories, proving that all was not well. But English church councils before Oxford 1222 do not advert to clerical education at all. Nor, so far as I know, is there yet any sign of elementary examinations in the reading and understanding of the liturgy when clerks were ordained or presented to livings. Gerald complained that prelates neglected to examine ordinands.[1] The earliest example I know of examination of the presentee to a living is the record on the Curia Regis rolls of a presentee rejected by Richard Poore, bishop of Salisbury, in 1219, because he was illiterate.[2]

Once instituted, an ignorant parson or vicar could not be easily displaced. He might put off the evil day by appeal to Rome or—if we could believe Caesarius of Heisterbach's edifying stories—might get dispensation from an even higher authority. For Caesarius tells [3] how Archbishop Thomas Becket suspended a priest for illiteracy. The only service the priest know how to recite was the mass of the Blessed Virgin Mary. Because he recited this daily, Our Lady ordered the archbishop to re-instate him, and the archbishop did so.

Prelates had to tolerate ignorance among the clergy, if not by heavenly command, by force of circumstances. For probably there were not enough educated men to go round, and not enough schools to train them.[4] Moreover, many

---

[1] *Opp.*, ii. 334–5, iii. 368.   [2] *CRR*, ix. 196.

[3] *Dialogus miraculorum*, dist. 7, c. 4 (ed. Strang, 1851), ii. 5–6. Full references to other versions of this tale are given by T. F. Crane, *Liber de miraculis s. dei genetricis Mariae* (Cornell, 1925), p. 86.

[4] See Maurice de Sully's summary of what every priest ought to know, in C. A. Robson, *Maurice de Sully and the mediaeval vernacular homily* (Oxford, 1952), p. 80, cf. p. 56.

benefices were miserably poor and would not attract able and ambitious men : as late as 1222 the minimum salary for vicars was fixed at only five marks. Rectors and vicars, it is true, appear in private charters and the public records with the title of 'master'. But they were few compared with the whole number of parish clergy. Probably a high proportion of the masters were non-residents whose benefices supported them in the schools or in administrative office.[1] They made no direct contribution to the cure of souls.

The bishop's responsibility for his flock did not stop at the selection and appointment of the beneficed clergy. He was expected to exercise ordinary jurisdiction and discipline over all his subjects : that included, as well as rectors and vicars, the unbeneficed assistant clergy, the laity, and the inmates of all religious houses which were not explicitly exempt from his control. He fulfilled this duty in visitations and synods with injunctions and precepts ; and as judge-ordinary in ecclesiastical law-suits he could hold court wherever he might be, *sedens pro tribunali*, and could delegate his judicial powers.

As for visitation, the old canon law which sanctioned it was hardly reflected in English practice before the last quarter of the twelfth century.[2] Then Becket's three immediate successors all used their metropolitan authority—and, on occasion, legatine authority—to visit cathedral churches and monasteries in various parts of England. Archbishop Richard began a visitation of his province soon after reaching England, by going to St. Paul's, London, in October 1174. We have traces of his presence on visitation in the dioceses of Bath, Chichester, London, Norwich, Rochester,

[1] Alexander III told the archbishop of York that absence for study was legitimate ground for non-residence (*Decretals*, 3,4,5).

[2] Archbishop Thomas II (1109–14) often visited monasteries of his diocese, according to Richard of Hexham (*The priory of Hexham*, i (Surtees Soc., 44, 1864), 53). The *Vita Wulfstani* of William of Malmesbury (ed. R. R. Darlington, pp. 36–7, 51–2) shows Bishop Wulfstan, already in the eleventh century, making regular pastoral tours of his diocese, preaching, confirming, and dedicating churches.

Winchester, and Worcester. He seems to have asserted his authority as legate and primate on these circuits.[1] His successor, Baldwin, visited the Welsh dioceses as legate and is reported at St. Werburgh's Abbey, Chester, in June 1187.[2]

Of Hubert Walter's visitations we have numerous records, though they are not sufficient to determine a complete itinerary. He visited all England as legate and, after his legation expired, visited the southern province as archbishop.[3] In 1195 he undertook a tour on explicit instructions from Rome.[4] He was in this year at Lichfield, where he made several suggestions for reform,[5] at York, where he deposed the abbot of St. Mary's,[6] and at Thorney, where he deposed the abbot.[7] Probably it was on another tour of East Anglia that he visited Norwich, Castle Acre, and Ely.[8] At Ramsey he was accompanied by Bishop Hugh of Lincoln and various abbots, and with their agreement delivered written injunctions (which survive) for the temporal management of the abbey.[9] On several journeys in the west country he visited Evesham and Lanthony, where he issued injunctions about meat-eating.[10] With Archbishop Hubert, moreover, we have one of our earliest indications of the visitation of parishes. At some time unspecified, he summoned the clergy and people of certain Suffolk parishes to undergo his visitation at Moulton, within the deanery of Bocking, a peculiar of the archbishopric.[11]

---

[1] *Gesta Henrici*, i. 80–1 ; R. de Diceto, i. 395–6, 398 ; Thorpe, *Reg. Roffense*, pp. 347, 350 ; *Chron. mon. de Bello*, p. 167 ; Jocelin of Brakelond, *Chronicle* (ed. Butler), p. 4.

[2] A. W. Haddan and W. Stubbs, *Councils*, i. 387–8 ; *Annales Cestrienses* (Lancs. and Chesh. Rec. Soc., 1887), p. 36.

[3] Cf. *PL*, ccxvi. 1231 for his monastic visitations by ordinary authority.

[4] R. de Diceto, ii. 146–7.   [5] Wilkins, i. 500.

[6] Hoveden, iii. 294. He visited some houses in the diocese by deputy (Gervase of Canterbury, i. 529).

[7] *SLI*, pp. 41–5.

[8] Jocelin of Brakelond, pp. 81–4 and *PUE*, iii. 571.

[9] *Cart. mon. de Rameseia*, ii. 204. Apparently the first nine articles are the archbishop's (cf. ii. 212).

[10] *Chron. abb. de Evesham*, pp. 106–7, 119, 129 (in 1197, 1201, and ?1203) ; *Calendar of papal letters*, i (ed. W. H. Bliss), 42.

[11] He overlooked the fact that the parishes of Isleham and Freckenham

English diocesans were not, it seems, prompt to follow their archbishop's example. Bartholomew of Exeter and Hugh of Lincoln are reported to have visited their dioceses.[1] The bishops of Worcester and Chichester visited certain religious houses in their dioceses around the year 1200.[2] These examples are far from indicating a regular system of visitation, nor did England come near to seeing such a system until late in the thirteenth century. All that can be discerned at the end of the twelfth century are the first stirrings of activity in this form of discipline.

It is not surprising that this aroused opposition and complaints about expense from those who were visited. Archbishop Richard was said to have travelled with a burdensome retinue,[3] and an attempt was made to discredit Archbishop Hubert at the Curia on the ground that he had been an oppressive and extortionate visitor.[4] In 1200 Hubert's own Council of Westminster (c. 5) reiterated the decree of the Third Lateran which fixed a maximum retinue for each rank of visitor, and declared, in accordance with the canons, that prelates should not take hospitality or procuration fees where they did not visit.[5]

The complement of pastoral visitation was the provincial council and the bishop's synod. There has been a tendency to regard the Fourth Lateran Council, which demanded (c. 6) annual meetings of these assemblies, as a starting-point in the revival of an ancient practice. But in England the development began a generation earlier. Archbishop Richard of Canterbury held the first English council to be called ' provincial ' in 1175. This council promulgated important canons, some of which found their way into the

were peculiars of Rochester within Canterbury's peculiar (*Reg. Roffense*, pp. 444–5).

[1] Below, p. 167 and *Gesta Henrici*, ii. 231–2.
[2] *Chron. abb. de Evesham*, pp. 109–10, 115–16, and *PL*, ccxiv. 975 ; *Calendar of documents . . . in France* (ed. J. H. Round, 1899), pp. 332–3.
[3] *Gesta Henrici*, i. 80–1.   [4] Jocelin of Brakelond, p. 85, *PUE*, iii. 572.
[5] Wilkins, i. 506. The above details correct the dating of the development in my *Episcopal visitation of monasteries in the 13th century* (Manchester, 1931), pp. 32, 36.

corpus of English church law and were glossed by Lyndwood in the fifteenth century as canons of Langton's successor, Archbishop Richard le Grand. Lyndwood's error has encouraged the view that the English church law which preceded Langton was archaic and inapplicable in later times. In fact, this council of 1175 contained up-to-date decretals on ecclesiastical discipline, had something to say about the law of marriage, and enumerated the recognized prefaces to the mass. It was, in its way, important.[1] Then, for twenty years, there was no sign of conciliar law-making in England until in 1195 at York and in 1200 at Westminster Archbishop Hubert promulgated more canons. These draw largely upon the decrees of the Third Lateran, but they are much more than mere reiteration of papal decrees. The canons are concerned with the behaviour of the clergy, religious Orders, and lay folk, and with the administration of the sacraments. They contain more of the didactic element than is found in earlier English conciliar law : they are the precursor and exemplar of synodal statutes of the thirteenth century, in particular those of Salisbury c. 1220.

To what extent the bishop's synod supplemented these infrequent councils, publicizing their canons and uttering additional statutes, it is hard to say. Recently a Swedish scholar has put forward the view that diocesan synods in their later form were a creation of Innocent III and the Fourth Lateran Council. This is claiming too much greatness for a great pope. Mr. Gagnér's arguments do not bear scrutiny.[2] We can say confidently that in twelfth-century England the synod was a regular institution in most, if not in all, dioceses. And while there is no long series of English synodal statutes earlier than the Fourth Lateran,

---

[1] Wilkins, i. 476–9, and see *EHR*, L (1935), 385–8.

[2] Sten Gagnér, ' Zur Entstehung der europaïschen u. der schwedischen Diözesansynode ', *Kyrkohistorisk Årsskrift*, 48 (1948), 1–31. Besides ignoring the English material M. Gagnér depreciates unduly the evidence for Odo de Sully's authorship of at least some of the Paris statutes preserved under his name.

The evidence which I adduce here modifies my view of the matter in *English synodalia of the 13th cent.* (Oxford, 1941), p. 31.

the *Gesta Regis Henrici* preserves one piece of statute-making in the preceding generation. *s.a.* 1186 the chronicle reads : ' Hugh, bishop of Lincoln . . . in his synods ordered that all his subjects, both clerical and lay, in virtue of their obedience should inviolably observe these decrees.' [1] There follow eight short precepts and prohibitions, directed against irregularities on the part of archdeacons and other officials and parish clergy.

These brief *decreta* are the only survival, to my knowledge, from twelfth-century England ; and one dubious piece of statute-making after the year 1200 occurs in an early manuscript of Archbishop Hubert's canons : [2] its five chapters must come from some English diocesan before 1215. Beside this evidence may be set references to decrees issued in synod. As early as 1136 Pope Innocent II provided that the abbot of Cirencester should send one of his canons to the bishop's synod ' who should hear and receive the episcopal customs (*consuetudines episcopales*) and report them to the other brethren '.[3] It would seem reasonable to interpret these *consuetudines* as statements of law rather than demands for money. In the dispute between Archbishop Richard and St. Augustine's in 1182-3, the obligation was laid upon priests to attend synods and hear *prohibitiones et precepta sinodalia*.[4] Finally we recall that Gerald of Wales, telling his story of the parish priest who absent-mindedly repeated ' Swete lamman dhin are ' at mass, declares that this caused the bishop of Worcester, William of Northall

---

[1] *Gesta Henrici*, i. 357. These decrees are paralleled by *decreta* for the diocese of Saintes (1141 × 1166) discovered by Dom Jean Leclercq : see ' Les decrets de Bernard de Saintes ', *Revue du moyen âge latin*, ii (1946), 167-70.

[2] British Museum, Royal MS. 7 C. vii, fo. 55. These statutes may not have been issued in a synod.

[3] *PUE*, iii, 152 (' si quando diocesanus episcopus sinodum celebraverit . . .').

[4] Gervase of Canterbury, i. 303. This is the title given to the synodal statutes of Paris ascribed to Odo de Sully (1196-1208). For the obligation to attend synod and receive *precepta* cf. *EYC*, iv. 1 (before 1086) and *Antiq. cartularius ecc. Baiocensis*, ed. V. Bourrienne (Soc. de l'hist. de Normandie, 1902), i. 113 (*c.* 1144).

(1186–90), to have it proclaimed in synods and chapters that the singing of such songs was forbidden.[1]

The bishop's synod was not only a place for statute-making. In the twelfth century it was used more for exhortation and correction, for giving publicity to the endowment of churches, for litigation. This introduces the bishop as judge ordinary. During the middle part of the century, as earlier, ecclesiastical suits of all kinds were often conducted in synods.[2] Towards the end of the century this procedure is still found, but only seldom : the insistence on a stricter procedure and the increasing professionalism of the bishop's clerical staff may well have led to formal court sessions outside the time of the synod. Unfortunately our sources give no details. But the bishop's and archdeacon's official appear for the first time, rural deans are more active than before, and we get the impression that the work was being delegated and placed in professional hands.[3]

Dr. Zachary Brooke suggested that after the time of Thomas Becket ' the bishop's court became much less important, and so did his functions as judge ordinary ; on the other hand, he commonly had to act on papal instructions as judge delegate.'[4] Evidence does not exist for a quantitative comparison between pre-1170 and post-1170 ; but on general grounds, it is hard to believe in a decline of the bishop's court, even though appeals to Rome often removed cases from his hearing. The evidence of their activity is scattered. Among the surviving papal letters which arose from appeals to Rome some refer to cases terminated before the ordinary. Cartularies, formularies, and casually preserved letters furnish other indications that the metropolitans and the bishops still used their judicial powers. A valuable series of letters and drafts survive from the time of Archbishop Hubert in the muniments of Christ

---

[1] *Opp.*, ii. 120.   [2] See Appendix III (i).

[3] This trend may be observed in France in the curious and learned work of Canon Edouard Fournier, *L'origine du vicaire général et des autres membres de la curie diocésaine* (1940), pp. 106–12.

[4] *The Engl. Church and the papacy*, p. 214.

Church, Canterbury [1]—valuable not so much for the persons and events they record as for the evidence of the judicial action of the archbishop, usually operating by deputy or delegate. They include cases of marriage, of testaments, of brawling in church.

It is evident that church government was more intensive than it had been, and the bishop had become busier, both as ordinary and as agent of the pope. As he came to exercise more regular control over the appropriation and the ministry of parish churches, as elaborate procedure *ordine iudiciario* came to replace the casual judicial proceedings of the synod, the bishop found himself in need of a larger clerical staff, trained to conduct the formal business and write the formal documents which now accompanied every institution, judgment, or report to Westminster or Rome. But the bishop did not only need a larger staff. He needed trustworthy deputies, especially when secular affairs took him away from home. He had his archdeacons, who were his recognized deputies, each in his own *provincia*.[2] The archdeacon maintained a relatively direct oversight in the parishes, over the morals of the parochial clergy and laity, the fabric of the churches, the filling of vacant churches.

From the middle of the twelfth century, at latest, the English archdeacon was holding his assemblies of the clergy under a variety of names : senate, synod, and provincial chapter.[3] There are a few indications, as the century advances, that he was expected to visit the parishes,[4] but we usually hear of this only because some archdeacons were

---

[1] Cf. Cheney, *Engl. bishops' chanceries*, pp. 130–1, 157–8, and below, Appendix III (xii–xiv).

[2] *Ibid.*, pp. 7–9. For vice-archdeacons, *ibid.*, pp. 9, 143–6.

[3] Singularly little is known of the composition of these gatherings, and it is not always easy to distinguish between the ruri-decanal chapter and the synod of a whole archdeaconry. From a letter of Bishop Herbert Poore of Salisbury to Archbishop Hubert it is clear that attendance sometimes fell far short of what was thought desirable (Hist. MSS. Comm., *MSS. in various collections*, i. 234).

[4] C. of Westminster (1200), c. 5, after reiterating III Lateran Council, c. 4, requires archdeacons to see that churches are properly furnished.

burdensome in seeking hospitality. The archdeacon of
Nottingham was reproved on this account in 1171, and the
archdeacon of Chester at some time in Alexander III's
pontificate.[1] The decree of the Third Lateran Council
(c. 4) which restricted retinues was explicitly mentioned in
later privileges for English religious houses,[2] so that we may
infer that archidiaconal visitations were a reality.

But the archdeacon's position was ambiguous. Even if
the lawyers sometimes treated him as having *cura animarum*
in a jurisdictional sense, this was something less personal
than either the pastoral duty of the parochial incumbent or
the paternal authority of the bishop. All his duties, without
exception, could be performed by deputy. An archdeacon
was tempted to treat his office purely as a source of income
and pursue a career elsewhere, leaving an underling to
discharge his duties. So, quite apart from scandalous cases
of neglect of duty,[3] the archdeacon often acted on the
bishop's business outside his own archdeaconry or, like Peter
of Blois, archdeacon of Bath and chancellor of Archbishop
Richard, took service with another prelate or with the king.
If he were a man of mark, he would appear on papal commissions of judges delegate. During the vacancy of a see,
he might carry many responsibilities of a diocesan, as the
records of Lincoln show.[4]

At a lower level, and within a smaller range, the rural dean
had come to play a quite considerable part in the machinery
of church government.[5] He was beneficed and resident on

---

[1] *Monasticon*, viii. 1314 ; *Decretals*, 1,23,6.

[2] E.g., *PUE*, i. 585-6, iii. 555.

[3] In 1202, G. de Pertico, archdeacon of Northumberland, was alleged
to be absent continuously from his archdeaconry and to be drawing
£100 p.a. from two churches which he had appropriated (*PL*, ccxiv.
1170-1).

[4] For institutions to benefices in dioc. Lincoln, *sede vacante*, by archdeacons see C. W. Foster in Assoc. Archit. Societies' *Proceedings*, xxxix
(1928-9), 179-89. The archdeacon of Derby acted in the vacant see of
Coventry, 1208 × 1215 (*Reg. antiquiss.*, iii. 49).

[5] While the archdeacon claimed to appoint rural deans, the bishop
sometimes established direct control. Cf. Gerald of Wales, *Opp.*, i.
222-3.

the spot. The archdeacon often passed on to him episcopal mandates to enquire concerning the patronage of churches, and so forth. He may sometimes have had the title of vice-archdeacon. Recent work on the activities of rural deans suggests that in this period they were handling more matters, executive and judicial, than ever before or since.[1] Much business fell to them which in a more highly developed bureaucracy went to full-time officials. According to the Council of Oxford (1222) they were venturing to hear matrimonial cases, which were beyond their competence.

The archdeacon and rural dean were already long-established. In this period the central government of the diocese was strengthened by the creating of a new official, an ' official ' *par excellence*, whose function was simply to be the bishop's deputy. In the third quarter of the twelfth century the *officiales* of bishops are mentioned in general terms. Then, in the last two decades named individuals appear with the title. According to Peter of Blois it was Richard of Ilchester, bishop of Winchester (1174–1188), who introduced the bishop's official into England,[2] and the other evidence is not incompatible. By about 1210 the bishop's official is found in most English dioceses, and before that date the archdeacon commonly has his official as well.[3] Probably he was partly occupied with judicial business from the first, but certainty is difficult to come by without court records or commissions. In the records which do survive the twelfth-century official usually appears as the person who gives corporal institution or induction to heads of religious houses and to incumbents of other benefices. In addition, he deputizes for the bishop when he is not in his diocese. Already in Glanvill's time the official was to bring a clerk into

---

[1] See the unpublished thesis of James Foster (M.A., Manchester, 1955) on ' The activities of rural deans in England in the twelfth and thirteenth centuries '.

[2] Cited by R. W. Southern, *EHR*, liii (1938), 412, n. 7. Carl Schmalz, *De instituto officialis sive vicarii generalis episcopi* (Breslau, 1899), p. 10 held that the first traces of bishops' officials were to be found in England.

[3] Cheney, *Eng. bishops' chanceries*, pp. 20–1, 145–6.

the king's court if the bishop was not available ; [1] and when, some few years later, Archbishop Hubert's secular duties took him overseas, his official, Master Simon of Southwell, armed with the archbishop's counterseal, wrote in his name on provincial business.[2]   During the interdict on England the exiled bishop of Worcester, for one, left diocesan affairs to be carried on by his officials.[3]

But some of a diocesan's duties could not be discharged by either archdeacons or officials.   For he exercised a *potestas ordinis* acquired only by consecration.   In Angevin England, because of the absences of diocesans, the long vacancies of sees, and the periods when they were ruled by bishops-elect, there was always work for an extraneous bishop to do. Bishops of the Celtic fringe flitted across the English dioceses, not without causing scandal ; the archbishop of Nidaros (Trondhjem) fled from King Sverre of Norway in 1181 ; [4] the archbishop of Ragusa, driven out by his Dalmatian flock, found refuge at the court of Richard I and eventually received the see of Carlisle in 1203 ; [5] the exiled archbishop of Nazareth stayed at Ramsey Abbey in 1203.[6]   These men were available to ordain clerks,[7] to confirm children, to

---

[1] *De legibus*, lib. iv, c. 9 : ' si nullus fuerit ibi episcopus '.   This might refer to a vacant see.

[2] Gerald of Wales, *Opp.*, iii. 216–17.   Canon Fournier, dealing with the official in France (*op. cit.*, pp. 113–77), regards the judicial rôle as his original and essential occupation (pp. 134, 143–7).   This is not confirmed by the English evidence (which Fournier ignores) and the fact weakens his thesis.

[3] *BJRL*, xxxi (1948), 311.   A few signs show penitentiaries for reserved cases in English dioceses before IV Lateran Council (c. 10 cf. K. Edwards, *The Eng. secular cathedrals*, p. 156).   A ' generalis diocesis confessor ' is mentioned in C. of York (1195) c. 16.   Hugh, bishop of Lincoln, sent a Buckden woman to the prior of Huntingdon : ' illarum videlicet partium penitentialem ' (*Magna vita S. Hugonis*, pp. 268–9).

[4] *Gesta Henrici*, i. 268–9.   He was billeted by the king on the vacant abbey of St. Edmunds and then on the vacant see of Lincoln.

[5] *SLI*, p. 54.

[6] *P.R. 5 John*, p. 6, cf. p. xviii.

[7] In 1207 the archbishop of Armagh was sent ' ad exequendum episcopale officium ' to the vacant bishopric of Exeter (*Rot. litterarum clausarum*, i. 88a), and celebrated orders at Evesham (Brit. Mus., Cotton MS. Faustina B. i, fo. 24r).

dedicate altars and consecrate or reconcile churches.[1] In the circumstances of the age auxiliary bishops were necessary ; but their *bona fides* was sometimes called in question [2] and they sometimes conferred ordination irregularly.[3]

Diocesan government, as it appears in action towards the close of the twelfth century, had one defect in common with papal government : for want of a well thought out and acceptable fiscal system, the administration had to resort to all manner of shifts, honest and dishonest, to make both ends meet. Diocesan finances, like the finances of the papacy, can explain much in the history of the Church. Time and again monetary considerations led to the condoning of abuse, the stifling of reform, the discouragement of zeal. We can remark their effects without being able in the present state of knowledge to give any adequate account of a bishop's budget.

The revenues of the English bishoprics varied greatly, but every bishop derived most income from the returns of land, the profits of jurisdiction, and the usual feudal incidents. He could also claim procuration—that is, hospitality—or a fee in lieu, from churches which he visited in his diocese. When parish churches fell vacant, he probably (as in later times) took some part of their sequestrated revenues. As patron on a large scale he could meet the expenses of administration in part by collating his officials, archdeacons, clerks, and chaplains to livings in his gift. He also inherited from earlier times customary fixed payments from the parish clergy and people, known as synodals, pentecostals, and *cathedraticum*.

These dues, regarded as customary and legitimate, were seemingly comprised under the general title of *episcopalia* or

---

[1] Bishop Albinus of Ferns dedicated a chapel and altars at Waverley, 1201 and 1214 (*Annales monastici*, ii. 253, 282).

[2] See Gerald of Wales, *Opp.*, iii. 368 and Archbishop Richard to his suffragans (Peter of Blois, ep. 53, *Opp.*, ed. Giles, i. 160-2).

[3] M. Paris, *Chronica maiora* (RS), vi. 41 ; *Reg. Malmesburiense* (RS), i. 375.

consuetudines episcopales, reserved to the bishop in twelfth-century papal privileges.[1]   One cannot, in many instances, be certain of the precise meaning to be attached to the general title.   Often it implies functions as well as profit. The situation became complicated during the twelfth century by the frequent assignment of duties and dues to arch-deacons.   The nature and value of this part of the bishop's income remains obscure, and until a thorough study has been made it is rash to risk any general statement.   But the subject is so important that something must be said briefly about it.[2]

Synodals were paid by the parish clergy, presumably when they assembled in diocesan synods.[3]   At first they were doubtless due to the bishop, but in some dioceses they had been alienated in favour of dignitaries or clergy of the cathedral.[4]   Pentecostals, linked with the annual visit to the mother church by clergy and laity of the diocese, probably went more often to the cathedral chapter than to the bishop ;[5] the proceeds, moreover, tended to be diminished by exemption (for other great churches besides the cathedrals had their Whitsun processions).[6]   The due most difficult

[1] E.g., *PUE*, i. 426 (1178) and 489 (1183).

[2] Cf. J. R. H. Moorman, *Church Life in England in the xiii cent.* (Cambridge, 1945), pp. 120–1.   On ' episcopal customs ' see Barlow, *op. cit.*

[3] Churches belonging to St. Paul's Cathedral were said in 1181 to pay 18*d.* at the synod after Easter and 18*d.* at the synod after Michaelmas (*Domesday of St. Paul's*, p. 147).

[4] Bishop Ernulf had granted his synodals to the monks of Rochester (Thorpe, *Reg. Roffense*, p. 7).   Archbishop Geoffrey ordered the archdeacons to pay the customary 100*s.* a year of ' our synodals ' to the chancellor of York (*EYC*, i. 129).   At Chichester in the thirteenth century the synodals were divided (*Chartulary of the high ch. of Chichester* (Sussex Rec. Soc., xlvi. 1946), no. 690, cf. pp. 308, 336).

[5] See *Reg. antiquiss.*, i. 257–9.

[6] E.g., Southwell took pentecostals in Nottinghamshire (*Monasticon*, viii. 1313–14), St. Albans in Hertfordshire (*Gesta abb. S. Albani*, i. 503, cf. *PUE*, iii. 279), Reading Abbey in the deanery of Reading (*Reg. Simonis de Gandavo* (Canterbury and York Soc., xl. 1934, p. 453).   Celestine III told the abbey of Fécamp, in 1193, that her parishioners must obey the ancient custom of Normandy whereby on Whitsun day from every household one person went in procession to the cathedral church or sent a penny by his priest (Loewenfeld, *Epp. pont. rom. ineditae*, p. 406 no. 251).

to distinguish is *cathedraticum*. Occasionally this appears to be payable by parish clergy to the bishop,[1] but in these instances may be identical with synodals.[2] More often it was a perquisite of the archdeacon,[3] and seems sometimes to have served as a convenient cover for illicit exactions.[4]

Apart from these periodic and customary revenues, both the bishops and their archdeacons asked their subjects for charitable aids on special occasions. The Third Lateran Council (c. 4), in condemning tallages and taxes, allowed moderate aid in case of need. The evidence for these aids, though slight, is enough to suggest that they were not altogether unusual in England. St. Frideswide's Priory obtained from Alexander III a special letter to prelates who had sought from them taxes under the name of gifts, ' preter debitum canonem ' ;[5] and about the same time contributions of one shilling towards an episcopal aid and of sixpence towards the archdeacon's were considered suitable for the churches belonging to Kenilworth Priory.[6] Rather later, Archbishop Geoffrey of York is said to have raised opposition from clergy and laity when he tried in 1193 to tax his subjects heavily.[7] This did not prevent him from seeking another aid for expenses incurred in exile.[8] His contemporary at Durham, Bishop Philip, was accused of overstepping his rights by demanding aids from the clergy of the cathedral priory's churches.[9] By contrast, when in 1194 the saintly Hugh of Lincoln involved himself in a debt of 2,000 marks

---

[1] The bishop of Coventry established his right to 2*s.* a year as *cathedraticum* from the rector of Manchester between 1198 and 1208 (*Magnum reg. album of Lichfield* (Wm. Salt Archaeol. Soc., 1924), p. 177).

[2] *Decretals*, 1,31,16, cf. Moorman, *op. cit.*, p. 120, n. 6. See also *Dictionnaire de droit canonique*, s.v.

[3] *Epp. G. Foliot*, i. 363 (ep. 266), cf. below, Appendix III (viii).

[4] See below, p. 153.   [5] *PUE*, iii. 447.   [6] *Ibid.*, iii. 411.

[7] Gervase of Canterbury, i. 520. As elect of Lincoln he had taxed his clergy, according to Walter Map (*De nugis curialium*, dist. v, c. 6) but cf. Gerald of Wales, *Opp.*, iv. 364.

[8] *PL*, ccxv. 613 (before 1205). The *auxilium* of churches and parsons in Durham diocese (*P.R. 8 Rich. I*, p. 256) and the *talliagium* of Exeter bishopric mentioned in 1208 (*Rot. lit. clausarum*, i. 110a) may be royal exactions *sede vacante*, but equally may be episcopal taxes.

[9] *Hist. dunelmensis scriptores tres* (Surtees Soc., 1839), p. 18.

L

to the Crown, he only reluctantly had recourse to his clergy. The clergy themselves voted the money and the bishop insisted that individuals should assess their own contributions.[1] How the assessment was usually reached is not known.

The evidence for archdeacons' aids speaks only of excesses. As early as 1161 Archbishop Theobald, in his last illness, had ordered a customary aid to be abolished : the archdeacon of Canterbury had benefited from this custom and Thomas Becket, as archdeacon, drew from the archbishop a remonstrance for opposing its abolition.[2] Some twenty years later the archdeacon of Essex was said to be demanding annually a subsidy of two shillings from each church and twelve pence from each vicar.[3]

Archdeacons, indeed, come badly out of these records. They were ill-provided with regular income and had plentiful opportunity to wring money out of their subjects. So is explained the evil repute from which archdeacons always suffered, as men who sold the sacraments, took bribes to connive at immorality, and practised many refinements of extortion. And no sooner has the bishop's official emerged into historical daylight than he is tarred with the same brush. We might suspect those eloquent archdeacons, Peter of Blois and Gerald of Wales, to be guilty of unfair harshness ; [4] but Gerald actually condemns his fellow archdeacons just as freely.[5] It is, however, significant that the evils attracted general condemnation ; even if corruption was widespread and could not be eradicated, at least there was unceasing effort to restrict it.

Archbishops Richard and Hubert, and Stephen Langton after them, all issued canons against the taking of fees for

---

[1] *Magna vita S. Hugonis*, pp. 185–7 (cf. *P.R. 7 Rich. I*, pp. 159, xxvi).

[2] *MTB*, v. 10–11.

[3] Coll. Wigorn., iii. 40 (p. 108). Cf. an earlier complaint about archdeacons in the diocese of Chester, John of Salisbury, ep. 69 (*Opp.*, ed. Giles, i. 91) and a later complaint about the archdeacon of Northumberland (*PL*, ccxiv. 1170–1).

[4] Peter of Blois, ep. 25 (*Opp.*, ed. Giles, i. 91) ; Gerald, *Opp.*, ii. 329.

[5] *Opp.*, iv. 329, cf. iii. 325.

inductions to benefices, for ministration of the sacraments, for burials.[1] Supervision of the morals of the clergy and people tempted archdeacons to make profit in such a way as to bring upon them royal rebuke in the Inquest of Sheriffs 1170 (c. 12). Archbishop Hubert, Hugh of Lincoln, and Gerald, archdeacon of Brecon, all forbade subordinates to accept gifts for the doing of justice.[2]

There was evidently a tendency among archdeacons to take advantage of an old and discredited custom. In the eleventh century and earlier parish priests paid an annual due to the mother church when they came in Holy Week to collect consecrated chrism for use in baptisms throughout the ensuing year.[3] But strict churchmen smelt simony in this, some English diocesans remitted the payment,[4] and it was condemned by the Council of Westminster 1125 (c. 2).[5] Nevertheless, chrism-money re-appeared as an exaction, usually by archdeacons, in the latter part of the twelfth century, sometimes described as a mid-Lent [6] or Easter [7] offering, sometimes levied under the name of some legitimate charge, synodal [8] or *cathedraticum*.[9] The occasion of the levy was objectionable, but the needs of administration probably

---

[1] C. of Westminster (1175) c. 7 and 8, York (1195) c. 3, Westminster (1200) c. 4 and 8, Oxford (1222) c. 2 and 18 ; cf. III Lateran c. 7 and IV Lateran c. 63 and 66. For bribes and fees taken by English archdeacons see *Decretals*, 5,3,20 and 36.

[2] C. of York (1195) c. 11 and 18, Westminster (1200) c. 12 ; *Magna vita S. Hugonis*, pp. 187–8 and *Gesta Henrici*, i. 357 ; Gerald, *Opp.*, i. 251. Cf. C. H. Haskins, *Norman institutions* (Harvard, 1918), pp. 330–1 and *PUE*, i. 508.

[3] See *The Domesday monachorum of Christ Church, Canterbury*, ed. D. C. Douglas (Royal Hist. Soc., 1944), pp. 6–8.

[4] *Historians of the ch. of York* (RS), ii. 191–2 (York, 1121) and below, Appendix III (iv).   [5] Wilkins, i. 408.

[6] Innocent III, writing to Archbishop Hubert (1199. *PL*, ccxiv. 657), accuses suffragan bishops of this practice. In 1181 the church of Caddington (Herts) rendered 12d. to the archdeacon in mid-Lent ; this was in addition to synodals (*Domesday of St. Paul's*, p. 147).

[7] E.g., *Cart. mon. de Rameseia*, ii. 152 (1160 × 1176), cf. Coll. Wigorn., iv. 16 (p. 111 = *Decretals*, 5,3,16) ; *PL*, ccxiv. 657.

[8] Coll. Wigorn., iii. 40 (p. 108) (1179 × 1181) ; *PUE*, iii. 523 (1191).

[9] Alexander III to the bishop of Norwich and dean of Chichester : ' Si vobis constiterit quod denarii qui occasione crismatis vel olei a clericis solebant exigi nunc mutato nomine pro chathedratico exigantur,

called for some such charge.   Certainly some of these payments had become well-established customs in later centuries.

Our conclusion must be that the mechanism of diocesan
government, however imperfect, shows a distinct advance
upon the conditions of the mid-twelfth century.   The
Church in the twelfth century had a programme of improv-
ing the discipline of the clergy and curtailing the rights of
laymen over churches.   She had to cope with the survival of
old ideas of proprietary churches and family livings, and with
the growing privileges and influence of religious Orders.
She dealt with this problem by enlarging the supervisory
power of the bishop and by giving him more deputies and a
larger office staff.   Angevin England seems to have produced
men for the task who were at least efficient.   They brought
to their duties as bishops and archdeacons legal education
and practice, and experience of the corresponding trend of
lay government in this age.   They were in constant touch
with Rome as petitioners, litigants, and delegates, and were
skilful enough to dodge, if they could not settle, the differences of Church and State.   What one misses in most of the
surviving sources is evidence of genuine evangelical activity.
The author of the *Gesta Regis Henrici* says [1] that St. Hugh,
bishop of Lincoln, ' lived in his diocese, edifying his flock by
his good life and words of fatherly exhortation '—as though
this was not what the world expected of a bishop.   Yet it
would be impossible to prove that bishops had been habitu-
ally in closer touch with their flocks in the first half of the
twelfth century.   The evidence is wanting.   It remains open
to doubt whether the men most influential in the Church, in
developing thus the mechanism of her government, did much
to strengthen the personal influence of the clergy as pastors
of the people.

archidiaconum illum qui hoc fecerit a tam nefaria exactione com-
pescatis.'   E. Friedberg, *Die Canonessammlungen zwischen Gratian u.
Bernhard v. Pavia* (Leipzig, 1897), p. 57.   Also cases cited in notes 7
and 8.

[1] *Gesta Henrici,* i. 357.

VI

THE LAITY

THERE is a synodal statute of the bishop of Worcester, dated 1229, which reads : [1] ' Laymen are not to sit in the choir among the clergy, nor carry cross or candle in processions, except as a matter of necessity.' The layfolk must be taught their place ; only the clergy have the right to be in the sanctuary. The two orders worship in separate compartments of the church, divided by screens of stone or wood. The separateness is emphasized by the rector's obligation to repair the chancel of the parish church, an obligation which remained when the duty of maintaining the nave was firmly put upon the parishioners. [2] It was a clear reminder that the function of the laity in the Church was to be obedient to the clergy in matters of dogma and discipline. They must do as they were told with submissive heart. Stephen Langton, preaching at St. Paul's on his return from exile in August 1213, tells his congregation : [3] ' Because you are layfolk, it is your business to believe that your prelates are men who do all things discreetly and with counsel.' The view of the Church as the community of the faithful was not lost sight of by the theologians. But in the government of the Church and in everyday speech, the Church was equivalent to the clerical order.

The clergy were the shepherds, the laity sheep. The Church could not therefore be expected to make much use of laymen in her government. The injunction of Deuteronomy xxii. 10 was held to be applicable : [4] ' Thou shalt

---

[1] Wilkins, i. 625, cf. *Decretum*, 3 (de cons.), 2,30.

[2] An early instance of the division is seen *c*. 1185 when the rector of St. Peter's, Northampton, is obliged to roof the chancels of his churches : Brit. Mus., Harl. ch. 44 H. 34.

[3] G. Lacombe, ' An unpublished document of the Great Interdict ', *Catholic Hist. Review*, xv (1930), 417. [4] *Decretum*, 2,16,7,22.

not plow with an ox and an ass together.' The old law of
the Church declared that a layman had no power of ordering
things (*statuendi*) in the Church : he had the obligation to
obey, not the authority to command.[1] It was in keeping
with this principle that Innocent III condemned an unrea-
sonable custom prevalent in the diocese of Passau whereby
in ecclesiastical cases the decision of the whole assembly,
both literate and illiterate, was treated as final.[2] We may
guess that in twelfth-century England the presence of laymen in the bishop's synod, seeming to participate in synodal
judgments, provided one reason for the gradual withdrawal
of lawsuits from the synod.

We have already seen how, during the twelfth century, the
theologians and canonists strengthened the *esprit de corps* of
the clerical order.[3] I revert to the matter now to point out
briefly that doctrinal and legal developments were reducing
the rôle of the laity in the administration of the sacraments.
Baptism could indeed be performed by layfolk, but the
earliest synodal statutes of the thirteenth century provide
that the priest shall always intervene afterwards to ensure
that rites connected with the sacrament were fittingly celebrated.[4] Again, although marriage was a sacrament celebrated by the contracting parties, and the validity of it did
not depend on a priest's presence, the Church legislated
rigorously against clandestine marriages, not celebrated *in
facie ecclesie*, and discouraged them by all penalties short of
annulment.[5] Finally, the doctrine of penance laid such
stress on the power of the priest to bind and to loose that the
ancient discipline of confession to laymen was pushed to the
background. Huguccio regards the layman grudgingly as
the last resort, *in articulo mortis*, if no priest, or deacon, or

[1] *Decretum*, 2,16,7,23, cf. *Decretals*, 3,13,12.
[2] *PL*, ccxiv. 526 (*Decretals*, 1,4,3).
[3] Above, pp. 103–6.
[4] Wilkins, i. 505, 576.
[5] C. of Westminster (1175), c. 17 and (1200) c. 11. Cf. IV Lateran
Council, c. 51 and A. Esmein, *Le mariage en droit canonique* (2nd ed., 1929),
i. 205–9.

subdeacon is available.[1] It is not always realized what a revolution this constituted in the twelfth century.

In theory the laity could not participate in church government. But just as the Angevin kings exercised a good deal of control over the Church in their dominions, so in relation to individual parishes and religious houses, local notables among the laity enjoyed customary rights and pulled ecclesiastical strings.

To return for a moment to the synodal statute of 1229. This reappears in a revised form at Worcester in 1240 : [2] ' Laymen are not to stand in chancels of churches during divine service, saving however the respect due to patrons and persons of rank (*sublimium personarum*) '. Bishop Robert Grosseteste made a similar order at about the same time : [3] he would admit only patrons to the chancel, ' out of respect or for some other reasonable and evident cause '. The patron was a force to be reckoned with. His station in the chancel, where his body might afterwards be buried, was symbolic. To the parson of a parish, the patron was not only the original giver of his benefice, he was usually a near neighbour, immeasurably superior in wealth and social standing, in a position to help or harm exceedingly. The Reverend Mr. Collins and Lady Catherine de Bourgh must have been familiar characters in the twelfth century, though their manners may have been less polished than in later days.

Even cathedral canonries, which in later times came within the bishop's collation,[4] were as yet sometimes under lay patrons. The king claimed the patronage of the prebend of Moreton-on-Lugg in the church of Hereford in 1200.[5] The Kyme family retained the patronage of the Lincoln prebend of Carlton by a charter of 1208,[6] and at a rather

---

[1] Quoted by P. Anciaux, *La théologie du sacrament de pénitence au xii siècle* (Louvain, 1949), pp. 588-9.
[2] Wilkins, i. 666.   [3] *R. Grosseteste Epp.* (RS), p. 162.
[4] Edwards, *Engl. secular cathedrals*, pp. 120-4.
[5] *CRR.*, i. 262, but cf. *PUE*, ii. 362-3.
[6] *Reg. antiquiss.*, i. 142, cf. ii. 241.

later date (1220 × 1228) awards by ecclesiastical arbitrators
put the Salisbury prebend of Shipton-under-Wychwood in
the patronage of Sir Adam of Brimpton and that of Blewbury
in the patronage of Hugh of Sanford.[1]

Monasteries, also, had their patrons.   How important the
relationship appeared both to the monasteries and to their
patrons emerges clearly from Mrs. Wood's monograph on
the subject.[2]   Patrons of monasteries included (with the
king, bishops, and earls) many lesser barons and country
gentlemen.   Even when they were not richer and more
powerful than the religious houses, they could be of material
assistance to them in courts of law and elsewhere.[3]   Moreover, patrons usually preserved some right in the appointment of heads of houses.   In 1201 and 1202 Roger de Lascy
appealed to Rome on two occasions and established in court
christian that priors-elect of Nostell and Pontefract must be
sent to him for confirmation ; if he approved, he joined with
the canons in presenting the elect to the diocesan.[4]   Roger
also brought into question the pension payable from Pontefract to the mother house of La Charité-sur-Loire.   The
abbey had claimed ten to fifteen marks or more, instead of
the one mark which was due.   Roger, as patron, defended
the priory against this burdensome tax, and won his point.
In the year of the Nostell case (1201) a still more important
patron, Earl Hamelin de Warenne, reached agreement with
the abbot of Cluny, an agreement arranged by distinguished
arbitrators : the archbishop of Canterbury, the bishop of
Ely, and the justiciar of England, Geoffrey fitzPeter.   This
safeguarded the earl's patronal rights in the election of priors

---

[1] *Charters and docts. of Salisbury Cathedral* (RS), 102–5, 123–4 and
Register of St. Osmund (RS), i. 327–8.
[2] S. M. Wood, *Engl. monasteries and their patrons in the thirteenth century*
(Oxford, 1955).   I do not discuss advocates of monasteries, of the
continental sort, as distinct from patrons who were the founders or
their heirs.   Examples in England are scarce, though the word *advocatus*
is found (Wood, pp. 17–18).
[3] *EYC*, viii. 123, cf. Wood, *op. cit.*, p. 144.
[4] Public Record Office, Anc. deeds D.L.25/46 (Pontefract) and
1223 (Nostell).

of Lewes and limited the annual pension due from Lewes to Cluny. It is significant that the award, like an interim settlement twenty years earlier, was made by a mixed clerical and lay body. It is also significant that, although this award was later condemned by Pope Gregory IX in a judgment incorporated in the *Decretals*, the condemned procedure still persisted for another hundred years.[1]

Then there was the question of custody of vacant monasteries, which a patron claimed in the same way as a feudal lord, who took his tenant's land into custody during a minority. When religious houses came under the royal patronage of the Angevins, the Crown exercised custody of their temporalities during vacancies and derived profit from them ; but this right seems to have been less thoroughly enforced by other lay patrons, though the right was safeguarded (probably against the Crown's encroachment) in Magna Carta (c. 46).

It was rare, but not unknown, for a patron to intervene for the maintenance of discipline in a monastery if it became notoriously corrupt. King Henry II seems to have initiated the visitation which purged and reformed the nunnery of Amesbury in 1177.[2] In 1207 King John instructed the bishop of Bath to enquire into the condition of the Cluniac priory of Montacute (Somerset), which was of the king's patronage—' so that our dignity be in no way diminished '. As a result Prior Durand was deposed and paid £100 to have the king's good-will ; the abbot of Cluny paid to be exonerated ; and the monks of Montacute paid £40 to stop the king from sending Durand back.[3]

But the rights and the influence exercised by lay patrons over churches only affected the upper classes of the laity and

---

[1] *EYC*, viii. 119–22 with references to other documents in the case ; cf. R. de Diceto, ii. 173, and see Wood, *op. cit.*, pp. 57–9.

[2] *Gesta Henrici*, i. 135–6, 165.

[3] *Rotuli litt. patentium* (Record Comm.), p. 78*a* ; *P.R. 9 John*, p. 60, *P.R. 10 John*, pp. 108, 110, *P.R. 11 John*, pp. 8, 100, *P.R. 12 John*, p. 72. For royal intervention in religious houses in the thirteenth and fourteenth centuries cf. K. L. Wood-Legh, *Studies in church life in England under Edward III* (Cambridge, 1934), ch. i.

affected them only to a strictly limited extent. Before the
end of the twelfth century, the old secular idea of lay proprietorship had yielded place to the ecclesiastical idea of
patronage. We are left with the general impression that
in the thirteenth century lay influence counted for more
than lay rights.

Patrons apart, lay society was excluded thoroughly from
the sphere of church government. In the English parish of
the early thirteenth century there is no trace of the church-
wardens,[1] the common parish fund, the communal action by
the parishioners which are found in and after the fourteenth
century. There may have been some lay control over the
money collected for the fabric of cathedral and parish
churches ; but if so, the records are wanting.

Layfolk, in short, had more duties than rights, and foremost among their duties was the material support of the
clergy. The Church represented this as a privilege, for it
was a kind of atonement for the sinful life they led. To
quote a chapter of the *Decretum* attributed to St. Jerome :
' They are allowed to take wives, till the land, . . . put
offerings on the altar, render tithe.' [2]

When we speak of the wealth of the medieval Church we
mean—as to nine-tenths of it—the amount which layfolk
have given to support and enrich the clergy. (In return, of
course, the clergy not only exercise the cure of souls but
also have certain moral and legal obligations towards the
sick and needy layfolk.) Some of the Church's wealth
comes by direct, compulsory taxation which a layman must
pay to avoid immediate censure. If he refuses to pay tithe,
he will be excommunicated, and the spiritual penalty is in

---

[1] For the earliest traces see the excellent essay by the late Charles
Drew, *Early parochial organisation in England : the origins of the office of
churchwarden* (St. Anthony's Hall Publications no. 7, 1954).

[2] *Decretum*, 2,12,1,7 : ' His concessum est uxorem ducere, terram
colere, inter virum et virum iudicare, causas agere, oblationes super
altaria ponere, decimas reddere, et ita salvari poterunt, si vicia tamen
benefaciendo evitaverint.'

itself a means of exacting material penalties. For the man
who is excommunicated for tithe, and who does not submit
to the Church and pay his dues along with legal costs, may
find himself put into the king's prison until he does submit.
There are other payments made by parishioners to their
rector or vicar—for example, churchset and mortuaries—
which are so rooted in custom as to be compulsory. In
addition, the clergy expect fees, more or less fixed in amount,
to be paid on the occasion of baptisms, burials, marriages,
and so forth. These must be voluntary payments if the sin
of simony is to be avoided. But the Church uses all its
powers of admonition to ensure that such ' laudable customs ' are maintained.[1]

The original endowment of the parish church, it is true,
usually provided the incumbent with some land, and occasionally the glebe was so extensive as to put him in the rank
of substantial farmers. In this way the clergy (at least in
country places) shared many of the cares and occupations of
their parishioners. But probably they relied mainly for their
living on seasonal and casual offerings, in money and kind :
the ' parochialia iura et de vivis et de mortuis ' of a Merton
Priory document of 1180.[2] Like episcopal revenues, these
offerings form a subject which deserves further investigation.[3] The enquirer may hope for some light from the
ordinations of early vicarages and from lawsuits and complaints about the withholding of dues.

So, in 1212 (during the general interdict) a jury of six
priests met in Wexham church (Bucks) to assess the value of
the vicarage in the neighbouring church of Upton, appropriated to Merton Priory.[4] They reported, among other
things, that the vicar drew 30s. in lesser tithes, offerings

---

[1] Cf. Innocent III in *PL*, ccxv. 472 and IV Lateran Council, c. 66.

[2] A. Heales, *Records of Merton Priory* (1898), Appendix, p. xx.

[3] Dr. J. R. H. Moorman has already brought together valuable details
in *Church life in England in the 13th cent.*, pp. 110–37. A wealth of information about offerings on the continent, especially in France, is contained in Georg Schreiber's *Gemeinschaften des Mittelalters* (Münster,
1948).

[4] Heales, *op. cit.*, p. 67, cf. *Liber antiquus Hugonis Welles*, p. 18.

worth 30s. at Christmas, Candlemas, Easter, and other feasts, and the money paid at confessions. Appropriating monasteries and rectors were careful to regulate the share their vicars took. At Henlow (Beds.), late in the twelfth century, a priest named Hacon held the vicarage from Lanthony Priory.[1] He took one third of the proceeds (*obventiones*) due from the whole village except for the tithe of the canons' demesne ; but when his successor, Hugh, was appointed, by a readjustment of obligations Hugh received ' all the altar-bread and all the cheese '. Again, at Painswick (Gloucs.) early in the thirteenth century, the resident rector was assisted by Richard the son of Robert of Stroud, a priest, as his vicar ; it was agreed that for part of Richard's recompense he should receive the offerings of the rector's household, the mass-penny at burials, ' reasonable ' legacies of parishioners, and ' half of his confessions '.[2]

When a vicar's whole stipend might be worth as little as five marks, these offerings were not inconsiderable. They meant much to a poor incumbent, and more to a poor parishioner. They must have been a constant concern and, in the case of lesser tithes especially, the difficulty of determining the obligation must have given rise constantly to evasion and dispute and ill-feeling. As Mr. Pantin says of tithe-paying,[3] ' it must have required the tact of a saint to make the system run smoothly.'

Compulsory or quasi-compulsory charges throw little light upon the people's response to the demands of church government. In order to discover that, it is more instructive to observe the ways by which the Church encouraged good works and the material expressions of piety : the endowment

[1] See Appendix III (x).

[2] See Appendix III (xvi). ' Oblaciones domus rectoris prefate ecclesie ' is rather puzzling ; and I am not sure whether in this case ' legatum ' should be taken as the equivalent of mortuary.

[3] W. A. Pantin, *The English Church in the 14th cent.* (Cambridge, 1955), p. 204.

The lack of a fixed rule about mortuaries and the attempt of a rector *c.* 1200 to establish a rule is seen in *Chartulary of the high church of Chichester*, no. 28.

of religious houses with landed property, the offerings at
shrines of saints, the response to appeals for church-building.
Sinful man seldom thinks that he is on the way to regenera-
tion unless he is expending toil or money. It is a common
saying that people do not value what they get for nothing.
And so a man who obtained an indulgence, or who wished
to share the merits of a monastic Order by taking the
cowl on his death-bed, or who looked for help through
the intercession of some particular saint, gave a *quid pro
quo*.

Homilists, to be sure, insisted on the importance of the
godly intention behind the good works. ' God has no regard
for the works of a bad Christian, for neither he nor his works
please Him . . .' preached Maurice de Sully ; [1] ' what profit
can it be to him to go on pilgrimage and travel far from his
village if he does not travel far from his sin and vice ? ' ' At
times ', wrote Pope Innocent III,[2] ' the evidence of works
is unreliable and deceptive, as for example in hypocrites.'
But these reminders were necessary just because the Church,
in her appeal to the masses, encouraged the contrary belief.
The inner life must find outward expression. The pilgrimage of the Christian's life on earth became a pilgrimage to a
shrine, the soldier of Christ became a Crusader against the
enemies of the Church, and the pious laid up store for themselves in Heaven by furnishing God's houses, the churches
here below. One could multiply examples. As Sir Maurice Powicke has put it : [3] ' An excitement of the senses accompanied the appeal of the spirit.' The clergy controlled
nearly all the usual practices of devotion and, incidentally,
disposed of the proceeds.

The religion of the people was bound up so much with
external observances that a historian who wishes to discover
its trends may hope to find a good many clues in records,
monuments, and surviving *objets d'art*. But there are serious

---

[1] C. A. Robson, *Maurice de Sully and the med. vernacular homily*, pp. 108–9,
cf. the rest of sermon 14 and pp. 34, 82.
[2] *SLI*, p. 28.   [3] *The Christian life in the Middle Ages*, p. 12.

difficulties in interpreting the evidence. The first and most serious arises from the fact that in the Middle Ages religious observance was a function of society, so that we often cannot distinguish between inner impulse and social pressure as the motive for a pious act. Motive in these matters was too complicated a thing for us to assess, with our imperfect data and measuring instruments. It is a commonplace that people went on crusade for all sorts of reasons, some the reverse of spiritual. And how can we tell which was the Pharisee and which the sincere penitent among subscribers to a building fund?[1] The solitary who acquired a reputation for holiness might be an impostor, like the Yorkshire knight who turned hermit in the reign of Richard I and attracted Robert of Knaresborough to his side. When the king died, says Robert's biographer, a trifle crudely,[2] ' the knight returned to his wife and children like a dog to its vomit '. He had fled to the woods simply for fear of the king, whom he had offended.

A second difficulty of interpretation lies in the very abundance of evidence as compared with the materials from the early Norman period. On the one hand, we have new ordinances for the paying of pentecostals and numerous complaints about wicked men who withheld tithes and dues. Do they indicate that the laity were more antagonistic to the Church's demands or that prelates were becoming more efficient and kept better record of their subjects' obligations? On the other hand, pilgrimages to local shrines and miraculous happenings at the intercession of the saints are more copiously recorded than before. But was there really any increase? The records may be explained by the formalizing of canonization. The pope demanded written evidence of the wonders that occurred : hence collections relating to Thomas Becket, to Wulfstan of Worcester, Gilbert of Sempringham, Hugh of Lincoln, and Osmund of Salisbury, all

---

[1] Miss M. D. Anderson quotes appositely the fifteenth-century *Dives and pauper* to this effect (*The imagery of British churches* (1955), p. 13).
[2] *Analecta Bollandiana*, lvii (1939), 369.

chronicling events in these days.[1] Earlier hagiographers simply had not learnt to be equally business-like.

Despite these difficulties of interpretation and the impossibility of arriving at definite conclusions, it is worth while considering, if only briefly, the ways in which people's devotion was expressed. First of all, the parish church—and to some extent the cathedral church—provided the ground for common worship, with the many-coloured liturgy of the Christian year and homilies to elucidate its significance, with the sacrifice of the Mass, with the commemoration of the dead, and special devotions in honour of the Blessed Virgin. The better furnished church provided visual instruction in the image of a saint or a picture of the Doom.[2] But many churches were poor and poorly served. Parish clergy often lacked the education and the means to make the church services edifying and dignified. What proportion of churches were well furnished, how many parsons or vicars delivered homilies, how many parishioners attended the church regularly—we shall never know. Church-goers had the opportunity then, as now, to show their piety by providing for the fabric. It is precisely in the 1170's that we meet first with a confraternity of the fabric in one of the greater English churches.[3] The earliest known was founded by Gilbert Foliot, about the years 1174–5, for the completion of St. Paul's Cathedral. Others followed at Lincoln and Salisbury. This period was a great age in the re-building and enlarging of cathedral and parish churches, and the evidence remains in stone.

[1] The ' miracula S. Thome ' of Benedict was probably written before the canonization though it was not actually sent to Rome (cf. E. Walberg, *La tradition hagiographique de S. Thomas Becket* (Paris, 1929), pp. 55–73). But the cardinal legates had doubtless seen at least part of the collection, and the pope justified the canonization in part by well-attested miracles (*MTB*, vii. 546).

[2] E.g., the painting at Chaldon, (Sussex), *c.* 1200, and see E. W. Tristram, *English medieval wall painting* (12th and 13th cents.) (Oxford, 1944–50).

[3] Rose Graham, ' An appeal about 1175 for the building fund of St. Paul's cathedral church ', *Journal Brit. Archaeol. Assoc.*, 3rd series, x (1945–7), 73–6 ; C. R. Cheney, ' Church-building in the Middle Ages ', *BJRL*, xxxiv (1951), 20–36.

Written records more often introduce pious laymen of the richer sort as the founders of chapels in the remote parts of large parishes and in their own homes. These chapels were supposed only to be established with the bishop's consent.[1] For this reason, and because disputes often arose about their status in relation to parish churches and their patronage, they are often better documented than are more important churches. An instance of the chapel founded for the benefit of an isolated group is that of Saddleworth, built about the end of the twelfth century on the Yorkshire moors by William de Stapleton.[2] It lay within the parish of Rochdale (Lancashire), but the parish church was fully ten miles away, across rough country. The idea of the proprietary church still lingered in attenuated form, and gentry who could no longer treat the parish church as a private possession set up chapels for their own households in their own houses. Between 1178 and 1185 Gilbert de Vere, brother of Aubrey III, earl of Oxford, had a chapel and chaplain within his house (*curia*) of Rainham (Essex).[3] A few years later, St. Hugh, bishop of Lincoln, ratified an arrangement by which the rector of Allexton (Leicestershire) agreed with Peter, son of Hasculf the forester to allow his chaplain to serve in Peter's oratory in his house.[4] Another example, of the same period, comes from Norfolk, where the parson of Great Hingham granted Robert de Cantelu, his patron (*advocatus*), a chapel in his house.[5] About 1200 Ralph, son of Simon of Wessington, in Derbyshire, arranged for his household chapel (' quam feci in atrio meo ') to be served by an Austin canon or by the canons' chaplain of Crich.[6]

---

[1] C. of Westminster (1138) c. 12 (Wilkins, i. 415).
[2] *Coucher book of Whalley Abbey*, i (Chetham Soc., x, 1847), 147.
[3] *CRR*, v. 147.
[4] *Sir Christopher Hatton's book of seals*, ed. L. C. Loyd and D. M. Stenton (Oxford, 1950), no. 163, pp. 118–19.
[5] Bodleian MS. Norfolk ch. a. 2 (no. 167).
[6] *Cart. of Darley Abbey*, ii. 439–40. For interesting details of the services provided in the chapel of Hundridge (in Chesham, Bucks) in 1200, see *CRR*, i. 459, and in William de Cantelupe's chapel of Water Eaton (in Bletchley) in 1211, see *Pedes finium* (Rec. Comm.), i. 247.

There is little sign, so early as this period, of privately
endowed chantries in parish churches. But a story told by
the St. Albans chroniclers [1] about Bishop Bartholomew of
Exeter (who died in 1184) is relevant to the theme. Bartholomew was on visitation of his diocese. One night when he
slept in a house adjoining a village church and its cemetery
he arose about midnight for matins. In the darkness he
heard a child's voice say in English ' Riseth op, alle Cristes
icorne. Levenoth ure fader of þis wrold fundeth (Rise up,
all Christ's chosen people. Levenoth our father is departing
from this world) '. Thereupon a chorus of children's voices
replied : ' Woe upon us, woe upon us. Who will now pray
for us and give alms, or celebrate Masses for our salvation ?
Levenoth our benefactor is passing away.' When morning
came the bishop discovered that a parishioner named
Levenoth had died that night. He had been a great giver
of alms and had maintained at his expense a priest to celebrate daily prayers and Mass for the departed. The voices
the bishop had heard were of the souls in purgatory whose
bodies lay in the adjoining churchyard. It is a nice example
of provision for a mass-priest.

Hermits and anchorites of both sexes formed a distinct
class of devout persons, neither wholly clerical nor wholly
lay. They were sanctioned by the Church and supported
largely by the alms of layfolk. Many of them only appear
as the recipients of regular grants from the Crown recorded
year after year on the pipe rolls. Occasionally we have
fuller information about these recluses and their patrons.
Just as St. Wulfric of Haselbury had been kept by William
fitzWalter in Henry I's reign,[2] so St. Robert of Knaresborough was provided (towards the end of the twelfth century) with a church dedicated to St. Hilda and land to
cultivate at Rudfarlington in the vale of Knaresborough.[3]

---

[1] Roger Wendover in M. Paris, *Chronica maiora* (RS), ii. 216–17 and M.
Paris, *Hist. Anglorum*, i. 312–14. A similar story is connected with
St. Edmund Rich, in the Lanercost Chronicle.

[2] *Vita S. Wulfrici*, ed. M. Bell (Somerset Rec. Soc. 47, 1933).

[3] ' Vitae S. Roberti Knaresburgensis I ', ed. Paul Grosjean (*Analecta*

M

His benefactress was a noble lady, Helen, who was probably of the family of Percy. When Robert's hermitage was disturbed by robbers, Helen gave him shelter and maintenance adjoining the church of Spofforth. Later in Robert's life the powerful William de Stuteville was converted by a vision from being his persecutor to be his protector, and gave him land and stock in another place, and alms to distribute to the poor.

I turn to consider briefly the laity's attitude to the religious Orders, though it is impossible to do justice to a subject which deserves close investigation. The records are confusing. For if some suggest that monasticism was failing to attract recruits of the same number and quality as in the past, the evidence is insufficient to prove it. And if the monasteries' acquisitions of lands are more often by purchase or exchange than by free gift, they may have received large gifts in other forms. Scarcely any new Benedictine abbeys are founded, but other Orders continue to expand, well into the thirteenth century. King John, prompted by Archbishop Hubert, endows the Cistercian abbey of Beaulieu as an act of penance. Archbishop Hubert himself, like his friends and relations among the wealthy gentry and official class, encourages the Orders of regular canons. But it is noticeable that as a rule the public was not generous to these foundations : few of them enjoyed great prosperity. Nevertheless, the monasteries were commonly the burial-places of the saints, and notable relics attracted pilgrims. The treasurers' accounts of Christ Church, Canterbury, which begin in 1198, show the great popularity of this unique shrine.[1] Many less important places of pilgrimage testify to the people's lively faith. Religious zeal was quickened by miracles at the tombs of St. Modwenna in Burton Abbey (1201), of St. Frehemund in Dunstable Priory (1213).[2]

Bollandiana, lvii. 1939). See also *The metrical life of St. Robert of Knaresborough*, ed. Joyce Bazire (Early Eng. Text Soc., orig. series, 228, 1953).

[1] C. E. Woodruff, ' The financial aspect of the cult of St. Thomas of Canterbury ', *Archaeologia Cantiana*, xliv (1932), 13–32.

[2] *Annales monastici*, i. 209, iii. 39.

Miracles worked by the merits of St. Amphibalus provided money to build the west front of St. Albans.[1] The tomb of William the baker of Perth, who was murdered by robbers when on pilgrimage to Canterbury in 1201, enhanced the reputation of Rochester Cathedral.[2] Such facts are testimony equally to the enterprise of the monks who owned the bones and to the faith of the people who brought their maladies and their offerings to the shrines.

There was a general disposition to look for signs and wonders. The rumour of miracles at the tomb of the young King Henry in 1183 was put about for political reasons.[3] Other cults, engineered by disreputable clerics for their own profit, had to be condemned by ecclesiastical authority.[4] But the clergy were in general ready enough to encourage these acts of reverence and to give credence to miracles and prodigies. William of Newburgh, the shrewd Austin canon, derides false miracles, but he believes the story told by Stephen, archdeacon of Buckingham, about a restless ghost whom St. Hugh of Lincoln laid by opening his coffin and placing a written certificate of absolution on the breast of the corpse. He is also prepared to believe that King Sverre of Norway brought about the destruction of King Magnus's fleet (1186) by invoking the devil.[5] As we read Ralph of Coggeshall we get a glimpse of the world of fancy in which the Cistercians of this time lived ; and able men among the secular clergy were just as prone to accept uncritically the marvellous and mysterious. John of Salisbury, Ralph de Diceto, Roger of Howden all expected the prophecies of Merlin to come true.[6]

[1] *Gesta abb. S. Albani*, i. 219.
[2] *Acta sanctorum : Maii*, tom. v, pp. 268–9.
[3] Coggeshall, *Chron. anglic.*, p. 267 ; Wm. of Newburgh, in *Chron. reigns Stephen*, etc. (RS), i. 234.
[4] Bishop Hugh of Lincoln condemned superstitious respect paid to a murdered plunderer of the Jews : sensible folk had scoffed, but it had been favoured by clerics for the profit they gained (Newburgh, *loc. cit.*, i. 311). Archbishop Hubert condemned the cult of William fitzOsbert in London (*ibid.*, ii. 473).   [5] *Ibid.*, ii. 474–5, i. 231.
[6] John of Salisbury, ep. 176 (*Opp.*, ed. Giles, i. 284–5) ; R. de Diceto, ii, p. lvi ; Hoveden, ii. 47.

When the pastors' faith was salted with such ingredients it was natural that the laity should show a taste for the miraculous. Revivalist preachers might reasonably hope for audiences and results. Little enough is known of the ordinary preaching *ad populum* in twelfth-century England, but we have reports of the English preaching tours of a French abbot, Eustace of St. Germer de Flay, in 1200 and 1201.[1] Eustace invited people to repentance and to take the Cross, for the Fourth Crusade was then being planned. According to Roger of Howden he also worked some truly astonishing miracles. On his second tour, he came armed with a letter, written in the name of Jesus Christ, which had been found, so he declared, on the altar of St. Simeon in Golgotha, at Jerusalem. This pious fraud, which had long antecedents,[2] condemned the profanation of the sabbath and of holy places. As a result of Eustace's sermons at least nineteen Sunday markets were moved to week-days, and miracles brought retribution upon numerous breakers of the sabbath.

Eustace, and others like him who excited piety among the people by working wonders, did not always have ecclesiastical authorization.[3] And the saints who had a popular appeal were not always canonized by Rome. But Innocent III might decree in the Fourth Lateran Council (c. 62) that relics must not be sold, that the veneration of new relics could only be authorized by the pope, that pious frauds must not be tolerated ; the clergy in the provinces remained content with fairly low standards of criticism in weighing merits and miracles. They were more indulgent than was the court of Rome to popular enthusiasm.

---

[1] J. L. Cate, ' The English mission of Eustace of Flay, 1200–1 ', in *Études d'hist. dédiées à la mémoire de Henri Pirenne* (Brussels, 1937). Eustace was preceded in his appeal for a stricter sabbath by an anonymous old man who warned Henry II at Cardiff in 1172 (Gerald of Wales, *Opp.*, v. 289–91).

[2] See *Dict. d'archéol. chrét. et de liturgie*, s.v. ' Christ, Lettre du ' and for references to recent literature of the subject, C. Brunel, ' Versions espagnole, provençale, et française de la lettre du Christ tombée du ciel ', *Analecta Bolland.*, lxviii (1949), 383–96.

[3] It is unlikely that Innocent III sent Eustace (Cate, *loc. cit.*, pp. 4–5, 8–9).

Talking of pilgrimages and the response to preachers like Eustace of Flay, we are bordering on the subject of the Crusades. Here again we encounter a baffling insufficiency of records. What England contributed in men and money to the Crusading movement deserves closer investigation than it has yet received, even though the findings can hardly be conclusive. I must confine myself now to pointing out that England was moved more in this period by the idea of the Holy War than before or since. She made a far greater contribution to the Third Crusade, with her king and soldiers and resources, than to any of the earlier expeditions. Close study might reveal that there were more English Crusaders in King John's reign than has been suspected.

Many Crusaders did the right thing for the wrong reasons, but the movement as a whole remains the greatest manifestation in that age of religious enthusiasm—the sudden gust of devotion which bowled men over and made them resolve on meritorious action without worrying overmuch about the economic and social consequences. And although the Crusades were controlled in actual fact by kings and noblemen, who restricted clerical intervention as much as they could, the movement was essentially sanctioned and sponsored by the pope. And whatever the other advantages which a Crusade offered to its participants (they included the Church's protection for Crusaders' property) the essential spiritual reward resulted from papal indulgences.

What did the laity think about this system of church government? Only one generalization is safe—that comparatively few thought about it at all. Beyond this we cannot go very far. Record sources shed practically no light upon the matter, apart from a few which show some sympathy with the king in resistance to papal claims. The chroniclers are all clerks or monks, and their testimony is confined to examples of piety rewarded and impiety punished. Literary works are seldom of service : even those on secular subjects and those which breathe secularism are generally written by clerks. The authentic voice of the layman is missing.

There is one biography of a layman of this period, composed in the vernacular a little later, to all intents and purposes by a layman. I refer, of course, to the *Histoire de Guillaume le Maréchal*, written about 1226 on the basis of information from the Marshal's squire, John d'Erlée.[1] This is the picture of a pattern of chivalry and a man of distinguished character. In the last years of his long life he worked in close, friendly co-operation with the papal legates in England and the archbishop of Canterbury. But what does his biographer tell us of his sentiments towards the Church ? Practically nothing. The Marshal goes at his king's command on pilgrimage to Jerusalem ; he goes also as a pilgrim to the three kings of Cologne. At various times in his career and on his deathbed he makes substantial, but not over-lavish, gifts to religious houses. He leaves his body to the Templars, and he is admitted to the confraternity of the Cistercian Order. He makes a pious ending after receiving a plenary indulgence from the legate Pandulf. But with these exceptions, the Church and the clergy hardly appear in the 19,214 verses of the biography. One remark made by William during his last illness has been often quoted. A knight present at William's bedside irritated his master by reminding him of the doctrine that a man cannot be saved unless he restores what he has taken from others. The Marshal, who in his time had beaten five hundred knights in tournament and appropriated all their gear according to the rules of the game, replied : ' The clergy are too hard on us : they shave us too close . . . Either their argument is faulty or no man can be saved.' [2] This is revealing, but does not show desperate anti-clericalism. Perhaps the most interesting bits of the *Histoire*, for our present purpose, concern the Marshal's appointment to the regency of England and

---

[1] Discovered in 1881, it was edited by Paul Meyer in three volumes, Soc. de l'hist. de France, 1891–1901. It is used extensively by Sidney Painter, *William Marshal* (Baltimore, 1933).

[2] vv. 18481–2, 18495–6.

his resignation of it. He only accepted office when the papal legate assured him that it would gain him remission of his sins ; and he resigned the kingdom to God and the pope, his feudal superiors.[1] The Marshal was an exceptional man, and his biography would no more justify a generalization about the attitude of the laity to church government than Jocelin of Brakelond's chronicle a generalization about monastic observance. But perhaps it helps to define the limitations of the evidence.

The nature of the people's faith in Christianity, the extent of paganism, are matters beyond our discovery. Thirteenth-century preachers, by their tirades, leave no doubt that besides much gross ignorance there was much indifference, and superstition, and incredulity. How much is another matter. The Church made it clear that she was ready to resort to force against unorthodoxy, and in England the unorthodox did not raise their voices. But the laity, whether or not they thought deeply about these things, seem to have accepted clerical government in matters of religion ; they conceived of no other sort of religious system, and paid the clergy their due with more or less complaint and evasion. It did not depend upon the piety of the individual. Catholic Christianity and the hierarchy were integrated in the social order. Although the layman's duty was to obey, obedience implied active membership of the Church. The Church, it is true, failed signally to convince the people and their lay rulers by the logic of her argument that politics came within her province, but she had succeeded in establishing her concern with every other social activity. It was her strength and her weakness. Every Englishman was, in the wider sense of the word, a Churchman.

This course of lectures has been concerned with one aspect only of church history : not the history of religion, of spirituality, theological learning, or popular faith. I have concentrated on questions of church government. I have

---

[1] vv. 15550–8, 18047–52.

treated the Church not as the community of the faithful but as an organization and an authority, which provided a discipline for the Christian life and provided it in a society where everybody (barring the odd Jew and Muslim) was supposed to be a Christian.   Some may associate this subject of church government chiefly with the ideals of the Gregorian reformers and the lofty projects of Pope Innocent III.   To them I must have seemed to smear grand designs with crude, commonplace colours.   The picture certainly shows a disorderly scene, which has its harsh and discordant tones. For the problem that the men of this time were concerned with was not merely the problem of Church and State : it was the wider, the perennial, problem of the Church and the world.   Besides the papacy's response, we have had to consider that of the clerical administrators at lower levels. They were not all imbued with the same principles and were not all heroic.   They were engaged in remoulding an ecclesiastical system which had grown up with and within a social system.   The quality of the clergy and the nature of English society in the twelfth century alike modified the result.   I have not tried to estimate the degree of success which this system of government achieved or to consider in detail whether it was well adapted to the needs of the age.   That would involve the whole history of the Church.

It is not uncommon for an administrative machine to be designed with an eye to certain conditions, only to reach formal perfection when changes have made it out of date. Some criticism of this sort may come to mind when we consider the method of utilizing church endowments, or the fixing of parochial boundaries in town and country.   Perhaps too little account was taken of an increasingly literate laity, of economic changes, and shifts of population.   The religious problems of the thirteenth century, it might be argued, were going to be faced by the friars rather than by the older institutions of the Church.   On the other hand, it is arguable that the friars could only achieve what they did achieve within the existing framework of church government, which was flexible enough to include them, bending them to the Church's purpose. But these reflections take us far beyond my subject.

Whatever the judgment passed upon the system, the period we have been considering was a time of unexampled activity in building the machinery of church government. The business of government became the work of professional administrators, more impersonal, more complicated, and more uniform than before. In the course of the later Middle Ages the Church went much farther along the same road ; but already, by about the year 1200, the main lines of the system had been drawn, as it concerned both the internal government of the Church and the day-to-day relations of Church and State.

Sir Maurice Powicke, in his closing lecture on Stephen Langton, directed the attention of English scholars to ' the history of the reconstruction of the Church in England after the interdict, in accordance with the Lateran decrees '. He said : [1] ' Historians of the English Church tend to overlook the fact that this was no insular movement, but a general attempt to give force to the decrees of a great council.' In 1927, when that was written, the warning was salutary. But since then so much historical writing has emphasized the importance of Innocent III and the Fourth Lateran Council that it is necessary to pay more attention to Powicke's following remarks. He observed that ' these decrees [of the Fourth Lateran] were not counsels of perfection issuing from the brain of a great pope ; they summed up the work of previous councils, of a generation of papal legislation, and of ceaseless discussion by theologians. . . . English experience had provided much of the material, suggested many of the problems which had led to the great work of definition.' [2]

---

[1] *Stephen Langton*, p. 151.
[2] It is worth noting how often the decrees of IV Lateran were concerned with practices, good or bad, which were said to prevail in certain provinces or regions. Maybe the pope condemned an English practice in prohibiting drinking-bouts ' ad equales potus ' which were the vogue ' in certain parts ' (c. 15) ; he certainly laid down no new rule for the

Recent work in the history of government seems fully to confirm this view. When Bishop Hugh de Wells of Lincoln assigned vicarages ' by authority of the council '—meaning the Fourth Lateran—he was doing no more than his predecessors had done without that authority. When Bishop Richard Poore of Salisbury composed his synodal statutes, he borrowed from the canons of Archbishop Hubert Walter. More generally, we may say that the law of the decretals was being applied in England in the last decade of the twelfth century much as it was applied after 1215 : the Council made no break and caused no change of direction. The interdict of 1208 to 1214 had indeed been, as Gerald of Wales said, a serious wound upon the body of the Church, but it had not produced ecclesiastical anarchy. The machinery had not been wrecked. It was in working order when the exiled bishops returned, so that the age of Langton inherited and built on a strong tradition of orderly government.

That was not a very old tradition in Langton's time. Impossible though it is to attach precise dates to the development, we can say that in all manner of ways the character of English church government was transformed between 1170 and 1213. Gratian had declared the doctrine of the pope's judicial supremacy but it was the popes from Alexander III to Innocent III who elaborated the procedure of appeals and gave directives to judges-delegate. Becket and his contemporaries on the English bench had been aware of their rights and duties according to current canon law ; but it was left to the next generation of bishops, and their archdeacons and officials, to work out ways of enforcing the law, ways of establishing its validity as against the less strictly canonical procedure of earlier times, ways of compromise

English Church when he extended ' the special custom of some places to other places in general ' in the matter of banns of marriage (c. 51). The decree to set up provincial chapters of religious Orders had been anticipated by a mandate for the Austin canons of the province of York in 1207 (SLI, pp. 84–5 : PL, ccxv. 1128), which may, however, have remained a dead letter.

with the lay power. Both in Rome and in England bureaucracy was, for good and for ill, coming into its own. The
movement was towards uniformity and definition, to the
disadvantage of old immunities and irregularities ; it im-
pressed the pattern of diocesan government on the Church.
As for the parish clergy, we must not over-estimate the
scanty evidence, for we know very little about them. Doubtless, as of old, they usually took on the colour of their sur-
roundings and did not even try to disengage themselves from
the social order and economic system in which they found
themselves. But in many a parish the grant of the parson's
rights to a monastery made a difference to the social status
of the incumbent on the spot. And gradually, throughout
England, parsons and vicars alike submitted to the influences
which emphasized their standing as clergy and brought
them, as clergy, under a stricter ecclesiastical supervision.
The change was only beginning in Becket's time ; by the
time Langton returned to England it had proceeded far.
The Church had put into effect her determination that the
clerical order should manage its own affairs.

APPENDIX I

PROVIDEES AND ITALIANS IN ENGLISH BENEFICES
(see pp. 76–82)

GENTILE, nephew of Pope Alexander III, held (in addition to his prebend of Lincoln, noted on p. 80) the church of Eynsford (Kent).[1] Another nephew, THOMAS, was admitted to Caxton (Cambs.) in 1190 or 1191.[2] LAURENCE, nephew of Celestine III, was a canon of St. Paul's Cathedral in 1192.[3] S., nephew of Innocent III, held the prebend of Leighton in Lincoln Cathedral in 1213.[4] In 1178 MASTER AIMERICUS DE PARTIMACHO, clerk of the legate Hugh Pierleone, held a church of Merton Priory at the request of Alexander III.[5] MASTER ELIAS OF CHIEVELEY obtained a mandate from Pope Celestine III to the abbot and monks of Abingdon, asking them to give him the church of Chieveley (Berks) ' notwithstanding any promise made contrary to the rules of the Lateran Council without our command '. Master Elias presumably anticipated trouble, for he got a papal letter to two bishops to execute this mandate. That was not enough, for the monks sent to Rome, the bishops wrote for further instructions, and the pope reiterated his previous mandate. Elias eventually got his church, but after enjoying it peacefully for some time (according to his own account) he was forced to resign it and had recourse to Rome again in 1199.[6]

HUGUICIO LOMBARDUS held the prebend of Warminster in the church of Wells in 1200.[7] MASTER BRITIUS, a papal notary, held for about ten years the church of Hessle (E.R. Yorks.) ; the priory of Guisborough had conferred it upon him at Innocent III's command.[8] In 1201 John, a Roman nobleman, was a prebendary of York.[9] This was probably that MASTER JOHN

[1] *Epp. Cantuar.*, p. xlviii, n. 1. [2] *PUE*, i. 567.
[3] R. Newcourt, *Repertorium* (1708), i. 144 note f.
[4] *Rotuli litt. clausarum* (Record Comm.), i. 156b.
[5] *PUE*, i. 424–5 : ' ad mandatum domini pape et ad preces domini regis '. [6] See *SLI*, p. 15.
[7] A. Potthast, *Regesta pontificum*, no. 984 ; cf. Hist. MSS. Comm. *Wells MSS.*, i. 55, dated by the presence of Master Philip the notary.
[8] Potthast, *Regesta*, no. 1459, and *PL*, ccxvi. 374–5.
[9] Potthast, *Regesta*, no. 1281. John Romanus witnesses an act of the dean and chapter in that year (*EYC*, ix. 201, cf. i. 42, 196, 245).

LE ROMEYN who is often mentioned as a canon and in later years became subdean (1228), archdeacon of Richmond (1241) and treasurer (1249), dying in 1255. He was father of Archbishop John le Romeyn.[1] The fact that in 1249 he made a gift in alms for the souls of King Richard and his own parents suggests that Richard I may have had something to do with bringing him to England.[2]

Between 1202 and 1205 a papal nominee was concerned in litigation over the church of Woodhorn, Northumberland ; and the case, while obscure in its details and unrecorded as to its outcome, illustrates the conditions which might prevent a provision from taking effect. Innocent III wrote to St. Albans, as patrons of the church of Woodhorn, to assign this church to H., NEPHEW OF JOHN, CARDINAL BISHOP OF ALBANO, and a student at Paris. The pope had learnt that the church was vacant on the death of Master Roger of St. Edmund. But the abbot replied that Roger had been improperly instituted in the church by the bishop of Durham, as a result of pressure from the Crown ; the abbey's presentee (G.) had obtained a papal letter against Roger and had for six months past had custody of the church *causa rei servande*. Was the church vacant? The pope replied on 1 Feb. 1203 that if G.'s only right depended on his presentation and on this temporary custody, he was not to press his claim : the mandate in favour of the cardinal's nephew should be executed. He appointed the bishop of Ely as executor.[3] Two years later, however, the case was still unsettled. The cardinal's nephew had been instituted by the bishop but the prior and convent of Tynemouth, who claimed to be patrons of Woodhorn and who got royal confirmation of their patronage on 25 Feb. 1204,[4] complained to the pope that this was in disregard of their appeal to the pope. They said that the prior had acted under duress, on the order of the abbot of St. Albans (his superior), whose order was the consequence of the papal mandate of 1 Feb. 1203, obtained *tacita veritate*. Their case was heard by an auditor in the Curia. The cardinal's nephew, or rather his proctor, said that he had been violently despoiled of the church of Woodhorn to which he had been instituted : on this ground he sought restitution, without prejudice to the

---

[1] *Register of John le Romeyn, archbishop of York*, ii (Surtees Soc., 1917), pp. v–viii.

[2] *EYC*, ii. 182.   [3] Appendix III (xii).

[4] *Rotuli chartarum* (Record Comm.), p. 120.

question of right. It was at this stage, in March 1205, that the pope wrote to the bishop of Worcester, the abbot of Chester, and the dean of York, ordering them first to reinstate the cardinal's nephew and then to hear and settle the case. Two months later, he wrote again, allowing them to leave the final decision to Rome.[1] I have found no trace of further action.

While the case of Woodhorn was proceeding another Roman, MASTER JOHN DE COLONNA, the nephew of a cardinal, found it necessary to get a papal letter to the archbishop of Canterbury to protect his rights in the church of ' Gotesdon '.[2] Some ten years later, when he was cardinal-priest of S. Prassede, he claimed a pension of two marks in the chapel of Nympsfield (Gloucs.).[3] In 1204 a NEPHEW OF GREGORY, CARDINAL OF S. GIORGIO let at farm a prebend at York, where the prebend of Langtoft was held by CARDINAL JOHN, THE PAPAL CHAN-CELLOR, from 1205 (at latest) until his death in 1213. The pope then provided his relative, LEONARD, to the vacant prebend and invested him with it personally.[4] At his death Cardinal John was also drawing income from the church of Conisbrough (Yorks.) which the pope granted to his relative, PTOLEMY.[5]

A few of these individuals may have received their benefices by other means than papal request and command. Other foreign holders of benefices in England held them by the king's gift, directly or indirectly. For while King John paid pensions to cardinals and other influential persons,[6] just as he paid money fiefs to Flemish knights, he often provided that these should be paid from churches. Already in the 1170's, St. Augustine's, Canterbury had granted a pension of 4 marks to Master Franco, at the request of the papal chamberlain ; the king asked for a pension of 12 marks for him and the whole sum was secured to Franco by making him parson of Milton.[7] In 1200 the king granted to Master Philip, papal notary, an

---

[1] *PL*, ccxv. 591-2, 625-6. The register reads ' Chichester ' : I suggest Chester is intended. It is worth noting that both the other judges held their offices by papal authority, Mauger in the see of Worcester, Simon in the deanery of York.

[2] Appendix III (xiii).

[3] *Cart. mon. de Gloucestria* (RS), ii. 43-4 (probably 1213 × 1214).

[4] *Rotuli litt. clausarum*, i. 90 ; *Rotuli chartarum*, p. 147*b* ; *SLI*, p. 148 (*PL*, ccxvi. 860).

[5] *PL*, ccxvi. 876.

[6] See *Rot. litt. clausarum*, i. 156, 168*b*, 180 ; *Rott. litt. patentium*, p. 69, 118.

[7] William Thorne, in Twysden, *Scriptores decem*, col. 1829.

annual fee of 30 marks ' until we do better for him in an ecclesiastical benefice '.[1]   In 1214 Nicholas, a clerk of Ugolino,
cardinal bishop of Ostia, had royal letters of presentation to
two churches (Easthorp and Great Birch) in Essex, in the king's
gift ; [2] and the cardinal himself received four hundred marks
a year ' for a nephew of his until provision be made for him
in some benefice '.[3]   Another cardinal's nephew, John Pierleone,
was to receive a pension ' from the next ecclesiastical benefice
in our gift to fall vacant '.[4]   John of Colonna, who has been
noted above as the holder of an English benefice, was described by a royal clerk, writing to the king from the Roman
curia in March 1215, as ' fidelissimus amicus vester '.[5]   Most
of our information belongs to the period when John was courting
the cardinals in 1213-15 ; but it is clear that the practice was
not new.   It was said that Bishop Hugh Nonant, in evicting the
monks from Coventry, intended to attach prebends of his new
church to certain Roman cardinals' titles ; so that the revenues
of the prebends would induce them to support the bishop in
the Curia.[6]

[1] *Rot. chartarum*, p. 61*b*.   [2] *Rot. litt. patentium*, p. 123*b*.
[3] *Rot. litt. clausarum*, i. 180.   [4] *Rot. litt. patentium*, p. 118.
[5] *Foedera*, I. i. 120.
[6] Richard of Devizes, in *Chron. reigns of Stephen*, etc., iii. 440-1.

APPENDIX II

EARLY VICARAGES IN THE DIOCESE OF LINCOLN
(see pp. 131-3)

THIRTY of the vicarages in the *Liber antiquus* are described as
' ex dudum ordinata '. Although in a few of these the ordinations may belong to the first years of Hugh de Wells,[1] others
so described or said to be *ab antiquo* (p. 27) or *antiquitus ordinata*
(p. 51) may belong to an earlier time. That is very probable
in Cassington (p. 3) which Bishop Hugh I had appropriated to
Eynsham Abbey *c.* 1198, providing for a vicarage of five marks
to be assigned by the monks ;[2] it is certain in Maxey (p. 31),
as an entry in *Rotuli H. de Welles* (i. 90) shows, and in Henlow
(p. 22) as witnesses the document printed here below (p. 192).
Outside the ' ex dudum ' category, the entries for Spalding
(p. 65), Chesham, second moiety (p. 18), Marton (p. 68) suggest
old arrangements. At Swinstead one of the two ordinations
may precede the time of Hugh de Wells (pp. 46, 65). According
to a statement made in 1225 the vicarage of St. John the Baptist,
Peterborough (p. 31), ' longo tempore talis extitit '.[3]

The *Liber antiquus* never mentions an earlier ordination than
the one it copies ; but there certainly were earlier ordinations
in some of these places. At Henlow (below, p. 192) the record
shows an ordination undergoing change before the end of the
twelfth century. At Pulloxhill (p. 20), according to an entry
in the annals of Dunstable, written before 1215, a vicarage was
assigned by the authority of Bishop William in 1204.[4] The
cartulary of Ramsey Abbey furnishes details of an earlier ordination for Hemingford (p. 27), between 1192 and 1200.[5] By a
distinctly irregular transaction Roger the priest, son of Thurstan
the priest of Hemington, became vicar of the church for life
when Geoffrey, bishop-elect of Lincoln (1173-81), appropriated

---

[1] Nuffield (Tonfeld, *Liber antiquus*, p. 11) was only appropriated to
Goring Priory in Sept. 1215 (*ibid.*, p. 80). But even here the preceding
rector may have employed a vicar on the same terms.
[2] *Cartulary of Eynsham Abbey* (Oxford Hist. Soc. 1907-8), i. 47.
[3] *Rot. H. de Welles*, i. 209, ii. 126.
[4] *Annales monastici*, iii. 28.
[5] *Cartularium mon. de Rameseia*, ii. 177.

the church to St. Neot's Priory. Thurstan had given the church
to St. Neot's in 1149 on condition that his son should hold it
of the monks for an annual render of two shillings.[1] Naturally,
a new ordination was made after Roger's death. There is also
the less certain evidence provided by Bishop Hugh I's charters
of confirmation. When he confirmed to various monasteries
the churches of Stainton (? le Vale) and Thornborough and
moieties in Chesham Bois and Ulceby, he safeguarded ' a competent vicarage ' in each.[2] Whether he approved a detailed
arrangement for each church does not appear. In short, we
cannot be sure that an ordination by Bishop Hugh de Wells is
anything more than the revision of an existing vicarage, unless
we have proved that it was he who authorized the appropriation.

The *Liber antiquus*, moreover, is no guide to the number of
perpetual vicars in the dioceses of Lincoln in Hugh de Wells's
day. It only seems to record ordinations made by him, or
inspected and approved by him, on the occasion of a vacancy
in an appropriated church. It does not include vicarages in
churches held by individual rectors.

The same sort of record-material which adds to the information about certain churches in the *Liber antiquus* shows that
vicarages had long been established in other churches not specified
in the *Liber*. The earliest have been mentioned in the text
above (pp. 16, 18). In the document concerning Newport
Priory, Bishop Robert de Chesney, between 1151 and 1154,
safeguarded the *vicariae* without specifying their details ; but
the vicars were to be presented to the bishop for institution and
were, therefore, not removable priests.[3] A vicarage of the same
sort, involving a pension of half a mark, may have been established in the church of Milton Ernest before the time of Hugh I ; [4]
likewise one in the church of Puttenham (rendering only 12*d.*),
where Nicholas de Sigillo, archdeacon of Huntingdon, instituted a perpetual vicar.[5] The same archdeacon instituted a
vicar at Offord, who was to pay the rector one mark annually
by way of pension.[6] Bishop Walter (1183–4) instituted a vicar
when he appropriated Minster Lovell church to the abbey of

[1] *Facsimiles of early charters from Northants. collections*, ed. F. M. Stenton
(Northants. Rec. Soc. IV, 1930), pp. 62–4, 69–70, cf. *Liber antiquus*,
p. 32.
[2] *CRR*, v. 145 ; Cheney, *Eng. bishops' chanceries*, p. 79 ; *CRR*, vii. 72 ;
Reg. antiquiss., ii. 277–80.
[3] *Calendar of docts. preserved in France*, ed. J. H. Round, p. 444.
[4] *CRR*, vii. 135. [5] Appendix III (vii). [6] *CRR*, i. 340.
N

Ivry and ordained a vicarage which was to be one half of the lands and obventions.[1] At Checkendon and at Ripton he provided simply for fixed annual pensions to be paid to the rectors.[2] When he appropriated four churches to St. Paul's Cathedral, he provided that perpetual vicarages should be created.[3]

Bishop Hugh I stipulated at Nocton and Dunston that there should be ' honesta sustentacio vicariorum ', and this was apparently fixed, if not immediately, within the bishop's lifetime.[4] In appropriating Long Bennington church to Savigny *c.* 1190, he specified in detail the portion to be given to the perpetual vicar.[5] At Kingsey, where (about 1190) he admitted William the clerk of Eye to the perpetual vicarage, he laid down that the vicar's portion should consist in all the tithes but sheaves, the altarage, and two marks a year.[6] The Ramsey cartulary preserves the elaborate details of his ordination of Shillington vicarage,[7] and the Bardney cartulary details for Edlington.[8] The latter, as we know from an early charter of a vice-archdeacon, was not the first ordination of a vicarage in this church.[9] The perpetual vicar of St. Michael on Northgate, Oxford, when he was instituted by Bishop Hugh (1191 × 1195), received all the church's revenues subject to a pension of two marks due to St. Frideswide's Priory, the parsons.[10] A few years later a similar arrangement was made at Souldern when a vicar was instituted.[11] Other similar cases are found at Stonesby, Saddington, Kibworth Beauchamp, and Hardwick.[12] Bishop Hugh I also instituted vicars, stating their obligations, to Cranwell[13] and Gedney.[14] A pension-paying vicar of Maid's Moreton (*c.* 1200-3) may have been instituted by him.[15] At

---

[1] *CRR*, iv. 260.

[2] *Boarstall cartulary* (Oxford Hist. Soc., 1930), pp. 4-6 ; *Cart. mon. de Rameseia*, ii. 179.

[3] *Early charters of St. Paul's*, pp. 229-30.   [4] *CRR*, iii. 111-12.

[5] *Cal. of docts. . . . in France*, p. 307.   [6] *Reg. antiquiss.*, iii. 21-2.

[7] *Cart. mon. de Rameseia*, ii. 176.

[8] Brit. Mus., Cotton MS. Vesp. E. xx, fo. 32v.

[9] *Reg. antiquiss.*, vii. 206.

[10] *Cart. of St. Frideswide's* (Oxford Hist. Soc. 1894-6), i. 160-1.

[11] *Cart. of Eynsham Abbey* (Oxford Hist. Soc.), i. 135.

[12] *Rotuli Hug. de Welles*, i. 272, 265 (cf. *EYC*, v. 97, n. 5), 265, *CRR*, iv. 73. The last two churches had individual rectors.

[13] Brit. Mus., Cotton MS. Vesp. E. xx, fo. 231v.

[14] Foster Library, Lincoln, copy of Wrest Park cartulary of Croyland, fo. 107v.

[15] *Newington Longeville charters* (Oxon. Rec. Soc. 1921), pp. 37-9.

Deene, before 1191, the bishop instituted a parson on condition that the perpetual vicarage of Simon the clerk was respected so long as Simon lived.[1] He made a similar proviso at Wing.[2] Gerald of Wales complained to Bishop Hugh of the excessive provision for the vicar of Chesterton.[3]

Bishop William (1203–6), besides ordaining a vicarage at Pulloxhill in 1204 (see above) made a perpetual vicarage in All Saints, Oxford, whereby the vicar took the revenues and paid the parsons, St. Frideswide's, a pension of three marks.[4] Another of this bishop's ordinations, at Great Hale, is recorded in the register of Bishop Oliver Sutton, two generations later.[5]

In addition to these records the rolls of Bishop Hugh de Wells occasionally mention a vicar who was instituted by the bishop's predecessors : at South Kilworth, Swinford, Whitwick, and Great Glen.[6]

[1] Westminster, Dean and Chapter mun. 16144.
[2] Brit. Mus., Cotton MS. Faustina A. iv, fo. 40v. [3] *Opp.*, i. 259–68.
[4] *Cart. of St. Frideswide's* (Oxford Hist. Soc.), i. 282.
[5] *Register of Oliver Sutton*, i (Lincoln Rec. Soc. 39, 1948), 7.
[6] *Rot. Hug. Welles*, i. 242, 251, 265. Some of the details of this appendix I owe to the thesis (B. A. Manchester) on St. Hugh of Lincoln by my former pupil, the Rev. James O. Colling. Some were already assembled by Fr. Herbert Thurston in *The Life of St. Hugh of Lincoln* (1898), pp. 319–21, 616–17 where (pp. 320–1, 325) a warning was given against post-dating the institution of vicarages which should have been noted above, p. 132.

APPENDIX III

i *(see p.* 144)

Brit. Mus., MS. Harl. 3650, fo. 37r.

Ricardus dei gratia Coventr' episcopus universis sancte ecclesie fidelibus in domino salutem et benedictionem. Questus est nobis Ricardus de Hasting', custos rerum que per Angliam ad Templum Ierosolimitanum pertinent, quod canonici de Kenill' ecclesiam de Cobinton' in suo feodo sitam iniuste occupatam detinerent, illis econtra respondentibus quod ad ius eius vel Templi Ierosolimitani sive ad quemlibet illius fundi dominum illa nullatenus ecclesia pertineret, utpote que capella erat ecclesie sue de Wotton'. Post multas hinc inde allegationes eo tandem fine quievit eorum altercacio : quod ego veritatem rei per clericos provinciales diligenter inquisitam cognoscerem et, legitimo provincialium testimonio certificatus, quod utrique parti super hoc innotescerem, id ipsi ad litis decisionem absque omni reclamatione susciperent. Convenientibus itaque de more ad sinodum in nostra presencia tocius provincie clericis et quanta decuit diligencia super predicta controversia requisitis, venerunt in medium venerabilis frater et coepiscopus noster Godefridus episcopus de Sancto Asaph et frater Bald' canonicus de Kenill', Willelmus decanus de Radeford', Robertus presbiter de Bedewrd', et Turkillus de Essesho presbiter, constanter asserentes et probare parati quod pie recordationis episcopo Rogero eidem sinodo residente ante annos circiter xxx^{ta} per testes legitimos, ipsis videntibus et audientibus, probatum est et ordine iudiciario pronunciatum quod prenominata capella de Cobinton' iure parochiali ecclesie de Wotton' est et debet esse subiecta. Nos itaque pro debito nostre sollicitudinis ecclesiastice paci providere cupientes que ante nos gesta sunt ne in litem veniant recidivam, scripto comendare curavimus, quod per viros bone opinionis et integre fame legitime testificatum est, et certis indiciis declaratum, ratum atque inconcussum manere statuentes. Hiis testibus Willelmo abbate de Lilleshall,[1] Laurentio priore de Coventr', Hugone priore de Eaton', Edmundo archidiacono

[1] MS. Lillesham.

de Coventr', Rogero archidiacono de Salop' et clericis tocius sinodi, Hugone de Ardena et Radulfo de Sudleg', Ivone de Allespedr'. [date ? 1161 × 1165]

The text is in a cartulary of Kenilworth Priory. The place-names almost all belong to Warwickshire : Cubbington, Leek Wootton, Radford, Bedworth, Ashow, Allespath (Meriden). Hugh de Arden and Ralph de Sudley may be the knights named in 1166 (*Red Bk. of the Exchequer* (RS), i. 295, 325) ; Ivo de Allespath was a tenant of the Earl of Chester (W. Farrer, *Honors and knights' fees* (1924), ii. 280).

This document is followed in the cartulary by another notification by the bishop, of which the witness list includes the four first witnesses named above. It confirms to Kenilworth the church of Harbury by the testimony of seven named priests (fo. 37v).

Another document in the volume (fo. 43v) is the certificate of Bishop Godfrey of St. Asaph, which shows that he was a monk of Coventry at the time of the synod, which took place in the reign of Henry I.

ii (*see p.* 7)

Norwich, Dean and chapter muniments, Norwich charter N.596.

.H. rex Angl' et dux Norm' et Aquit' et comes And' episcopo Norwic' salutem. Precipio quod monachi Norwic' habeant et teneant bene et in pace et iuste et libere ecclesiam Sancti Iohannis ante portam castelli et sicut Wodewinus presbiter eam eis dedit. Et nisi feceris, archiepiscopus Cant' faciat. Teste episcopo Cic' apud Rothomagum. [date ? 1156 × 1166]

Original, measuring approx. $6\frac{3}{4}'' \times 1\frac{3}{4}''$, sealed *sur simple queue* with narrow strip below for a tie. Remains of seal of brown wax, showing sword and sword-arm on obverse, arm and orb on reverse. Later endorsements : Sancti Iohannis ante portam. ·xxiii A·

iii (*see p.* 7)

Westminster, Dean and chapter muniments, no. 3777.

.H. rex Angl' et dux Norm' et Aquit' et comes And' Osberto de la herlotere salutem. Precipio tibi quod iuste habere facias priori de Herleia et monachis decimas suas de Meidencota sicut eas melius habuerunt tempore regis H. avi mei. Et nisi feceris, I. Sar' episcopus faciat ne amodo inde clamorem audiam pro penuria recti. Teste Petro de la Mara apud London'. [date ? c. 1164]

Original, measuring approx. 5¾″ × 3⅜″, sealed *sur simple queue*, with badly mutilated remains of seal. Printed by F. T. Wethered, *St. Mary's Hurley in the Middle Ages* (1898), p. 94 no. 13.

The church is the Benedictine priory of Hurley (Berks), the tithes those of Maiden Court, in East Garston (Berks).

A writ in similar terms, written in the same hand, is addressed to William de Lond' concerning other tithes in East Garston (muniments, no. 2272, cf. William's grant of the tithes to Hurley in Madox, *Formulare*, p. 251 no. 425).

iv (*see p.* 153)

Brit. Mus., Cotton MS. Vespasian E. xx, fo. 38r.

R. dei gratia Linc' episcopus omnibus fidelibus dei salutem. Noverit universitas vestra nos perpetuo remisisse clericis omnibus per episcopatum Linc' constitutis et ecclesiis paschalem consuetudinem quam crismatis denarios vocare consueverant. Pensionem quoque quam de eadem consuetudine archidiaconi nostri nobis sive predecessoribus nostris annuatim solvere consueverant omnino remittimus.   Prohibemus igitur sub anathemate quod nullus ullis temporibus iam dictam consuetudinem cum admodum prava sit et sacrorum canonum auctoritate prohibita in episcopatu Linc' presumat exigere.   Teste Waltero abbate de Kirkestede, Radulfo abbate de Luda, David abbate de Barling', Magistro Gilberto de Sempringham, Baldrico archidiacono Leicr', Martino thesaurario Linc' ecclesie, Radulfo subdecano Linc', Willelmo Clemente, Willelmo de Amundavill' dapifero.   [? 1163 × 1166]

The text is in a cartulary of Bardney Abbey.

v (*see p.* 89)

Westminster, Dean and chapter muniments, no. 2857.

.R. dei gratia Herefordensis episcopus et A. eadem gratia abbas Eveshamensis omnibus ad quos litere iste pervenerint salutem.   Noverit universitas vestra quod causa que vertebatur inter priorem de Luffeld et Hamonem filium Menfelini nobis a domino papa delegata, in presentia domini regis taliter terminata est : quod prior et monachi petitionem quam habuerunt super cella predicti H. de Bradewella et monacho et eclesiis[1] de terra H. eidem H. et heredibus suis omnibus remiserunt et iuri quod se in eis habere asserebant in perpetuum renuntiaverunt.

[1] MS. *sic.*

Sepenominatus vero .H. assensu uxoris sue et heredis sui prefatis
priori et monachis et ecclesie de Luffeld decimam tocius panis
sui de dominio lucro suo dedit et in perpetuum concessit et
ecclesiam preterea de Torneberga eis dedit liberam et quietam
cum omnibus ad eandem ecclesiam pertinenciis. Nos autem
utriusque sigillo certificati hanc compositionem prescriptam
sigillorum nostrorum munimine confirmamus.

[1174 × 1184]

Original, measuring approx. 7½″ × 2⅜″, sealed *sur double queue*
with the seals (badly mutilated) of Bishop Robert Foliot (the counterseal inscribed : ' Sigillum Roberti ') and Abbot Adam.   Hamo's
grant is printed in *Monasticon*, iv. 350 : ' decimam totius panis domus
meae ubicumque in terra mea fuero de proprio lucro meo . . .
ecclesiam de Thorneberga '.   For *decima victualium hospicii* see *ibid.*,
v. 350.   Luffield Priory was in Northants., and Bradwell and Thornborough (Bucks) are nearby.

vi (*see p.* 115)

Maidstone, Kent, Archives Office, Ul 20 Q 13.   Cartulary of
Leeds Priory, fo. 7v.

Ricardus dei gracia Cantuariensis archiepiscopus, tocius
Anglie primas, omnibus Christi fidelibus ad quos presentes
litere pervenerint illam que est in domino salutem.   Ad universitatis vestre noticiam volumus [1] pervenire controversiam
inter dilectos filios nostros canonicos de Ledes et David de
Tymberdene clericum et Walterum presbiterum super ecclesia
de Crundale motam, de consensu partium amicorum inter-
veniente consilio, in presencia nostra sub hac composicionis
forma conquievisse.   Predictus siquidem Walterus [2] qui in
predicta ecclesia perpetuam habet vicariam solvet annuatim
predicto D. de eadem ecclesia nomine pensionis duas summas
frumenti, quarum alteram idem D. sibi retinebit, reliquam
vero predictis canonicis singulis annis persolvet infra octavas
Nativitatis Beate Marie Virginis.   Decedente [3] vero predicto
W. vel religionis habitum assumente, predictus D. tenebit
memoratam ecclesiam sub annua pensione viginti et quinque
solidorum sepedictis canonicis singulis annis solvendorum.   Ne
igitur super hiis que coram nobis acta sunt scrupulus dubita-
cionis emergat vel futuris temporibus aliquis maliciosus pre-
sumptor [4] hanc composicionis paginam confringere vel evacuare

[1] MS. volimus.   [2] MS. Waterus.
[3] MS. Decendente.   [4] MS. alicuius maliciosi presumptoris.

attemptet, eam tam scripti nostri patrocinio quam sigilli apposicione duximus communire. Hiis testibus, Magistro P. Blesensi archidiacono, Willelmo archidiacono Gloucestr', Magistro Henrico de Northampton', Magistro Roberto de Inglesham, Magistro Rogerio de Rolveston', Willelmo de Scotindon', Thoma de Nawesele, et aliis multis. [1182 × 1184]

This concerns Leeds Priory (O.S.A.) and the church of Crundale, both in Kent. The priory was not the patron of the church, though the composition here described may have followed some claim to the patronage. This shows how a payment due to a third party might become a charge on a parish church : 25s. was still paid from Crundale to Leeds in the sixteenth century. The witness-list shows some important members of Archbishop Richard's *familia*. Probably the title of Peter of Blois's archdeaconry (Baton') has been omitted by the copyist. Thomas de Nawesele appears in other documents as of ' Newsole ' or ' Niewesole '.

vii (*see p.* 133)

(*a*) Brit. Mus., MS. Egerton 3033, fo. 51r.

Nicholas archidiaconus Huntind' omnibus clericis per archidiaconatum [1] suum constitutis salutem. Universitati vestre constare volumus nos ad presentacionem prioris et canonicorum de Esseby instituisse Ricardum de Trimuge [2] clericum perpetuum vicarium ecclesie de Putteham solvendo eis annuatim nomine pensionis xii denarios in festo nativitatis Beate Marie. Hiis testibus.

(*b*) Public Record Office, Anc. deed B. 2967.

Nicholas archidiaconus Hunt' omnibus clericis per archidiaconatum suum constitutis salutem. Noverit universitas vestra nos ad presentationem Ricardi filii Galonis instituisse priorem et canonicos de Assebi personam ecclesie de Puteham cum omnibus pertinentiis suis, presente Ricardo eiusdem ecclesie persona. Ita tamen quod Ricardus solvet annuatim nomine predicte ecclesie prefatis canonicis xii denarios in festo nativitatis Beate Marie. His testibus, Humfrido capellano, Benedicto capellano, Adam de Ameri, magistro Hamone de Wint', Radulfo de Amblia, Willelmo filio Ricardi, Ricardo clerico, Gaufrido clerico, Waltero de Triaingnel. [3] [? 1167 × 1185]

---

[1] MS. archideaconatum.
[2] MS. *sic*, probably for Triunge (Tring).
[3] Cartulary omits witnesses.

Both texts are in a cartulary of Canons' Ashby Priory (O.S.A., Northants). (*b*) Survives in the original, measuring approximately 5⅝″ ×4″, with step for sealing *sur simple queue* and tie below. The church is Puttenham (Herts.). If Richard of Tring in (*a*) is Richard the parson of (*b*) these documents were probably issued together and represent an attempt to appropriate the church and transfer the tenure of the existing parson into that of a perpetual vicar. The archdeacon, Nicholas de Sigillo, was probably acting during a vacancy of the see of Lincoln. In the event, these acts were not confirmed : the bishops instituted rectors in the thirteenth century.

viii (see p. 151)

Brit. Mus., MS. Egerton 3033, fo. 10r.

Omnibus ad quos presens scriptum pervenerit Savaricus archidiaconus[1] Northampton' salutem. Noverit universitas vestra me intuitu pietatis et favore religionis concessisse et presenti carta confirmasse canonicis de Esseby hanc libertatem qua ipsi diu gavisi sunt, scilicet ut eorum ecclesia de Essebya et capella de Atteniston' que est de parochia eiusdem ecclesie libera sit et quieta a cathedratico et ab omni exactione et consuetudine excepto quod annuatim solvent pro denario Sancti Petri quod solvere solebant tempore archidiaconorum[1] predecessorum meorum scilicet tantum duos solidos de parochia predicte ecclesie et capelle. Hiis testibus.

[1175 × 1192]

The text is in a cartulary of Canons' Ashby Priory (O.S.A. Northants). The church is that of Ashby, the chapel is of Adstone.

ix (see pp. 126–8)

Paris, Bibl. Nationale, ms. latin 3922*A*, fo. 153v*b*.

Celestinus III Wigorn' episcopo.

Nicholaus presbiter de Sancto Romano transmissa nobis conquestione monstravit quod cum ecclesiam Sancti Iohannis de Hortona tue diocesis canonice sit adeptus, N. filius Antonii qui proximo ante ipsius ecclesie habuit personatum ad se vicariam ipsius ecclesie asserit pertinere. Quia igitur in ecclesia successiones in prelaturis et dignitatibus ecclesiasticis canonum statutis dampnantur, fraternitati tue per apostolica scripta mandamus quatinus, veritate diligentius inquisita, si tibi constiterit N. ipsum filium fuisse Antonii qui eiusdem ecclesie sicut premisimus proximo habuit personatum, omni contradictione et appellatione

<hr>

[1] MS. archideac . . .

cessantibus super eadem vicaria silencium perpetuum imponere
non postponas. Dat' Laterani, pontificatus nostri anno iii.

[14 Apr. 1193 × 13 Apr. 1194]

The text is from a decretal-collection (' Rotomagensis I ' written
very early in the thirteenth century). It occurs in corrupt forms
in other collections, finally in Gregory IX's *Decretals*, 1,17,13 (JL
16616). Their principal variants may be seen in Friedberg's edition
of the *Decretals*. None of the texts except Rotom. I gives either address
or date. Most other texts read ' Michael ' for ' Nicholas '. I am
obliged to Dr. W. Holtzmann for full collations of ' Gilbertus ' and
' Estensis '.

This case, where a parson had installed his son as vicar, provides
variant of the usual prohibition of hereditary succession. The
church is probably that of Horton, Gloucs.

x *(see pp.* 162, 182)

Public Record Office, Chancery Masters' Exhibits, Lanthony
cartulary A. I section x no. 75.

Inquisicio facta per R. decanum de Langeford' super vicaria
de Henlowe.

Hec est inquisicio facta per R. decanum de Langeford et
totum capitulum sui decanatus super vicaria de Henlowe apud
Wardon' in festo Sanctorum Crispini et Crispiniani proximo
post consecrationem Egidii Hereford' episcopi, scilicet quod
quidam capellanus Haco tenuit et habuit quo advixit nomine
vicarie terciam partem obventionum [1] tocius ville de Henl',
excepto de dominio canonicorum unde habuit terciam partem
tercie partis decimationum et unam acram et dimidiam ad
mesuagium. Diaconus vero qui ecclesie deserviebat procur-
abatur duabus septimanis in mensa canonicorum et tercia
septimana in mensa ipsius Haconis. Ipse vero Haco de seno-
dalibus et auxiliis archidiaconi respondebat [2] et de omnibus
aliis consuetudinibus que ad ecclesiam pertinent excepto quod
si episcopus posuisset auxilia per episcopatum suum canonici
responderent pro duabus partibus, Haco vero pro tercia parte.
Cui de medio sublato Hugo capellanus successit, presentatus
in sinodo apud Bedeford' per magistrum Moysen, tunc pro-
curatorem canonicorum in partibus illis, et per cartam illorum
eandem vicariam continentem quam Haco habuit, preter quod
ipse Hugo habuit totam panem altaris et totum caseum et ipse
debebat diaconum suis sumptibus totaliter exhibere, quam etiam

---

[1] MS. oventium.   [2] MS. *om.* respondebant.

cartam in morte ipsius Hugonis predictus R. decanus in scriniis eius presentibus multis clericis et laycis dixit se invenisse. Quod ne cuiquam longevitate[1] veniret in dubium, voluit capitulum hoc scriptum ad peticionem canonicorum conficere et ei sigillum R. decani apponere. Huic inquisitioni faciende interfuerunt Robertus de Potton', Fulco de Tamiseford, Hugo de Herdinton' et plures alii. [25 October 1200]

The church is Henlow, appropriated to Lanthony Secunda (Gloucs.). It lay in the rural deanery of Langford (Beds., not Oxon.), dioc. Lincoln. The other place-names belong to the vicinity. When a new vicar was instituted to Henlow *c.* 1219, the terms of the vicarage (stated in *Liber antiquus*, p. 22, to be ' exdudum ordinata ') were given briefly in *Rot. Hugonis de Welles*, i. 108. The document above provides more interesting details, shows the provision for the assistant deacon, and shows the habit of enquiry in chapter. Master Moses and Hugh, priest of Henlow, were the first witnesses of a grant to Wardon Abbey *c.* 1190–1200 (*Cartulary of . . . Old Wardon*, ed. G. H. Fowler (Manchester, 1931), pp. 41–2).

xi (*see p.* 136)

Westminster, Dean and chapter muniments, no. 2254.

Omnibus Christi fidelibus ad quos presens carta pervenerit Herebertus dei gratia Saresburiensis episcopus eternam in domino salutem. Pastorali convenit sollicitudini virorum relligiosorum [*sic*] inopiam, qui vigiliis nocturnis et laboribus diurnis cordis contriti sacrificium pro benefactoribus suis devotas deo offerunt oraciones, beneficiis sublevare. Nos igitur attendentes honestatem et relligionem dilectorum nobis in Christo prioris et monachorum de Hurleia, concedimus eis et auctoritate episcopali confirmamus omnes decimas garbarum de Waltham que ibi per annum provenient et preterea oblaciones que similiter in die Sancti Laurencii a quibuscumque fidelibus offerentur, ad officium sacristie sue convertendas. Quicquid autem residuum fuerit tam de capella de Warefeld cum omnibus pertinenciis suis tam in domibus quam in terris, quam in pascuis et pasturis et omnibus libertatibus et liberis consuetudinibus suis, cum omnibus minutis decimis et oblacionibus de predicta ecclesia de Waltham provenientibus, cedet in usus perpetui vicarii qui ad presentacionem eorundem monachorum de Hurleia per nos vel successores nostros in predicta ecclesia fuerit instituendus, qui vicarius sustinebit debitas et usitatas consuetudines

[1] MS. *sic.*

episcopales, in ceteris vero omnibus honeribus que ecclesiam illam variis de causis contingere possunt, sicut vicarii vicinarum ecclesiarum pro vicaria sua respondebit. Prior vero et monachi de Hurleia sicut persone vicinarum ecclesiarum plenarie respondebunt pro porcione sua. Quod ut ratum sit et firmum, presenti carta et sigilli nostri apposicione duximus confirmandum, salvis in omnibus iure et auctoritate et dignitate Saresburiensis ecclesie et nostra et successorum nostrorum. Dat' per manum magistri Marciani de Wilton' apud Sunning' xiiii kal. Iulii, pontificatus nostri anno ix°. Hiis testibus, Hugone de Gaherst, Thoma de Chebbeham, Ricardo de Wdele, Marciano de Wilton', magistris, Petro canonico de Suwik', Bartholomeo, Abraham, Ada, capellanis nostris, Radulfo de Winesham, Hugone de Adintun', senescallis nostris, Waltero clerico, Benedicto dapifero, Willelmo de capella, Savar', Hugone coco, Waltero marescallo, et multis aliis.   [18 June 1202]

Original, measuring approximately 7″ × 6¾″. Episcopal seal and counterseal of green wax on white hemp cords. The document is inadequately calendared by F. T. Wethered, *St. Mary's, Hurley in the Middle Ages* (1898), p. 101.

Hurley Priory (Berks.) was a cell of Westminster Abbey ; Waltham St. Lawrence and Warfield (in the same county) lie a few miles to the south. Hurley was in the patronage of Geoffrey fitzPeter as representative of the Mandeville founders (cf. *Memoranda roll 1 John* (P.R. Soc., n.s. 21), p. 57). While the document is mainly of interest for its careful provision for a perpetual vicar and its reference to the vicarages of neighbouring churches, the mention of benefactors in the preamble should be noted, also the dating clause, and the list of witnesses.

xii (*see pp.* 179–80)

Canterbury, Dean and chapter muniments, Sede Vacante scrap-book, vol. ii, p. 102.

Innocentius episcopus servus servorum dei dilecto filio .. abbati Sancti Albani salutem et apostolicam benedictionem. Pro dilecto filio H. nepote venerabilis fratris nostri .. Albanensis episcopi, Parisiis commorante, tibi nostras litteras recolimus destinasse ut ei vacantem ecclesiam de Wdehorn' ad tuam donationem spectantem quam R. de Sancto Edmundo tenuerat assignares, denuntiantes [1] irritum et inane si de ipsa post receptionem litterarum nostrarum contra mandatum nostrum presumeres [2] aliquid attemptare. Postmodum vero tuis nobis

---

[1] MS. denutiantes.   [2] MS. *final* s *corrected from* t.

litteris intimasti quod cum dicta ecclesia vacavisset eam G. clerico contulisti instituendum diocesano episcopo representans, sed ipso presentatum clericum in monasterii tui dispendium instituere differente compulsus fuisti regia potestate dictum R. ad ecclesiam presentare quem diocesanus episcopus sine dilatione suscepit. Sed idem G. antea presentatus contra ipsum R. litteras apostolicas impetravit quarum obtentu anno dimidio iam elapso causa rei servande missus in possessione ipsius ecclesie perhibetur, unde non habebas pro certo an mandatum apostolicum de iure posses effectui mancipare. Unde venerabili fratri nostro .. episcopo Heliensi dedimus in mandatis ut de premissis inquireret diligentius veritatem, et nisi constiterit prefatum G. clericum per collegium presentatum ius habere in ecclesia memorata ipse non obstante huiusmodi possessione, causa rei servande sicut proponitur assignata, cum alius super ea nullam moveat questionem, mandatum quod fecimus pro nepote predicti episcopi Albanensis faciat appellatione remota effectui mancipari, contradictores ecclesiastica districtione compescens. Quocirca discretioni tue per apostolica scripta precipiendo mandamus quatinus mandatum quod dictus episcopus Heliensis tibi super hiis pro nepote memorati episcopi Albanensis duxerit faciendum sine contradictione qualibet suscipias et observes. Dat' Laterani, kalendis Februarii pontificatus nostri anno quinto.

[1 February 1203]

Original mandate, measuring approx. $7\frac{3}{4}'' \times 7\frac{1}{8}''$. Trimmed at foot, removing all trace of sealing. Ascribed by R. L. Poole (Hist. MSS. Comm. *Report on var. coll.*, i. 245) to Pope Innocent IV. The church is Woodhorn, Northumberland. Roger de St. Edmund, a chaplain of King Richard I, was claimant to the archdeaconry of Richmond, 1198–1202, and seems to have died in the latter year. Later stages in this dispute are described in *PL*, ccxv. 591–2, 625–6.

xiii (see p. 180)

Canterbury, Dean and chapter muniments, Chartae antiquae G. 187.

H. dei gratia Cantuar' archiepiscopus, tocius Anglie primas, dilecto in Christo filio W. Gernon salutem et benedictionem. Mandatum domini pape suscepimus in hec verba :

Innocencius episcopus servus servorum dei venerabili fratri .. archiepiscopo Cant' salutem et apostolicam benedictionem. Etsi omnibus ex suscepte servitutis officio facti simus secundum apostolum debitores eis tamen specialius in suo iure tenemur adesse quos honesta conversatio et litterarum sciencia recommendant et nobilitas generis nichilominus reddit claros. Ex parte siquidem dilecti filii magistri Iohannis de Columpna qui sue probitatis obtentu, intuitu quoque consanguineorum suorum quos sincera in domino diligimus caritate, carus est nobis admodum et acceptus, fuit propositum coram nobis quod W. Brueira cum quibusdam fautoribus suis ecclesiam suam de Gotesdon' per violenciam occupans fructus quos invenit ibidem contra iusticiam asportavit et ei restituere contradicit. Quocirca fraternitati tue per apostolica scripta mandamus quatinus dictum W. ut eidem fructus restituat memoratos et decetero ab ipsius indebita molestatione desistat monicione premissa per censuram ecclesiasticam appellacione remota compellas, et ipsum habens propensius commendatum, super reddituris quos habet in Anglia auctoritate nostra suffultus non permittas eum ab aliquibus indebite molestari. Siqui vero ipsum super hiis vexare presumpserint, tu eos omni occasione et appellacione cessante a sua presumptione compescas, faciens ipsos remoto appellacionis obstaculo tam diu ab omnibus arctius evitari donec sibi et vicariis suis passis iniuriam satisfactionem exhibeant competentem. Dat' Ferentini, idibus Augusti pontificatus nostri anno sexto.   [13 Aug. 1203]

Huius igitur auctoritate mandati tibi mandamus et monemus quatinus predicto magistro I. fructus quos de prefata ecclesia sua percepisti sine difficultate restituas, alioquin proxima secunda feria post festum Sancti Nicholai coram nobis compareas in ecclesia Sancte Marie de Lamh' memorato I. super premissis iuxta mandatum apostolicum responsurus et iuri paritarus. Vale.   [Late 1203]

> Original, measuring approx. $6\frac{1}{2}'' \times 4\frac{3}{8}''$, including steps at left foot for sealing *sur simple queue* and for tie. Master John de Colonna became cardinal priest of S. Prassede *c.* 1212. The church in question may be that of Little Gaddesden (Herts), which was appropriated to St. James's, Northampton and had a vicarage ordained in it by 1215 ; but this is far from certain ; nor have W. Gernon and W. Brueira been certainly identified.

xiv (*see p.* 145)

Canterbury, Dean and chapter muniments, ' Christ Church letters ', vol. ii, no. 253.

Venerabili in Christo patri H. dei gratia Cant' archiepiscopo et Anglie primati devotus filius suus I. decanus Hoylond' salutem

et debitam cum devotione reverentiam. Presentium lator I.
capellanus domini V. archidiaconi Salesberiensis qui ministrat
in quadam ecclesia sua apud Leverton' in Hoylond' conquestus
est michi quod cum quadam die dominica preparasset se ad
missam celebrandam et post aspersionem aque nuntiatum esset
ei de quibusdam inquietis et ebriosis impudenter sedentibus ad
tabernam ab hora nona diei sabbati usque ad horam terciam
dominice diei, violenter etiam trahentibus ad se euntes versus
ecclesiam ad servicium dei, unde tumultus factus est in populo
dei et scandalum magnum ortum est, et ipse vellet corripere
et castigare impudentes illos et perversos et ebriosos, insurrexit
in eum quidam iuvenis, litteratus quidem sed nescio si ordinatus,
Tomas nomine, et eum verbis contumeliosis et convitiis probrosis
affecit et dehonestavit et violentas manus in eum iniecit, et ad
tantam iracundiam provocavit quod non ausus est ad sacra-
mentum altaris accedere, nisi recessisset ab ecclesia qui eum
turbaverat et qui ecclesiam totam commoverat. Sed quia
noluit exire, exuit se vestimentis sacris quibus indutus erat et
cessavit[1] a celebracione divinorum. Ita consuevit ipse T.
adversari et obloqui verbo dei in preiudicium negotiorum
ecclesie dei, propter hoc autem vocatur in ius. Cum com-
pareret coram nobis in capitulo super prefatis excessibus responsurus, proposita querela presentium latoris et audita, ipse
iamdictus T. petiit indutias deliberandi utrum vellet cedere
an contendere super tot et tantis excessibus. Acceptis vero
indutiis canonicis, eum in alio capitulo ei prefixo comparere
super prememorata querela responsurus, presentium lator, I.
capellanus, presentiens eum velle apellare ad audientiam domini
nostri decani Lincoln' ut sic prolongaret iniquitatem suam,
prevenit eum et apellavit ad audientiam vestram, prefigens
terminum apellacioni sue diem lune proximam post invencionem
sancte crucis. Peto igitur a sanctitate vestra quatinus ita
corripiatur inpudens ille et puniatur ut et ipse cesset a per-
versitate sua et ceteri a consimili terreantur. Vigeat sanctitas
et salus vestra in domino, sancte pater.

[? 1201 × 1203]

Original, measuring approximately 5⅞" × 4", including step at left
foot for sealing *sur simple queue.*

John of Sutton, rural dean of Holland, appears in *Reg. antiquiss.*,
iv. 36, vii. 3, 22, 26 in documents *c.* 1200. The church of Leverton

---

[1] MS. secessavit.

(Lincs.) was divided, and Humphrey de Bassingbourne, archdeacon of Salisbury, was described as the last parson of a moiety in March 1240 (*Rotuli R. Grosseteste* (Canterbury and York Soc.), p. 49). Since appeal to the dean of Lincoln was contemplated, the case probably arose *sede vacante*.

xv (*see p.* 121)

Norwich, Dean and chapter muniments, Norwich charter 402.

Omnibus sancte matris ecclesie filiis Iohannes dei gratia Norwicensis episcopus salutem in domino. Noverit universitas vestra nos divine pietatis intuitu dedisse, concessisse, et assingnasse et presenti carta confirmasse dilectis filiis nostris monachis Norwicensibus ecclesiam de Wicton' cum omnibus ad eam pertinentibus ad officium cellararie sue in proprios usus inperpetuum possidendam, salvo nobis et successoribus nostris inperpetuum iure pontificali et parochiali. Indulsimus etiam quod si istam ecclesiam aliquo casu vacare contigerit, liceat predictis monachis vacuam possessionem ingredi hac auctoritate a nobis eis indulta et facient in eadem ecclesia competenter ministrari per capellanos suos pro rationabili voluntate sua amovendos et admittendos. Hiis testibus, magistro Willelmo de Linn', magistro Roberto de Gloucestr', magistro Roberto de Tiwa, Alano de Gray, Alano de Sancto Edmundo. Dat' apud Norwic' per manum magistri Galfridi de Derham, sexto decimo kal. Iunii pontificatus nostri anno quinto. [17 May 1205]

> Original, measuring approximately $7\frac{1}{2}'' \times 4\frac{1}{10}''$, fold at foot slit for sealing *sur double queue*. Endorsements : i. ' Con[firmatio] de ecclesia de Wictune'. ii. ' quadraplicatur." iii. 'D xli.' iv. The monogram of Archbishop Robert Winchelsey's notary, Hugh Musele (see *Reg. R. Winchelsey* (Canterbury and York Soc.), p. xix).
> The church is that of Wighton, Norfolk. Bishop John de Gray granted other churches to the cathedral priory on the same terms.

xvi (*see p.* 162)

Public Record Office, Chancery Masters' Exhibits, Lanthony cartulary A.I. section xvi, no. 19.

Omnibus sancte matris ecclesie filiis ad quos presens carta pervenerit Mau*gerius* dei gratia Wygorn' ecclesie minister humilis salutem in vero salutari. Ad universitatis vestre noticiam volumus pervenire nos ad presentacionem, peticionem, et assensum W. prioris et conventus Lanthon' patronorum ecclesie de Wyke et ad presentacionem Rogeri rectoris ecclesie de Wyka admisisse Ricardum clericum filium Roberti de Strode ad vicariam ecclesie de Wyka habendam et possidendam libere et quiete et honorifice inperpetuum, scilicet ut habeat conredium suum ad mensam rectoris prenominate ecclesie et unam marcam argenti pro stipendiis suis et oblaciones domus rectoris prefate ecclesie et denarium misse sue de corpore presenti et legatum suum rationabile et forragium equo suo et prebendam in itinere servicii ecclesie et medietatem confessionum suarum. Et ipse Ricardus predicte vicarie sicut sacerdos deserviet. Ut autem hec nostra donacio perpetuum firmitatis robur optineat eam presentis scripti etc.   [? 1203 × 1212]

The church of Painswick (Gloucs.) was given to Lanthony Secunda (Gloucs.) by Hugh de Lascy. The mention of ' W. prior ' suggests a date after Prior Geoffrey (of Henlow) became bishop of St. Davids in 1203 and before the death of Bishop Mauger in 1212, probably before the latter went into exile in May 1208.

o

INDEX

plenitude of power, 43-4, 48, 72, 76, 80, 82-3, 98
Plympton (Devon), Aug. priory, 109 n. 3, 122 n. 2
Poitou, Philip of, bp. of Durham, 151, 179
Pont l'Évêque, Roger of, archbp. of York, 11, 13, 28, 56, 58-9, 127
Pontefract (Yorks W.R., Clun.) priory, 158
Poore, Herbert, bp. of Salisbury, 27, 145 n. 3, 193-4 ; *familia* named, 194
Poore, Richard, bp. of Salisbury, 27, 138, 176
pope, as *princeps*, 44 ; as universal ordinary, 48 ; as *vicarius Christi*, 43 ; as *vicarius Petri*, 48 n. 3
Potton, Robert of, 193
Powicke, F. M., 106 n. 5, 163, 175
preaching, 34, 163, 165, 170
prebendal churches, patronage of, 157-8
precepta sinodalia, 143
Premonstratensians, 13, 38
princeps, 44
privileges, papal, 75, 85
procession, Whitsun, 150
procuration fees, 141, 146
prohibition, writ of, 34, 97, 107 n. 4, 110-13, 117-18
provision, papal, 80-2, 178-81
Ptolemy, relative of Innocent III, 180
Pucelle, Gerard, bp. of Coventry, 27 n. 1, 28, 46
Puiset, Hugh de, bp. of Durham, 56, 71, 110
Pulloxhill (Beds), 182
Puttenham (Herts), 183, 190-1

Radford, Radeford (Warw.), W. dean of, 186
Ragusa, *see* Bernard
Rainham (Essex), 166
Ralph, abbot of Louth, 188
Ralph, prior of Worcester, 9 n. 1
Ralph, subdean of Lincoln, 188
Ramsey (Hunts), Ben. abbey, 114-15, 116, 140, 182, 184
Rathbone, Eleanor, 47
Reading (Berks), Ben. abbey, 71, 89 n. 4, 150 n. 6
regnum et sacerdotium, 37 n. 2, 87-8, 107
relics, 170
rescriptum, 45 n. 1
Richard I, king, 10, 20, 25-6, 33 n. 4, 90-3

Richard, William son of, 190
Richmond, archdeacon of, *see* Chimeli, Honorius
Ridale, Askitillus de, 86
Ridel, Geoffrey, archdeacon of Canterbury, bp. of Ely, 22, 23, 27-8, 107
Ripton (Hunts), 184
Roches, Peter des, bp. of Winchester, 128, 131
Rochester, bp. of, *see* Ernulf, Glanvill (G.)
— cathedral priory, 169
— diocese, visitation in, 139
Roger, archdeacon of Salop, 187
Roger, bp. of Salisbury, 24
Rolleston, Mr. Roger of, dean of Lincoln, 120, 190, 197-8
Romans, 89 n. 3, 102-3
Rome, bribery and corruption at, 67-9
Romeyn, John le, canon of York, 178-9

S., nephew of Innocent III, 178
Sackville, William de, 54, 57
sacraments, administration of, 142
Saddington (Leics), 184
Saddleworth (Yorks W.R.), 166
St. Albans (Herts), Ben. abbey, 53, 85, 126 n. 1, 150 n. 6 ; abbot of, *see* Cella, Simon ; archdeaconry of, 122 ; rebuilding of, 169 ; and vicarages, 136
St. Davids, claim to metropolitan status, 31, 68, 73
St. Edmund, Alan of, 198
St. Edmund, Mr. Roger of, 179, 194-5
St. Neots (Hunts), Ben. priory, 123 n. 3, 183
St. Osyth (Essex), Aug. abbey, abbot and prior of, 69 n. 4
Saintes, *decreta* for dioc. of, 143 n. 1
Salford (Warw.), 135
Salisbury, bp. of, *see* Bohun, Poore (H. and R.), Roger, Walter (H.)
— cathedral, fraternity of the fabric of, 165 ; statutes of, 121
— diocese, statutes of, 142
Salisbury, John of, 11 n. 2, 19, 48 n. 3, 52 n. 2, 54-5, 73 n. 1, 79, 169
Sallay (Yorks W.R.), Cist. abbey, 113
Salop, archdeacon of, *see* Roger
Samson, abbot of Bury St. Edmunds, 62, 98
sanctuary, 33-4